D0467696

FOR
PACKRATS
ONLY

Also by Don Aslett

Other books on decluttering and personal organization:
Clutter's Last Stand
Clutter Free! Finally & Forever
The Office Clutter Cure
How to Have a 48-Hour Day
How to Handle 1,000 Things at Once

Other books on home care:
No Time to Clean!
Is There Life After Housework?
The Cleaning Encyclopedia
Don Aslett's Clean in a Minute
Don Aslett's Stainbuster's Bible
Make Your House Do the Housework
Who Says It's a Woman's Job to Clean?
500 Terrific Ideas for Cleaning Everything
Pet Clean-Up Made Easy
Painting without Fainting

Business books:
How to Have a 48-Hour Day
The Office Clutter Cure
Keeping Work Simple (with Carol Cartaino)
How to Be #1 with Your Boss
Everything I Needed to Know About Business I Learned in the Barnyard
Speak Up! A Step-by-Step Guide to Powerful Public Speeches

For professional cleaners:
Cleaning Up for a Living
The Professional Cleaner's Personal Handbook
How to Upgrade & Motivate Your Cleaning Crews
Construction Cleanup

To help you create:
Get Organized, Get Published!
   (with Carol Cartaino)
You Can... You Should...
   Write Poetry
How to Write & Sell
   Your First Book

FOR PACKRATS ONLY

How to Clean Up,
Clear Out, and Live
Clutter-Free Forever!

Don Aslett

Edited by Carol Cartaino
Illustrated by Craig LaGory

MARSH CREEK PRESS

Disclaimer

Many of those who read my cleaning and decluttering books imagine that I live in a concrete vault with whitewashed walls, almost no furniture, and one bare, 60-watt bulb. In other words, junk-free, or almost so. The truth is my wife and I live in a normal house (a big one, in the mountains of Idaho, but just an ordinary house). We have six now-grown kids with lots of kids of their own and scores of friends and neighbors, so there's always someone here. Our place is a major intersection of action—plenty of toys, noise, food, etc. Junk and clutter is what makes a house dull and sterile, because most of it is dead. Wouldn't you rather have one live decoration than half a dozen dead ones? So would we, and we do. Drop in for a visit!

P.S. This is an official disclaimer—just in case fifty lawyers' wives (inspired by this book) throw out their spouse's trial files, or forty farmers toss their wives' fruit jars. I'm not attempting to wrench away your wealth or divest you of your history or sterilize your dwelling. Nor am I trying to persuade you to pull the plug on any of your not-yet-moribund memorabilia. I just want to get you to subpoena your excess and start some civil action on it. I'll provide clues, appeals, and petitions (not to mention hard evidence) to get you to face and solve your own "case" (cases, probably) of clutter congestion, but I can't take responsibility for any lightheadedness, hernias, or landfill overflows that result from the heady act of decluttering.

For Packrats Only

Published by Marsh Creek Press,
PO Box 700, Pocatello, Idaho 83204.
1-888-748-3535; fax 1-208-235-5481.

Distributed by Betterway Books,
an imprint of F&W Publications, Inc.,
1507 Dana Avenue, Cincinnati, Ohio 45207.
1-800-289-0963.

Illustrator and designer: Craig LaGory
Editor: Carol Cartaino
Production manager: Tobi Flynn

LIBRARY OF CONGRESS CATALOGING IN PUBLICATION DATA:

Aslett, Don, 1935—
    For packrats only / Don Aslett ; illustrated by Craig LaGory.
        p.   cm.
    ISBN 0-937750-25-5
    1. House cleaning. I. Title.
TX324.A75833 1991
    648'.5—dc20

Contents

Introduction

If General Custer had as much general clutter as the average American of today—just to hide behind—the Indians would never even have nicked his neckerchief! Unfortunately, he didn't, so he was finished off completely.

But finishing off our clutter completely hasn't been quick or easy. It still rates as one of our chief problems in life; tossing that souvenir bullet out has been tougher than biting it. We still circle around our piles and heaps and closets full of junk and clutter with great war whoops and unfriendly intentions—but we never attack.

More than a quarter of a million junkaholics went out and bought my first book, *Clutter's Last Stand* (or got it as an anonymous gift from well-wishers or their mates). Thousands of prematurely buried junkers climbed out of their bondage as a result and wrote to me describing in dirty detail how they did it. These weren't the usual quick notes saying "thank you" or "I loved your book," but three- to five-page typed letters from doctors, lawyers, counselors, accountants, architects, and teachers, among others—all of them confessing their conversion and expressing the joy of being a born-again ex-junker.

Professors have used *Clutter's Last Stand* as a textbook for behavioral sci-

ence classes, and ministries and monasteries have used it like scripture for sermons. People have even sent me boxes of their select evicted clutter. (In fact I get more mail about clutter than I do about cleaning.)

All this made it clear to me that clutter was still casting its spell; there were still whole realms of junk out there to uncover. And more than a few million of you still hadn't managed to make the plunge into your plunder.

You obviously needed another booster shot and nerve builder, something to convince you to go the rest of the way and actually do it.

So now I've done a second volume. To give clutter addicts, who can all too easily backslide, a recharge of resolution, more compelling reasons to dejunk, more clutter cul-de-sacs to avoid, and a lot more on HOW to get rid of it. I've also included extracts from some of the most amusing and interesting communications I've received from readers about their dejunking experiences, frustrations, and triumphs. There's nothing like the warmly shared experiences of fellow sufferers—real live people we can relate to—to make us believe and move us to action. The stories, insights, and suggestions of real-life junkers—their further questions, their hard evidence, their amazing testimonies of cure and delivery—have helped me immeasurably to give new and better junk solutions in this book.

Good reading for good riddance!

Acknowledgments

YOU deserve all the credit for the contents of this book. So much of it is your thoughts, your wisdom, your philosophy, your confessions.... I just wrote it all down, most of it coming from calls, comments, and letters from readers of my first book on this subject, *Clutter's Last Stand*, and my television, radio, and cleaning seminar audiences.

I had the benefit also of some prime intelligence from college professors like **Britt Hargraves** and psychologists such as **Dr. Richard Silvestri** and **Dr. Sharon Katz**, as well as those professional organizers who live with their hands on the clutter pulse: **Gladys Allen, Stephanie Culp, Maxine Ordesky**, and **Paulette Ensign**. Other professionals, too, such as **Martha Cook** and the other librarians of North Idaho College Library and **Mrs. Captain Mary Lynn Rodal** of the Salvation Army, made important contributions to the material between these covers. I especially appreciate all those of you who sat down and wrote masterpieces we felt compelled to share, including **Theresa Cotter; Jane O'Reilly; Caroline Guthrie; Dawnelle Wood; Ginny Kent; Jean J. Pratt; Hazel Turner Hamblin; Lorraine Miracle; Avalyn B. Marquardt; Marjie Buffam; Ruth Bragg; Charles G. Langham**, Executive Director of SCROOGE; **Tabitha Scarpella; Robert Sheeler, M.D.**; and **Charlotte Limke**.

It all came in (sometimes a lot faster than the clutter was going out!)—tons of decluttering data—and none of it escaped **Tobi Flynn**, my director of operations, who saved and processed it. And then all of it, mine and yours, passed to the finest clutter connoisseur in the world (and no mean junker, either), my editor and clutter collaborator **Carol Cartaino**, who added to it, and blended and sprinkled it with perfect seasoning through the book. **Craig LaGory**'s art and layout made each page a pleasure to peruse (even while it loosens your grip on your grubby stuff).

Mentioning every single one of my helpers by name would be almost impossible, and more than a few wished to remain anonymous, in any case. But I'd like you all to know how much I've appreciated the assistance.

You unreformed packrats out there could take a few of those old cards you have saved and thank these people too, for what you are about to read and get rid of!

PART I

The Problem

CHAPTER 1

This Is an Emergency!

What's the Number-One Housework Problem?

Having computerized the comments of the hundreds of thousands of homemakers I've spoken to and heard from across the United States and abroad, I can tell you without hesitation that it's JUNK AND CLUTTER.

Across the board, rich or poor, mansion or bungalow, twelve kids or two, junk and clutter causes more headaches, strained backs, strained budgets, and strained relationships, more frustration, discouragement, guilt, embarrassment, chaos, and confusion than any other household challenge!

No matter how clean our house, we turn around and already there is junk and clutter on top of our refrigerator, in stacks on our countertops, clogging up our drawers, bulging from our cupboards and closets, overflowing our mailbox, and obstructing our hallways and stairways and littering our vehicles.

Where Does It All Come From? And How Do We Get Rid of It?

This book is dedicated to helping you discover the answer to those two questions.

Let me share a clutter adventure with you right here at the start:

The place was Phoenix, Arizona, a high school auditorium filled to its 600-person capacity. At the close of my three-hour seminar on professional cleaning techniques, I announced that today there would be a special attraction, a "Junk Contest," at a nearby bookstore. I'd autograph books and award a free professional upright vacuum for the most original, unique, worthless piece of junk anyone had been hanging onto.

I thought a dozen or so people might amble on down, but they came in droves! Like pilgrims to Mecca, wise men bearing gifts, worshippers bearing burnt offerings, they came holding their junk aloft, mumbling unintelligibly, eyeing each other's junk. What a sight! You wouldn't believe it! One woman had her kidney stones in a bottle (they'd been in there fifteen years now); someone else had a headless stuffed mallard and half a broken pool cue; someone even (believe it or not) had a leopard-skin-covered water heater made into a chair, with a lawnmower base!

Before I knew it, the store was jammed with junk and grim-faced owners competing for that new industrial vacuum. When I tapped the three bookstore clerks to help me judge, they edged to the back of the store. It was obviously going to be an impossible task–the junk was so good, so awful, so equal. But suddenly I was saved, as a couple brought in one last thing and handed it to me.

I held it up to the audience and asked them, "Okay, folks, what is it?"

"A johnny jumper?"

"No."

"A feed bag?"

"Nope."

"A parachute?"

"Uh-uh, no."

"An arm sling? A tool carrier?"

"Sorry, wrong, not even close."

The audience finally ran out of guesses, so I told them.

"This ladies and gentlemen, is a genuine *goat brassiere!*"

The audience tittered in amazement. "When mother goats freshen and have their kids, their udder expands and drags and flops. This straps on underneath to hold things up (use your imagination, folks)."

At this point the woman who brought this in was so excited by the possibility that her junk was going to win that she had her husband (much to his embarrassment) get up and demonstrate it. They did win! But folks, here's the kicker: they didn't own a goat! They had never owned a goat! Yet they stored the goat brassiere and shuffled it and moved it from home to home with them and even took it overseas with them—because they thought it might be valuable someday, because no one else they knew had one, and because they knew that famous old excuse "As soon as I throw it away, I'll need it."

How many of **you** have "goat bras" in among your junk? Let's do something about it, starting with Chapter 2!

3

Is It Really That Bad?

Your Personal Clutter Checkup Exam

People have tried everything from drugs to hot irons to hypnotism to get someone to tell all, to fess up. All to get a confession or information or hidden secrets out of others.

But all *I* have to say or do is ask about "your clutter" and immediately eyes roll, lips quiver, and the words just flow out! People will talk to anyone about it, announce it over national networks, write it up and sign it—the most personal things you can imagine—and they don't need any prompting once they get started. The deepest catacombs of clutter are laid open. And clutter is one thing people don't lie or exaggerate about because the simple truth is amazing enough. One day I just happened to mention that I'd discovered that about 40 percent of "housework" was actually nothing but picking up and maneuvering around junk and clutter. Gasps went through the audience. I'd hit a nerve.

The following are just a few statements from intelligent, well-educated, successful people like you and me—the **full** confessions are coming later!

"My mother saved everything. My father died ten years ago, and I'm sure he's in the bottom of the freezer."

"My parents bought me a new washer and dryer at Christmas. There wasn't any place in my clutter to set them up so the delivery people put them in the back of my pickup. I had to take a trip to Chicago (from Texas) and ended up hauling them there and back because I didn't have room to leave them in the house."

"I have three hundred tennis balls—and don't play tennis."

"I've had three hammocks for the last twenty years—and not a tree in sight."

"We opened a forty-year-old sealed package she'd been saving, and the contents were unrecognizable. I finally found a faded note on the bottom, identifying it as a piece of her sixteenth-birthday cake."

Don't think these are isolated incidences:

"My first husband saved rubber bands from the morning paper—that's 365 dried-up rubber bands a year. Our marriage didn't stretch any farther then they did."

"I just got my new L.L. Bean catalogue, so why am I holding on to the last ten years' worth of previous ones?"

"No matter what you need, I have three of them in all sizes—or I can get you one."

"But Don, it's good insulation."

"Well, we finally cleaned out the smokehouse. Two pickup loads of Cool Whip containers—twenty were full of nails all rusted together."

"We used to raise and show boxer dogs (whose tails are usually cropped), but we quit in 1940. Recently, I sorted through my cedar chest. We still have two dozen of the tails we cut off. [Can you believe that? I wonder if she occasionally takes them out and pets them.]

"That's nothing, Don. I have my husband's ex-wife's leg brace."

"I wanted to save my gallstones as a souvenir, but the doctor wouldn't let me. But I did get a picture of them, and I still have that."

Amazingly, I've heard the following confession over and over again, but this one has an added twist: "I still have the kids' umbilical cord ends. The dog got part of one, but I kept the rest."

"Eat your hearts out, America. I have not one, but *two* gallons of Mount St. Helen's volcano dust (and all six urinals from my visits to the hospital)."

"This, Don, is the hair I combed out of my special hairdo on the night of my junior prom. I've kept it in a box with a candy kiss that a date once gave me." (This woman is now 48.)

"Don, my husband has this old furnace motor, workability doubtful. We've not only kept it for over thirty-two years, but we've carefully moved it from New Jersey to Connecticut to New York to California to Kansas and back to New Jersey, then to Kansas again. We're now in Arizona (his allegiance isn't weakening, either)."

"I need help! All my drawers are junk drawers!"

"When I look over my junk kingdom, Don, it feels like I've eaten for thirty years and haven't sat down to digest anything yet—stuffed is the word!"

"'Don't hang up, don't hang up,' I was yelling as I searched frantically through my clutter trying to find my cordless phone."

"My wife is the only woman in Georgia who has her own neon 'Garage Sale' sign."

"There were two intelligent adults arguing over a bottle of dead lightning bugs collected the summer of '31—calling it a family heirloom."

"One thing I left behind when I moved was the 5-foot wrap that goes around the windshield and chrome mounting brackets of a motorboat (you never know, the guy moving in might need it)."

"We have five vacuum cleaners. Our first argument after we married was over whose mother had the best vacuum. So we have one like his mother's and my mother gave me hers. Then we bought various machines to do what neither of those would do. Then as each broke down and we couldn't find parts to repair them, we saved them to 'haul to Missouri' as our grandchildren's great-grand-mother's relics. They are family heirlooms now."

Traveling all over the U.S. and Canada and Great Britain and Australia, too, doing interviews on clutter, I've discovered something interesting: Clutter is probably the only thing on earth that's truly democratic.

It doesn't discriminate for race, creed, color, IQ, or economic status. And male and female are equally guilty—although it does seem clear from more than forty years of professional cleaning and all the confessions that've been sent to me that men seem to go for bigger, more expensive junk; women are somewhat ahead in creative excuses. Other than that, it's dead even!

Most of us will come right out and confess that we are indeed infected with the none-too-rare disease of junkitis. The holdouts, those who think they're above junkhood (an impossibility if you live in America), are really no different. I had a chance to demonstrate this when I was on a big talk show. Anticipating the fun and controversy of the subject, the camera crew went out and interviewed passersby—who really stole the show. Men and women executives in $600 suits were the worst. "Are you a junker?" "Certainly not, I have a neat, squared-away home and keep nothing." (We knew we would get this reply, so we got more specific.)

"Well, might you have any old dead flashlight batteries lying around?" The confident expression disappeared. "Well, maybe a few." "How many would you say is a few?" "Around twenty, I guess." "Are they any good?" "Well, no…." "So why do you keep them?" Silence.

The excuses that followed were amazing. One guy said the reason he kept them was when he got mad at his wife, he could go downstairs and put the batteries in a vise and crush them.

A classy, well-dressed, and well-educated woman was stopped and asked, "Are you a junker, ma'am?" In a crisp Canadian accent she said, "Absolutely not. There's nothing amiss or about in my home."

"Are you sure you aren't saving old pantyhose with runs?" she was asked. She grinned sheepishly, snapped her purse shut, and admitted to maybe a few in her dresser, a couple in her desk drawer at work, some at the vacation home, and of course a laundry bag full to make stuffed animals for the kids.

Another woman who denied all attraction to junk was asked, "Don't you even have any empty margarine containers around?" Instantly her arms extended like she was telling an Alaskan fish story. Why was she keeping them? She said she didn't know.

Now it's your turn.

Are you a junker?

Save your answer, we can make it easier.

We sometimes speak great truths by accident. "How are things?"

"Well, I'm down in the dumps today."

When you're living with clutter and junk, that's right on. No matter what all those piles around you are worth or how much good stuff they contain, the place is still a dump and produces a dumpy feeling, attitude, and appearance. Don't kid yourself: your surroundings regulate your life. You can't live above what you live with, especially if you created it. In time, you become just like it. Clutter plays no favorites, and it's easy to see why. Have you ever met a person who didn't want more? More is the name of the game. "More money will buy me more, comfort me, make me healthier, more popular. More will iron out my problems, my kids' problems, and my marital difficulties." The magic of "more" doesn't help our junk drive. There's nothing wrong with more if it's more education, more love, more kindness, more cleanliness, more flowers—more is better! Even when it comes to stuff, getting it is okay! It's progress! But *keeping all of it is clutter*.

"It is the preoccupation with possession, more than anything else, that prevents man from living freely and nobly."
—*Bertrand Russell*

Insurance adjusters say that the biggest thing holding up recovery payments isn't insurance company red tape or processing, but the owner's inability to remember and report all that was lost. For most people, accounting for what they have (or had) is almost impossible because they have so much.

From an NBC anchorwoman who lost one of her $200 glacier boots down a crevasse: "Don, I hate to admit this, but if and when I lose a limb, I've been praying it's the left leg."

Living is *doing*, loving and being loved—not *having*.

Why Do People Keep Junk?

This is one question I've been asked even more than "How did you become a cleaner?" (And I've been asked that plenty.)

One of the biggies is space to fill. Empty space bothers most people. Junkers and clutterers often have a compulsive streak in their personalities, too, and may like to live in the past. Junk and clutter, no matter how worthless, also give lots of people the illusion they are rich, have something to fall back on if hard times come. The more hardened junker's central drive is getting their money's worth out of things.

I've heard many other theories, too: heredity, lack of self-esteem (and need for personality reinforcement), fear of reality (and a desire for insulation from it), deprivation as a child, "I'm a Virgo and all Virgos are junkers," etc., etc. I've collected and compiled hundreds of reasons, as well as scholarly studies and speculation on the origin of the pieces. And I fed all of this into a computer to try and arrive at the reason why we collect and keep clutter. The answer is so profound I won't even keep the Nobel Peace Prize it will surely win (not even the box it comes in): By the time we emerge from the innocence of childhood, we firmly believe that things make us happy (be it toys, bigger and better homes, vehicles, collectibles, equipment, land, jewelry, etc.—or the money to buy the objects of our choice). If one little thing is fun and gives some pleasure, then surely more will increase our pleasure.

Things will even somehow change something inside of us. For instance, an object or possession will inspire or force us to perform better. "I'm slow; if I get a faster bike, I'll be faster."

"I'm always gaining weight; if I buy a house with a pool, it'll take those extra pounds off."

"I can't seem to practice—if I buy a better piano, the investment will make me play."

"I can't keep my lawn as nice as Larry's. A bigger, better mower is the answer."

"The kids won't study. I'm sure it'll help if we buy a computer or an encyclopedia set."

"I'm unpopular; a case of Head & Shoulders should do the trick."

Then, too, we gradually learn to measure our self-worth by how other people see us, so again we look for more and better things to make ourselves more impressive. We want to be happy and feel good and be liked, and so we keep getting and keeping things—more and more and more. (Just to have them, even if we don't use them, because somehow it will enrich our life and raise our level of living.)

> "After reading your books I feel more and more strongly about how much we own that we don't need at all. I've been giving things away right and left... a crockpot, a wedding gift espresso maker, our dusty wicker headboard. Some of my friends think I'm insane to be just giving these things away, but I know I never use them. (I almost feel guilty when someone takes them—a little like a drug dealer.)"

Let me report a phone call I received at one o'clock one morning (in New York where the call came from, it was three A.M.). An enthusiastic voice asked me to confirm that it was indeed Don Aslett she was speaking to. She identified herself and it seemed she'd just read my first book on clutter and was now a born-again dejunker. Her testimony, in brief, follows:

"Mr. Aslett, I'm 65, and live in a nice apartment in the city. My husband is an internationally known _____, retired. We are well-to-do, and for some time now I've had everything in life I could ever want. I spent my entire adult life getting and storing stuff. I lived to buy and bought to live. I'm the type who would pay $800 for a ring at a flea market—it was gradual, but it got that bad. Recently I unburdened myself of it all. For the first time in forty-five years I'm free. It's truly an unbelievable experience. I wouldn't have believed it could be this good even if God had told me. Now I can leave home and do other things."

Are you going to take the clutter cure now or later? Wait ten or twenty or thirty years more or start living now?

So much of human history seems to be a struggle to get out of bondage—captivity to some country, city, race, or nation. Many a life and limb has been lost fighting for rights and freedoms—for release, so we can get out and get on with living and enjoying life. We, of course, blame most bondage on "them"—the leaders, the government, the organization, the Lord, the society, the terrorists. Seldom ourselves; we're just the helpless victims. That might be so about 10 percent of the time, but the other 90 percent is all our own personal bondage or unhappiness. The situation is self-inflicted. We hold our own feet to the fire; our situation is what we make it or allow it to be. We could use those same feet to walk away. When it comes to clutter, *we* are at the root of most of what we're buried in right now. We allowed or even invited it (generally paid for it, too) to inundate us.

Sure "they" gave you plenty, those junk-bearing moms and dads and then grandpas and grandmas, those teachers and bosses. And don't forget the government. They all conspired to fill your life with clutter. But all of that was only a dribble compared to what YOU grew and sprouted and nurtured and cultivated to a giant redwood of deadwood clutter.

We spend a lot of time worrying about whether global warming is going to get us, or AIDS, or cancer.

But clutter isn't merely a statistical possibility; it's here right now and it's killing you. The "gonna" you should be concentrating on is *gonna get rid of it!* Clergymen, doctors, scientists, psychologists, and forty other "improvers" are telling you the same thing. When you get the junk out of your life, everything improves—mentally, physically, and emotionally.

For a long time clutter is just there–a nuisance and a struggle and an irritation—but suddenly it starts to blow your fuses.

You're finally sick of it. More of us change our behavior when we finally just get solidly sick of something, than for any other reason. Being bored, threatened, or economically affected may arouse a little interest and our sense of self-defense, but not action. Getting thoroughly sick of the stuff that hurts and plagues our life, however, will do it. One beautiful now-thin woman told me she'd tried every diet and exer-cise plan around, plus hypnotism, dieters' support groups, reducing drugs, and miracle milkshakes, without losing a pound. One day, undressing in front of a mirror, she looked at herself—and the sight made her sick. In five months, without any outside help, she lost it all.

A Bell Telephone executive once said to me, "Three marks of a great doer are curiosity, commitment, energy."

The very fact that you're reading this book means you have at least two of these things going for you already. Your curiosity about clutter control is aroused, and the time you're taking here testifies commitment. That you've gone this far says "serious" to me, and that spark of tingly excitement you feel when you think about going junkless will take care of generating the energy.

Your Personal Clutter Checkup Exam

1. When I see a garage sale, I feel:
A. Compelled to stop and at least look.
B. Embarrassed to leave with nothing.
C. Like asking to use their sign.
D. Sorry for the holders.

2. When I see an "on sale" sign, I:
A. Don't want to miss an opportunity to save.
B. Investigate to see if it really is a sale.
C. Check the list of gifts I need to buy for the next decade.
D. Ignore it completely.

3. When looking for a house or apartment, I always:
A. Consider storage space first.
B. Want to be sure there's plenty of closets in the floor plan.
C. See if it has a big project room.
D. Want to be sure it's good and far away from junk sources.

4. When hearing of a disaster, I:
A. Wonder if there's been any looting.
B. Call for the date of the salvage sale.
C. Start pricing water-and shockproof containers for my own stuff.
D. Send some of my excess to the needy.

5. When I do get rid of a piece of clutter, I:
A. Feel acute pain and depression.
B. Feel nagging remorse.
C. Only dream of it occasionally.
D. Feel nothing but freedom and relief.

6. When scraps of anything appear, I:
A. Snap up every single one of them.
B. Keep any that might possibly be useful.
C. Keep only those I know I'll use.
D. A scrap is a scrap—away!

7. When all those colorful catalogues arrive, I:
A. Hold checkbook and credit cards ready as I read.
B. Set aside a large block of time to read and study them.
C. Scan them quickly and make a mental note only of what I need.
D. Curse junk mail and ignore them.

8. When I see something neat but not really necessary, I:
A. Stay awake at night searching for an excuse to buy it.
B. Buy or take it just in case.
C. At least try it on or fondle it.
D. Walk right on by.

9. When the conversation turns to bragging about junk, I:
A. Dominate it.
B. Take part and take notes.
C. Listen for junk-source clues.
D. Read a Don Aslett book.

10. When someone gives me a piece of junk or clutter, I:
A. Keep it, or course—it was a gift.
B. Strive to find a use for it.
C. Put it in my "If I ever have a garage sale" pile.
D. Give a sincere thank-you and then dispose of it.

11. My favorite style of furnishing is:
A. Victorian.
B. Country or rustic.
C. Overstuffed, overfurnished everyday.
D. Modern, Japanese, Southwestern, Shaker, or just plan simplicity.

SCORING

If your answers include:	*You:*
6 or more A's	*Should be undergoing open storage-bin surgery*
6 or more A's and/or B's	*Are in big trouble*
Mostly C's	*Better watch out*
Mostly D's	*Can call yourself a Clutterbuster*

CHAPTER 3

Some Good Reasons to Get Rid of It

Does clutter affect the way we're treated, how much we're liked or loved? No doubt about it.

Most of us are pretty private people. We have lots of secrets no one knows about, not even our closest friends. We don't want anyone looking in our fridge, or into our finances. I call this our sacred space, and no amount of pressure or money could pry some of this information out of us. We've worked hard to develop our image over the years, our aura, our reputation. We may have the perfect front, and then along comes an indiscreet informer, worse than any double agent—clutter. It bares our heart and soul for the whole world to see. It reveals what we think, where our real intentions and attentions are.

I've often said you can tell a lot about how people relate to others by looking in their refrigerator. What they keep in there, and how long, is a good parallel to the way they run a relationship. If they stash and store and ignore until the big annual cleanup, they're also likely to stash and store up little irritations for a big family fight. Clutter is indeed our visual autobiography. People read us by what we keep and how long we keep it.

If it's yours, you wear it somehow. And just as if you showed up with red shoes and an orange purse, people notice and treat you differently. How do **you** treat a person who can't seem to get it together, can never find anything, is always hunting, digging, searching? You avoid them! When we dejunk, our friends, family, neighbors, lover, and even the IRS agent will change the way they treat us—and you can be sure it will be for the better.

If you don't think people treat you at the level of what you have, collect, and store, think again, Thelma! When a 26-cent stamp surrounded by eight 1-cent stamps shows up on your letter, they can't help but think "What a hoarder." If you fish in your purse for something for more than five seconds, they think "disorganized."

People are bound to treat you differently if:
• You constantly borrow because you can't find yours.
• No one can get into the back seat because your car is filled with stuff.
• You turn half or the rooms in your house into junk-storage stations.

- You have to make an aisle through the stuff to usher visitors into the living room.
- You build a third storage shed out back to enclose the overflow.
- You leave an old car or old sofa in your front yard for a month.
- You buy a junkyard.

Do We Offend Others with Our Junk?

Or is it just our imagination? A little while ago, I was waiting in the St. Louis airport. A true junker was a few seats away. He'd raided the souvenir shops and added several packages to the already too many bags he was carrying on the plane. His booty took up three seats, so an elderly woman had to walk over and sit in another section. He was so overloaded it took him forever to locate his tickets, so he held up the line of passengers loading. And as he struggled down the aisle he smacked every other passenger with his six bulky bags. Then he crammed all of this into more than his fair share of room in the overhead compartments, crushing someone's flowers and someone else's hat. And still he waddled up and down the aisle trying to find a compartment to hold his final bag (a bulging clothes bag that should have gone air freight). The captain came over the loudspeaker, "Ladies and gentlemen, we cannot taxi to the runway until **all** are in their seats." This guy now had 160 people waiting and two stewardesses opening and closing all the compartments trying to fit in his last bit of excess baggage. If dagger stares or muttered comments could have killed, his remains would have easily fit in one of the armchair ashtrays. (Yes, we can and do dump our stuff on everyone else.)

Not only is no man an island, few of us own the island to store it on! Your stuff is a stumbling block to many! Clutter causes fires and accidents, attracts vermin and vandals, and upsets neighbors. All of which affects others inside the family and out.

Clutter Steals Your Storage Space

When half the stuff in your cabinet is stuff you don't use, it isn't just innocently lying there—it's stealing 50 percent of your usable space. Go into your closet or kitchen with some masking tape, tape off 50 percent of the space in there, and sit back and look at it. That's exactly what junk and clutter is doing. It isn't just hibernating harmlessly in limbo; with all that stuff in your way you have to cram harder, look harder, and walk farther to get and use things. We'd ordinarily fly into an instant fit if anyone or anything took or encroached on our room, but clutter does it so cleverly we don't even realize it.

The one-third bad really hurts the two-thirds good. Just as a small haze can ruin the sharpness of a great picture, too much junk and clutter sprinkled in (like oversalting) can ruin the taste and appeal of the good stuff.

Clutter Accounts for the Lion's Share of the Cleaning!

When I started up my cleaning company more than forty years ago, people would call and ask "How much to clean my house?" We'd ask right back: "how big?"

We'd whiz through some jobs (exactly the same size and age home) in a half day, while others would take twice the time. We finally realized it wasn't our speed or skill that made the difference. When someone asked for an estimate on a floor, room, or house, we could bid much more intelligently if instead of asking "how big" we asked: can we find it? The amount of stuff in a house affects cleaning time more than anything else. In some (too many) homes most of our time was spent *digging past, carrying, relocating, and protecting* people's stuff. Getting to the wall or window often took three times longer than cleaning it. And was more work! As I said earlier about 40 percent of all the time it takes to "clean" a residence is just handling, getting around, and moving clutter and litter out of the way. That alone, folks, without any other reason, is enough to justify a jiffy dejunking. When you try to clean a clutter-crammed place you have no choice but to move discouragingly slow to get around things without breaking anything or tipping it over, and if you want to be thorough you must not only move the mass, but *replace* it all when you're done. Your vacuum cord hangs up on extra stuff, you drip or splash on it. And how often do you have to stop to search through the vacuum bag for that something-or-other you heard clinking up the hose?

But worst of all is how many more **things** it means you have to clean—all those extra fronts, backs, sides, tops, bottoms, fringes, ruffles, legs, shelves, dividers, stands, pedestals, edges, ledges, and curves. It's no exaggeration to say that a cluttered room has hundreds of times the amount of surface area to clean than an uncluttered one—and many more kinds of materials (which calls for a change of equipment and tactics for each one).

Cleaning will never go away, but at least 40 percent of it will dematerialize when your clutter does. Now that's incentive to incinerate!

All Clutter Is In Harm's Way!

Okay, so maybe you don't care; you're willing to die in your catacombs of clutter. What about the danger your stuff poses to others—and I don't just mean emotional or spiritual, or even the bad example it gives them. I mean the danger of actually harming their physical bodies. If I told you that right now you have stuff stashed about that could permanently scar, cripple, or even kill someone, would you take dejunking a little more seriously? Sure you would.

The Worker's Compensation case books are full of stories of maintenance crews who have been scalded with acids and the like as they dump our household garbage. All of us have some of this—it's called toxic trash, something we bought to unclog a drain, degunk an engine, kill a pest, treat a foundation, treat an ailment, or even do a cleaning job. Every year tens of thousands of Americans die (and many more are injured) by poisoning. Much of this is caused by clutter.

My grandson Alex was a natural-born hunting dog when he was a toddler. If I let him, he'd not only find anything and everything under, in, or on top of, he'd test it all by tasting it—as your little one does. We deserve the consequences of much of our clutter and junk, for being such hoarders and keepers. But who wants to be responsible for little ones (or anyone else) getting burned, maimed, punctured, or poisoned—all because we insisted on getting our forty dollars' worth by saving a few leftover pills? The potential dangers here are so great that there's simply no excuse good enough to keep this kind of clutter around. I can't send my grandson to sniff out yours, and I advise you not to wait until one of yours, or the neighbor's, finds your clotted pool chlorine or the 25 cents worth of brake fluid you were waiting to squeeze out of the bottom of the can, or the old DDT you couldn't bring yourself to dispose of. In order to store or keep something, a lot of us take it out of one container and put it in another, smaller one, such as a milk bottle, thinking we'll remember what it is. We seldom do, and then we spend years looking at that white powder or green liquid, wondering what it is, but not throwing it out because maybe it's valuable. We'll never use it, because we're not sure what it is, so we've created not just junk and clutter but a killer trap!

I remember vividly one case where no injury occurred (at least to people), but it could as easily have. I changed the antifreeze in my car and wanted to use the plastic jug to carry extra radiator water in the car, so I poured the antifreeze into a glass bottle that used to hold rug shampoo. It sat on the shelf for a month, and then one day it was gone. One of my crew returned from a carpet-cleaning job, shirt drenched with sweat. "Boy, that new rug shampoo was some-thing, Don. We never could get it to foam up." (At least the customer's carpet never froze up again.)

Tons of your garage and under-the-sink stuff is not only worthless, it's dangerous! Don't let your guard down just because three-fourths of it is gone—that little bit in the bottom, even one swallow, can do it!

You may have been smart or careful enough to dispose of all your potential casualty clutter, but just in case, here's a checklist:

❑ Any kind of acid—hard-water removers, concrete etching acids, brick cleaners, etc.
❑ Stain removers such as acetone or rust remover.
❑ Paint thinner, lacquer thinner, and other solvents.
❑ Paints (saved long enough, they look like pudding and make magnificent fire fuel).
❑ Old car batteries (battery acid is nothing less than life-threatening).
❑ Antifreeze and coolants (these are poison but taste sweet—which gets a lot of pets).
❑ Open cans of motor oil (can cause fires and pollute the environment).
❑ Mole or rodent poison (made of things like phosphorus and strychnine).
❑ Pool chlorine and other pool-treatment powders (can be a worse way to go than drowning).
❑ Ammonia cleaners (especially bad when mixed with something else, such as bleach—which will create poisonous gas).
❑ Old plastic bags and old refrigerators (can smother).
❑ Worthless old heavy metal parts (can smash or crush).
❑ Sharp-pointed tools—old blades for mowers and garden tractors, etc.
❑ Tangled rope (can strangle).

- ❏ Ancient canned goods (can give you more than a bellyache).
- ❏ Old medicines and pills of any kind (forget trying to create the impression you have a complete home pharmacy; it ain't worth it).
- ❏ Extra knives and scissors you don't really need.
- ❏ Heavy or precariously stacked stuff stored high up.
- ❏ Aerosols with the tops missing **still compressed** (which can become bombs if incinerated).

Amazing how much of this stuff you have, huh?

For safe disposal of toxic trash, call the Environmental Protection Agency in your city, county, or state for detailed instructions. They will have a brochure, sheet, or booklet on the subject (maybe even downloadable on the web, if you have a computer). Since the exact name of the department that concerns itself with hazardous waste may vary from state to state or city to city, you may have to call the main information or consumer assistance number of the government body in question first, to be referred to the right place. Many areas also have regularly scheduled collection dates, or dropoff points, for potentially dangerous household trash.

The University of Missouri Outreach and Extension, Office of Waste Management, is an excellent source of information of all kinds about hazardous waste, including how to organize a community "SWAP" so that potentially dangerous materials can be given to others who will use them up. Contact the Household Hazardous Waste Project, 1031 East Battlefield, Suite 214, Springfield, MO 65807. Phone 417-889-5000. Website: http://muextension.missouri.edu/xplor/wasteman/ww5000.htm.

> When a piece of junk injures us, physically or mentally, that ought to be a hint to move it to the top of the heave list.

The *Full* Cost of Clutter

A friend of mine was getting along fine, had his life on schedule, was making some good progress in paths he wanted to pursue. Then one fatal day someone gave him a chiming clock. He didn't need it (he had four fully functioning clocks in the living room already), didn't want it (chimes amplified in his hearing aid), but was touched by the thoughtful intent of the gift. So he hauled it home and wound it up, and like lots of junk and clutter, it began ticking away (our time!). Within a week it quit, and his wife nagged him to "do something" about it. So next morning, Saturday, instead of catching his little daughter's soccer game, he hauled it to the jeweler for a pre-op exam. Two hours later, he gave a one-hour explanation of the diagnosis to his wife and family. Early the next week the donor of the clock heard of its malfunction and dropped by for a thirty-minute talk about it during my friend's busiest part of the day. Two days later the jeweler called and informed my friend this was a rarer model than he had thought and parts would have to be ordered from Switzerland. "Is that okay?" "Sure, we've come this far, what choice do I have?" Then my friend worried quietly for three weeks about the cost of the parts and of getting them here. The parts arrived, and the bill came to $89! My friend drove in again and hauled the clock (which he never needed or wanted in the first place) home. They had a family argument over the bill that evening, the clock chimes reminding them all the while of the time and money and energy spent. Then it quit again! What could my friend do but haul it *back* to the repair shop so the jeweler could call Switzerland to complain about inferior parts? A month later and another bill, and it was fixed again. My friend brought it home again (by now everyone hated the clock but they had such an investment in it that getting rid of it was out of the question). The donor, hearing of its second incapacity, was distraught that he had given such a faulty gift and in a grand gesture of amendment went out and bought another clock for my friend. A full account of the fate and adventures of the second clock would fill the rest of this chapter, but in short, like the first, for no good reason, it took a lot from my friend's life. The second clock, as long as he kept it, kept him from the things that really mattered to him—of course he kept the first defective clock, too.

The Economy of Clutter

The following "confession" came forth in a college course in Behavioral Science that uses *Clutter's Last Stand* as a text:

After reading the chapter "The Economy of Clutter," I stopped to consider how much caring for our junk has cost us. In the last four years we have moved our personal belongings six times and our business five times. This spring the cellar we store the business assets in will become the new fire station. Now we must move for the seventh time.

My husband is an appliance repairman, a carpet and vinyl layer, a mechanic, and a bit of a carpenter. Therefore our assets consist of all the tools of each trade; old appliances, each in need of repair; business records and stationery; stuff that won't fit into the house; three old cars awaiting restoration; and a large collection of Chevy parts.

For each move, it has taken us at least a month to move and reorganize—let's say 160 hours per move. This next move will bring the total hours spent moving to 960. At $4 an hour, that comes to $3,840. Storage and power costs have totaled $1,697 to date. Estimating $20 gas for each move adds another $120. This adds up to a grand total of $5,657 for four years of junk storage.

All this stuff is supposed to make money. Assuming that to be true, I computed the possibilities. My husband normally gets $16 an hour for appliance repair. If it took forty hours to repair the used appliances he would realize $640 on appliance sales. If it took three forty-hour weeks to restore each car, each car would have an added worth of $1,920. The total money that could possibly be earned from our storage assets, calculating it this way, would come to $6,400. Subtracting the total cost of the stored assets from the possible income equals $743 for 400 hours of work. Four years of storing and moving has netted a possible income of $1.86 an hour.

These figures do not include time spent searching through the clutter for specific items that are somehow never found when needed. Nor do they reflect time and money spent protecting our clutter. These figures also don't take into consideration that my husband's earning potential is $16 an hour instead of the $4 allowed for moving wage. However, this project has helped me to realize the cost of owning things.

I surely felt the emotional drain of moving all our many belongings and knew it interfered with our income during the moves, but I didn't realize how much all this clutter was costing us in dollars and cents. I would love to report that I have hired someone to blow up the cellar containing these prize possessions, but I don't know of anyone in that line of business. Or report that we had a garage sale and sold everything so now we won't have to move again, but no such action was taken nor is it likely to. I can only report that I have learned that packrats don't prosper and why.

Since the letter you just read was written more than a dozen years ago now, folks, imagine what those clutter costs would be if updated to the new millennium!

The Extra Charges of Clutter

No one springs into action quicker than someone who suddenly discovers he's been charged twice for the same thing. Whether he's scanning a sales slip, an office order, a restaurant check, or a bank statement, if a double charge is spotted—even a few pennies' worth—the air resounds with roars of righteous wrath. The fact that someone else took our money makes it a matter of principle, not just petty cash. I've seen people make $5 phone calls, write four-page letters, and even travel a hundred miles to right or recover a two-dollar double charge. Paying twice for the same thing is undoubtedly the most un-American activity around.

So what height of fury would we reach if we stopped to consider that clutter charges us not once but at least a dozen times over for the same thing?

Consider the corner lot, for example, that my partner Mark and I bought several years ago on a commercial street, with the intention of building a new district office for our cleaning company. We paid $28,000 for it, and when we finally realized it was too small, we sold it for $35,000—to all appearances (and basic math) a nice clean profit of $7,000. But land, like clutter, has keeping costs. Eight years' interest on the money it cost to buy it came to $23,000, taxes were $2,700, maintenance and upkeep over the years we owned it came to $580, advertising to sell $400, Realtor fees $2,500. Like clutter and junk, the land just lay there all that time, and the bottom line was a loss of $21,000 on our investment. Startling, isn't it? Yet nobody snatched all that money away dishonestly. Overhead did it.

The extra costs of keeping clutter are much sneakier than adding an extra set of side-view mirrors or keeping down the weeds on a vacant lot. They're hidden in little phone calls, storage fees, relocation and repair of things we never use, and all the other operations we have to perform for our extra stuff. Cut your losses today!

> We all have a thing about waste —we don't throw anything away, any object, that is. All that expensive time, energy, and attention we waste doesn't horrify us or even occur to us… because it's intangible.

Packrat Rationalization #343: "If I get rid of it, I'm throwing money away."

You lose more money keeping unused and unloved things around. They occupy expensive space and valuable time. And the cost of space in your home can easily exceed $100 per square foot!

Save Now, Pay Later

We're all somehow under the impression that storage is free. Let's take a look at what it really costs to store something, in business or at home.

- Rent (for the part of your home devoted to storage, plus any storage bins elsewhere).
- Construction and purchase costs of storage devices (shelves, sheds, special storage structures, boxes, and containers of all kinds).
- Maintenance of the stored stuff (cleaning and organizing it, plus heat, lights, air conditioning,

humidifying, dehumidifying, pestkillers).
- Cost to move it from one location to another.
- Insurance and security service and devices (on the stuff and the place it's stored).
- Cost of your time to shop for it, argue over it, and eventually dejunk it.

A lot to pay for things you don't want or need!

The whole enormous array of storage devices isn't cheap either—those trays, bins, dividers, containers, chests, trunks, wardrobes, hooks, racks, garment bags, lockers, boxes, labels, file cabinets, file folders, hanging files, bookcases, additional shelves and cupboards and closets and dressers and storage sheds. And to keep what? It's easy today to spend more for the storage container than what it contains will ever be worth.

This excerpt from an ex-clutterer's letter highlights this often-overlooked cost of clutter.

"I found your message at just the right time…. We had become so involved with clutter that we'd literally run out of space and had called an architect to see if we could enclose some open porches and move a couple of walls to make more closet space and more bookshelves. He measured this and that and called back to tell us that our house was already over the maximum for the lot size in our area and he doubted we could get a permit to add on or enclose without a lot of hassle—so we were looking inward when *Clutter's Last Stand* entered our lives. Thanks so much for writing it. You have a rare ability to hit one's guilty area without bringing out one's defenses—it's nice to be inspired to action for a change."

A while ago my corporation was moving to a centralized accounting system, so we researched and studied and listened to salesmen, and finally with great anticipation bought an $85,000 computer. In our minds it was a magnificent, seemingly limitless machine. Three months later the head accountant brought some bad news: the computer was full to capacity. It couldn't take and digest the output any more. Every one of us was astounded. It couldn't be—but it was. Just as we finally reach our clutter saturation point, when our space and patience runs out, the computer had had too much, had maxed out. So now we had three choices:

1. A new and bigger computer (at a staggering cost).

2. A piggyback system for it (a mere $15,000), which would soon be filled up too.

3. Getting rid of some of the "stuff" in it to create more room.

The choice we considered last and the best one in the end is the same as the best answer for junk. Funny how we try to get around or accommodate or deal with a problem instead of eliminating the source.

> The cost of taking it with you is the same as sending it on ahead— *too much.*

Clutter Is a Constant Diversion

"You can't take it with you" summarizes the final packing-and-leaving reality, but it's in fact pertinent to this very minute of living. You're going places now whether you're 16, 22, 31, 43, 52, 64, or

75. You can't take it all with you today, never mind at the end of your life. Every time you leave (for college, a new job, to get married, to a new home), you can't simply up and go; you have a semi of junk pending at each location. This is a real energy smasher for you—an emotional, mental, and physical drain that makes it impossible to do anything quickly or efficiently.

Clutter is a constant diversion of thought, direction, and progress. It distracts and slows us up both physically and mentally. Out of sight, out of mind might be true with a lover or a landlord—but never with junk.

Clutter Usurps Your Affection

I've heard some amazing excuses over time for keeping carloads of clutter. One

gentleman, as I mentioned earlier, justified it as good "insulation." He was right in more ways than one. When we're building something we use insulation in walls, ceilings, floors, etc. Its effectiveness at blocking out heat or cold is called its "R" factor. Insulation creates dead air space that retards the transfer of temperature, moisture, and even sound, so the right kind of junk stacked deep enough, heaven forbid, could indeed be good insulation. But junk if far more than a weather barrier. It can even insulate us emotionally. The more stuff we bury ourselves in, the more things piled around us, the less warmth and feeling can be transferred to and from us, the less emotional vibrations can be felt or given off. Just as insulation shields us from the elements, so does it from affection. For someone to interact with us they have to hunt, dig, and blaze a trail to us. When we're well insulated we have a way of being oblivious to what the weather is outside. In a house that can be a great thing; in the matters of the heart, it's social suffocation. Waiting for a clutterer to come out into the open, rummage around and assemble themselves and find everything they think they need to operate can be a real turnoff. If you've been accused of being a little cold or distant, your stuff might be the real barrier. Another good reason to reduce your "R" (Rat) factor today.

> Ever notice that clutter has a yeast effect? Even if you just leave it alone it rises! It expands, seemingly by itself.

The Cost of a Free Mule

A country gentlewoman, for example, was given the gift of a fine mule to decorate and add authenticity to her small acreage. A year of mule ownership netted an interesting log of expenses. I asked her for a list of "possession payments" the mule had kicked up:

Calls and travel to inspect and research the animal before accepting it	$52
Purchase and installation of electric fence; repair of existing woven wire fence	545
Batteries for electric fence (per year)	40
Sheet cut up to make markers to hang on fence	20
Two new gates installed (for easy mule-visitor access)	177
Repairs on stall in old barn to house the mule	100
Water pan, feed bucket, salt block, curry set	49
Discing of pasture to remove mule footholes	135
Upgrade of pasture grass (vet nixed existing fescue for mules)	300
Lost income from field generally hayed for profit (per year)	120
Corral to move mule closer to house for viewing	450
Books on mule training	25
Mule-training starter kit: saddle, and bridle, lead rope, reins	407
Collar, harness, and mule cart	700
Finally hiring someone else to break the mule	350
Apples for mule treats, grain, hay (per year)	420
Wormers, hoof trim	47
Baby pictures/copies for unbelieving friends (per year)	120
Estimated orthopedic bills (for being kicked, tossed, and stepped on) (per year)	2,500
Time invested in one year of mule care (petting, viewing, brushing, feeding, watering, exercising, repairing electric fence, and removing manure)	5,400
One hour a day explaining "why you own a mule" (per year)	3,600
To make everything complete: one album of Bill Monroe's *Muleskinner Blues*	10
TOTAL FIRST YEAR COST OF A FREE MULE	**$15,567**

Walls adorned with pictures and paintings and trappings of every imaginable type, rooms laden with wall-to-wall furniture and statues and collections and decor, shelves and tables lined with trinkets and ornaments and souvenirs and bric-a-brac... they all have their cost, they all exact something from our lives, they all demand our attention and our investment. Do the returns justify the investment?

CHAPTER 4

It's Now or Never:

Time to Attack

At an auction, it's going, going, gone!

With our junk, it's going, going, going, going, going, going, going, going, going, gone? Well, maybe someday... Sigh!

When to Face Your Piles of Postponement (Junk)

For most of us, our sense of time was established as children, when time was timeless. As adults, we're not merely amazed but frustrated to see months go by now as days once did. Yet we all hold out hope that as the years crowded with family raising and intense living ease up and retirement is in sight, once again time will be forever. It doesn't work that way—time only accelerates and *years* flash by as days once did. I continue to ask audiences of adults, "Now that you're older, lots of you retired, how many notice you have more time than ever before?" I get a chorus of groans—never a nod.

It's now or never! There'll be *less* time after that four-week vacation, not more. And because dealing with that dungeon of doubtful assets we call clutter always comes in second to fixing, painting, redecorating, etc., we never get around to it. Junk is the germ of the disease of disorganization. Clean it out before you get caught up in other duties and a lot of those other duties will dematerialize. There's no time later, if you're counting on it. If you don't do it now you'll die with your thirty pairs of boots on.

Do It Now

Now is the time to launch into your private landfill. You've been in a holding pattern too long—circling, ever circling, like an indecisive buzzard, approaching, testing the elements. Stay too long in any holding pattern and you can count on running out of gas! Clutter cuddles so close to us that we get used to its presence, like weight slowly gained; delaying its departure one more day or a hundred would seem to have few alarming consequences.

But waiting until later almost always punishes us, with fines, late charges, missed flights, missed deals, memberships canceled, infection or secondary complications setting in. Don't you always cuss yourself for putting off Christmas shopping, for leaving the mower or bike outside till morning (got swiped), for not helping someone, or failing to mend a relationship before it was too late?

Wait Is Always Too Late!

Why does it always take trouble to inspire a cleanup action out of us?

When do people hit the Bible and the old prayer bones most enthusiastically? Seldom when things are going well; *always* when they're in trouble.

We don't throw things out of the fridge until they spill and stink and rot.

Few of us pay much attention to our teeth until they decay and ache.

We won't clean it up or move it out of the way until someone trips over it and breaks an ankle.

Only when things get hot for us do we seem to generate the steam to face them. Until then, our nature is to file it and pile it. Yet all this time we know we're going to have to face the problem someday—generally after it's been compounded by our procrastination.

Clutter accumulates so quietly and insidiously, so gradually, we usually don't even know it has us.

I remember reading a story about a woman who brought home (like clutter) an orphan lion cub from her brother-in-law's exotic collection. It was three feathery pounds of fur, so cute (like clutter) that she kept it (like clutter). It grew slowly into a pet, a favorite thing (like clutter), then became a big pet that took a lot of her time and strength to care for (like clutter). She was so close to it, so fond of it, that she didn't take the few cuffs and scratches she got seriously. She just never faced and comprehended its size and strength. And one fine day her friendship became nourishment for the once tiny animal she loved.

I bet right this minute your clutter is chewing on you a little, too. It may just be sampling you now; it will consume you later. If you leave this life early, it'll pounce on your family instead.

Clutter and cholesterol are a lot alike. Both are caused by too much "fat" and extras. Both plug the flow of life—very slowly but always deadly in the end. Both seem to go for the main arteries to the heart! We don't notice the pain either, because it's so gradual. And it doesn't put up any distress or panic flags—in fact it probably falsely flashes welcome signs instead. It cuts off our circulation and we never know how bad it is until the final showdown. The solution for excess clutter and excess cholesterol is about the same—for cholesterol it's **by-pass** surgery, for clutter it's **pass it by** (rather than buy it). Do it now!

Multiplication—Another Reason to Do It Now!

The longer you wait, the worse it gets! As long as clutter is there, it encourages more clutter. If there's one empty pop can on a vacant lot, another will follow and then a couple more, then whole bags of trash. Then the place becomes a trash site. Leave it and you'll soon have a landfill. And later, when you or your heirs have to hash it out, it's swelled to such enormous proportions that a bulldozer is about the only answer.

Once we get into the swing of things, we go on "automatic pile it." And like a sandstorm or a snowstorm, those little grains or flakes flying silently around don't look like much, but given a little time—overnight or so—and the whole face of the landscape is changed. And we're impressed with the amount we have to shovel away to find the driveway.

Now is the hour to make peace with your excess pieces and pounds of possession. Enough foreplay; its time for the act (or better yet, the **ax**!)

It's the Day of the Dumpster for junk, but for you it's new life—better, freer, with more time to do what you really want. You aren't winding down; you're breaking the bonds of clutter bondage. It's like a mini-resurrection for you, so why wait? Now is the long-awaited day of displeasure with our treasures. Why wait to be a winner? Remember, lingerers are losers.

A decision to make decluttering Number 1 is what will make you a Number 1.

> There won't be time later. There is no later with junk and clutter, only more.
>
> ---
>
> Saddest words of tongue and pen are "It might have been."
>
> ---
>
> Saddest word of junk and clutter… "someday."

Oh, for the Relief of It All!

Consider the story told to me by Helen Exley, one of my British publishers, when my wife and I were staying with her and her husband in their charming fourteenth-century cottage in the heather country of North Wales. On the mantel was a rather attractive plate. As my wife commented on it, Helen walked over to it and said, "It never was this beautiful before, to me. You see, this plate is worth untold dollars, it's two thousand years old. We wanted to, and did display it. But before we returned to London, on every one of our visits here, I always had to pack it up and take it home with us, and then get it out when we got home and put it back on display. It seems I was always tired when the time came to pack it, and I worried about it all the way to and from—the viewing was somehow never worth the handling each time. I did this for several years, and then one Sunday afternoon, as we were hurrying to get back to the city, the plate slipped from my hand and broke. It wasn't shattered, only glue-together broken. I was shocked at my inner reaction—instead of horror and anguish, a great flood of peace and relief came over me, and my subconscious said, 'Now I can glue it together (no one will know) and put it up on the mantel and *leave* it there for all to enjoy, including us.' It was a day of rejoicing instead of a black day. I was released from the burden of guarding it forever."

Haven't we *all* had things we clamped onto, that really clamped onto us instead—and one day when they were taken in a fire or a flood, the same big rush of relief came over us? Because when we had them, we also had the obligation to use them, or at least be constantly aware of them. It's like having a big home and fancy furniture when we really want to be alone most of the time. But we do just the opposite, invite and have people over to see the place constantly because of the fact that we have it. We *have* to use it, to feel justified that we got it. Start feeling relief today—start decluttering today!

> "I plan to sell the silver goblets that were given to me. They're always tarnished and are never used because they're too much work to clean. Then I think I'll work up to the silver tea service that has never been used and has been carted to at least four different addresses."

The Best Reason of All to Do It NOW

We're all in a daily struggle (if not turmoil) to be a better person, trying to kick our bad habits—to control our temper, lose weight, clean up our language, or even our morals, master a skill, measure up to an expectation. We often seem to fall short of the strength to pull these changes off in our lives, but we struggle and struggle and struggle. Most of the conquering or overcoming we're trying to do here is a simple matter of cleaning the clutter, getting the garbage out of our conduct or behavior—easy to say, but like all mental and emotional changes, tough, real tough to do. I promise you that when you start uncluttering your life by getting rid of the physical stuff first, you'll establish a habit and pattern that will quietly creep into all the other areas of your life and give you the strength and momentum to master the mental snags. Watch it work—it even beats therapy sessions.

You Say You're Suffering Packrat Hangups?

"*You* Might Be Able to Dejunk, Maybe, But Me, I'm a Confirmed Packrat!"

We might be stuck with the face or figure we have, but all that stuff all over the place? Never. It can disappear without a brain transplant or plastic surgery. Can it really? Can even I, the king or queen packrat, go from hopeless to junkless? You can indeed. What are you waiting for?

A sharp young man comes to mind. Shy all his life, he would gladly have chosen execution over speaking in public. He'd moved to our small community from New York, and he always sighed when he explained what a hopeless coward he was in front of people. He traveled with me to one of my speaking engagements once, and I asked him if he would say a few words to the crowd if the opportunity presented itself. He turned pale, so I told him to jot down just four little experiences he'd told me about; he could then stand up and relate those. When I called on him during my speech, he did stand up and start telling about himself and his family and some of the experiences he'd had in the big city. The crowd loved it, and they showed it; he felt it and kept talking and talking. When he was finished they mobbed him, and later at home tears of relief flooded his face. For all those years he'd been missing one of the biggest thrills in life, a chance to influence others and even change others' lives. He now speaks regularly all over the country! And all because of a simple little change he was sure he couldn't make.

Likewise, an employee who came to work for me in Sun Valley looked longingly at skiers shooting by at forty miles per hour, fearlessly schussing the mountain. "I couldn't do that in a million years," he said. Then someone talked him into a lesson on the bunny hill and one week later he whizzed by me at sixty miles per hour—down the most challenging slope at the famous resort. He'd had it in him all the time; he just hadn't done it.

You know how much fun it is in fairy tales, movies, and sit-coms when something is changed—zap—by magic? With a snap of the fingers something is done or gone or different or better. In play or pretend this is pretty thrilling, but we can do the very same thing in reality—the minute we quit waiting for something or somebody to change things, or for things to change themselves. After all, it's our stuff, yours and mine, not public property; we're the deciding judge and jury and fairy godmother of it and the only ones who can zap it.

Just think of all the changes that make you feel good: a change of sheets, a change of clothes, a change of scenery, a change of diet, job, vehicle. Think of how much younger, stronger, bolder, more positive and ambitious it made you feel. So get on with it—facing up to your stuff—and change it. Your life will change, in more ways than you ever imagined. You'll be out of the packrat race and back in the human race!

The No-Headway Syndrome

"I should," "I want to," "I've tried." Why have you failed in your decluttering so far, and why are you still sinking? Tossing junk and clutter it like going on a diet, getting religious, learning a new language—it's a fight and a struggle and often we don't seem to be getting anywhere. Some things set us up for failure in any worthy mission. A big one is expecting that it will be easy, that "it won't hurt a bit," that it's "no sweat." We may honestly believe—we may even be told—that we won't have to strain ourselves, and when we find that we do, we get discouraged.

I can still remember the first dentist I ever went to. I must have been seven or eight years old at the time and the dentist at least seventy, with a hand that shook like an elm in Kansas wind. In those days they melted the metal for a filling by putting a hot iron in your mouth. Any number of times old Shaky Hand burned my mouth or cut my lip up while my proud mother looked on. When the old fellow finished, she looked at me, smiled, and said, "Now that didn't hurt a bit, did it?" Of course it did! And so does lots of dejunking at first. Anyone who tells you it's easy isn't leveling with you. Letting go is one of the most mentally painful processes around, and oddly enough it can be even worse with things. We've usually had to face the fact that people live and then die, but we've never done that with our junk. In our hearts we've assumed it will live forever, and admitting otherwise is awful!

No doubt about it: Dejunking is an emotional drain. It's mental as well as physical work. It took a lifetime to round up your treasures, and so it might be hard to sleep at first, or to hear a room actually echo when the corral is empty or almost so. I know, "These are memories!" That's good! Memories are the feast of the future, a private pleasure we have earned and deserve. And some of what we keep for memories is profoundly positive stuff. But most of your memory mounds are a mess, doing you little good. A good enthusiastic dejunking raid is like trimming toenails, pruning trees, spading gardens: it puts old, dead, lost, forgotten memories to work again. I'm not asking you to always toss things—only to shift them into gear so they operate, do something useful, work for you.

If you can't find it, why have it?

Fear of REGRET: The Real Root of Retaining Rubble

I found reading a professional psychologist's analysis of why we junk ourselves up and keep ourselves junked

interesting and in fact in accord with my findings as a professional cleaner. I can give you the bottom line and save you the need to get a Ph.D. It's fear of regret. Weakness, greed, gifts, sincere intentions, etc., might be the reason we got something, but keeping it—well, it's primarily regret that we fear to face. If and when we get rid of it, we might want or need it. If we don't let it go, it's always there (somewhere) to be found and caressed. Even when we know our clutter is malignant and inoperable, if it's still safely in the rest home we are spared the pangs of remorse. The psychologists call this "avoidance"—which is not wanting to face something unpleasant, such as the thought of anything being gone forever. It's a thousand-to-one chance, but there is that chance. I might truly need it someday.

We always hear about the few success stories—the one piece of land or overlooked treasure that appreciated in value and sold for so much. And then we waste a ridiculous amount of worry on something that happens only very seldom. Since writing *Clutter's Last Stand* in 1984, I've asked millions of people on network TV, on radio, and in the newspapers, and tens of thousands of people in person at seminars, to tell me of something they or someone else kept that produced a great profit in pocketbook or life. Likewise, I've asked for any real regrets or unhappy consequences they're had from the act of decluttering. I have had one or two who regret some family record or notebook was chucked in an overzealous dejunking surge, but still in more than sixteen years now, with millions of people exposed to this question, no one has told me of any great or even tiny tragedy that happened because of dejunking—none. They may have heard of some hearsay, but as for real fact or something personally known to them—nothing. On the other hand, I can produce tons of evidence to show how keeping things destroyed marriages, relationships, mental states, and respect.

Risk? There is little or none to worry about. Don't waste your valuable emotion on imagined remorse. The reality of freedom outweighs the risk by at least a thousand times, so let go. One "maybe" isn't worth 200 cartons full of stuff.

Decluttering Anxiety Therapy!

If you can't shake decluttering anxiety, there is something you can do to reduce it. It's based on a proven psychological principle called pre-visualizing.

As Dr. Richard Silvestri of Glen Rock, New Jersey, suggests, sit yourself down and vividly imagine the act of dejunking before you ever do it. Imagine yourself going into the room or area and confronting your stuff. What exactly will you do? Put all the clear-cut junk into the trash, all the not-sures into a pile. How will you deal with the not-sures? Throw away some, keep some, etc.

Track your thoughts and feelings as you do this exercise, and every time you reach a point where doing one thing seems easy and doing something else seems harder, follow the track of what seems harder. In that direction you will uncover your underlying fears and doubts and anxieties.

Then take each fear or doubt—go for the worst case imaginable—and mentally find a solution or way to deal with it. What exactly *would* you do if you threw something out and found out later it was valuable? Or if someone came and asked you for it? What if you didn't examine something closely enough before you dumped it and then felt really mad or silly? What will you do or say to yourself when you discover you really did need it? What will you say to Mother when she discovers you *didn't* save and cherish it forever?

As you face these questions and work them over in your mind, you will gradually uncover the real issues involved and desensitize yourself to them. It's a proven psychological principle—the more you brood on and immerse yourself in something, the sooner it will lose its hold on you. You'll also become a master of the issues involved and begin to feel 100 percent ready to handle any challenge as to "why you threw **that** away." A feeling of mastery in anything makes us more willing and eager to do it. And as we confront and come to understand the forces at work here, we gain confidence and the sense that *we* are in command.

This same technique can be used to prevent and treat dejunker's remorse, or any regret, depression, or delayed negative reaction to having gotten rid of something.

Since dejunking can be anxiety-filled, it's best not to do it when you're in a high anxiety state—like right after or during family tragedy or hardship, or when you've been hit with a nasty surprise of some kind (other than what you're finding in the boxes).

Why Fear or Put Off Dejunking?

Lots of life's big accomplishments call for elaborate preparations or a big investment, but this one—the one that will most affect your life—takes:

- No special training or skill
- Very little equipment or supplies
- No machinery (except possibly a vacuum)
- No special location
- No money (in fact, it will save you money)
- No great physical stamina
- Little energy or fuel (just a little light bulb burning, usually)
- No particular weather, since most of it is done indoors
- No special time of day or night
- No help from anyone

You don't have any excuses not to do it!

Don't wait until your storage unit runs over and don't dejunk on the layaway plan. Bite the bullet and kick the habit!

How to Precipitate Dejunking

Changing our behavior, getting started doing something, especially something new or different, is always a test, a trial, a challenge. It takes a lot to get some of us to change or go straight.

"This is going to kill you, Harry, if you don't clean it out of your life." Does that scare Harry into action? Seldom! When the threat "it will kill you" doesn't necessarily move someone to action, change the way they eat, act, or collect... who or what can convince a junker to repent, or at least to begin the process?

Not a few people have suggested that the ultimate way to precipitate the dejunking process is to move. A determined junker, however, can perform transfer miracles at moving time and get a six-bedroom house worth of stuff somehow into a small apartment (with or without extra storage bins). And being forced to discard something is likely to launch them into a depression that costs more for psychiatry bills than staying in the big house would have.

Moving does often get us moving, but it's a forced situation, and no one is ever very happy with force. And it's all too easy to replace the lost with lots more. There are more workable ways to help get yourself to the point that you're willing to start. Here are my favorites for precipitating the junking process instead of wishing, waiting, etc.

1. Become aware—that it's worse than you think. If you emptied all the stuff in one room (or even just a couple of closets) in the middle of the floor and spread it out, you'd gasp for breath and wonder who multiplied it after you put it away. Few of us are fully aware of just how much we've got or how long we've had it. I made up an easy self-inventory sheet that will enable you to take a little sampling of what you have (and maybe uncover a few surprises, too). If you really want to rid yourself of hundreds of pounds of ugly house fat, just take this inventory. It'll be motivating, I promise!

The Home Excess Inventory Chart

Item	1 Number You Have on Hand	2 Number You Need and Use	3 Excess (Column 1 Minus Column 2)	4 Approx. Cost of the Excess	5 Space it Occupies
Sheets					
Suitcases					
Toys					
Scissors					
Knives					
Cookbooks					
Shoes (pairs)					
Belts					
Chairs					
Games					
Cars					
Cameras					
Barbecues					
Dish towels					
Pot holders					
Thermos bottles					
Coolers					
Extension cords					
Combs					
Cups and mugs					
Glasses					
Pots and pans					
Sets of silverware					
Toasters/toaster ovens, working & nonworking					
Coffeemakers					
Radios					
Televisions					
Umbrellas, regular and folding					
Flashlights, working and nonworking					
Framed (but unhung) pictures					
Books					
Scales (the kind you weigh yourself on)					
TOTAL					

My Clutter Bottom Line

If that doesn't quite do it, if you need even more of a catalyst for action, you can take the inventory idea a little further, as suggested by one of my readers, and literally inventory it all. (The result may remind you of when we hear a tape or see a picture or video of ourselves and exclaim, "No, that isn't me, no way, that's not me—is that really me?—you're kidding!")

"This works as nothing else does: **Make an inventory. Of everything**. When I say everything, I mean *everything*. Not just the big stuff like the furniture and valuables, but everything you ever bought or were given that now takes up space anywhere on your property.

"I've done such a project. I'm an artist and wondered where the fifty scissors I bought over the course of twenty years of married life had gone. Not to mention what all those keys on the dresser were for. So, at the rate of about two rooms per day, I opened drawers, emptied candydish catch-alls, looked under couches, counted shoes, and made a list of everything. I soon realized that every room has a catch-all of one sort or another, whether it's a dish, a drawer, a series of drawers, a cabinet, or the entire room. My inventory included the contents of the living room, dining room, upper and lower hallways, sun porch, garage, basement, toolshed, attic, back and front yards, back and side porches, the bathroom, and the kitchen, including all cabinets and the refrigerator. It ran to about 150 pages and became my husband's Christmas gift that year. Though it was valuable when our home was robbed, the real value was knowing all that we had, all that we didn't want, all that we didn't use, all that we wasted. The inventory made us more leery of making purchases on impulse and more set on using what we had. We finally

took out of the box the wonderful coatrack we bought in Germany, and hung it on a wall. We finally gave the gelato maker someone gave us (that we never used) to the church rummage sale.

"Just remember, list everything, even if you intend to throw it out immediately.

"And be sure to respect the privacy of *all* members of the family when you do this. Rooms, or portions of rooms, that are recognized as personal domains should be strictly off limits (if you would like to see these included in the general consciousness-raising, see if you can persuade the curators thereof to inventory their own private areas themselves)."

Lists, like accounts payable, always have more impact and reality than just thinking about doing something, or verbally hashing it over.

2. Consider how much of your time clutter consumes.

Converting ourselves to a dejunking program instantly would be simple if we could make a chart of how we've spent our lives in the past, such as the estimate below:

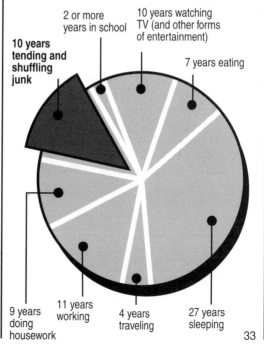

10 years tending and shuffling junk

2 or more years in school

10 years watching TV (and other forms of entertainment)

7 years eating

9 years doing housework

11 years working

4 years traveling

27 years sleeping

Dejunking our lives is the simple process of throwing out the waste and the worthless and using the space for new, live pursuits. What a great way to gain ten extra years and a thousand more things you've always wanted to do.

> "An earthquake can also be a great way to declutter. We had a 5.2 foreshock not long ago. That made me get really serious about preparedness. I made my husband reduce our shelving to waist-height shelves attached to the walls. For safety, nothing heavy can be placed higher than the first and second lowest shelves. Consequently, we got rid of lots of books and a heavy, outdated stereo system. We moved heavy, useless stuff off of every horizontal surface. We also got everything off the top of the fridge so that it couldn't fly. I moved my heavy bureau inside our closet. Now I think I don't need it at all. Now, unless our house collapses, there is virtually nothing that could fall on us... we don't have enough stuff around."

3. Let outsiders help you see it.

Isn't it amazing how much junk and clutter appears when company comes, or when we're having something installed or fixed by someone? Like dog or cat odor, it's not usually there, but as soon as we have guests, it comes back.

So order a new rug for the room or rooms in question, or invite someone you're in awe of to come stay for a week. I've seen would-be dejunkers start off totally discouraged and uncommitted, and then after a phone call from a special friend announcing a visit, become excited and eager to start. I've seen guys who never set foot in the garage until they're about to spring for a new truck or car. Then they can't wait to raid the side aisles and clear the floor.

4. Make a long trip (no matter what it costs, you'll save money).

We all deserve a couple of these in a lifetime. A world cruise, maybe Europe for a summer—something big (not a weekend in the Islands or you'll double your clutter). Something far off and extended triggers lots of little buzzers in our heads:

"Gee, I might not come back. Planes do go down."

"They say there are piranhas in these parts."

When packing and preparing for a big trip, we're in a totally different frame of mind than when we're just looking forward to a day or two somewhere. As we pack and go through things we might need in preparation, we end up looking in every drawer and closet and going through a lot of what we own. And the spirit of the upcoming adventure shifts our values from having and keeping to doing and seeing and being, so letting go is much easier. Trips put us into a spirit of condensation, too—a big trip is like a miniature move. Watch people pack for something like this. They're forced to acutely review and choose and reject, and the rejection is easy because it's offset by enthusiasm for the experience ahead. And because we secretly wonder if we'll ever be back, we can suddenly see a lot of things usually invisible to us—all the junk piled on the porch, for example, or the long-dead projects tucked here, there, and everywhere.

My wife and I go to Hawaii every winter for a couple of months, and the month before we leave, the dumpster fills up much more often.

5. Line up a good home for it before you round it up.

This one works wonders because yes, brothers and sisters, it's going to a better place.

We're all sentimental. *Something* can be loved as deeply as someone. We don't quit loving a person the minute life leaves them, nor can we always cast a chunk of stuff away without another thought—even after it's ceased to be useful. Feeling that "it deserves a decent home (or burial)" isn't romanticism, *it's reality.*

For example, I remember my cleaning company removing furnishings from a house that had had a fire. The insurance adjuster had determined that the front room was a total loss and everything had to be replaced. My strong-armed buddies and I just heaved the furniture brutally into the back of an old, wet truck, and they hit the truck bed with a crunch. The woman of the house winced and wept, as if we'd tossed her in along with it.

Don't we all feel like her about certain pieces of clutter? When we know our old house, car, appliance, or horse is going to have a "good home," it's 500 percent easier to let go graciously. Why do you think everyone always wants to know who the new owner will be? When we are told someone nice got it, we're regenerated and relieved—and then we can really let go.

Fear of waste and ungratefulness is one of the biggest reasons we don't part with things. Dejunking is easy when our junk has a decent place to go. So get a home for it (see page 164, and get on with it!

> "It will help someone through a bad time? Take it and take more right away!"

P.S. If all else fails, you can poke a hole in the water heater and flood the basement—or invite me to come visit.

You Know It's Time to Dejunk When...

- You read *Clutter's Last Stand* and that didn't do it.
- You can't carry your handbag for more than a block without shifting arms.
- You've been dating for several years and still haven't invited your date over.
- Your child's history class chooses your closet for their field trip.
- You still have a jar of Gerber's strained carrots and your youngest is nine.
- You only dare open your garage door after dark.
- You could never move—no one could mastermind such a major event.
- Your voice cracks saying the word "keepsake."
- You start your sentences with "I got" or "I bought" instead of "You know" or "Well."
- You put everything in see-through zippered bags so you can watch it.
- You have to get up and make a path for the meter reader.
- You are renting or using extra rooms just for stuff.
- You read the garage sale ads Sunday afternoon instead of the scriptures.
- Your closet's full but there's not much fit to wear.
- You can no longer convince yourself it'll all be valuable one day.
- You can see a use for a one-armed sweater.
- You catch yourself looking pensively at public dumps.
- You start pricing skids and pallets.
- You keep taking successful cuttings of plants you hate and nobody wants.
- You have three televisions: the one that works, the one that doesn't, and the one you're still too

busy to hook up (and its aerial system is already out of date).

- You have more empty jars than full ones.
- Yours is the only empty curb on Clean-Up Day.
- You buy three new pairs of bedsocks and find two packs you bought last autumn in the back of the drawer.
- Junk sorting is your biggest household chore.
- The owner holds the best stuff out for you before the garage sale opens.
- You know all the people in the first five yards of the flea market line.
- Your dream is to have the first pick of what's left from a move.
- You're discussing building a bigger house and the children are gone!

The choice is really clear. If you want to suffer and make sure others suffer, you don't have to do anything. If you have backbone and decency and any self-esteem, there's only one course to follow, by far the simplest and most rewarding—why not take it?

MARGE... MY LAST REQUEST.... BLOW UP MY WORKSHOP...

You have only three choices as to when to face it and do it.

1. Now (today)

You gain instant freedom, instant respect, and room for newer, more meaningful stuff. Everyone loves you and you save money—cash! It wards off other collections. You're available, open for action and growth, and you know you can't count on there being a later.

2. Later:

- The junk will have multiplied—doubled, tripled, or worse.
- You get more subjective, less decisive.
- All those other opportunities will have passed you by.
- You'll have less energy and lifting strength! (Your eyesight won't be as good, either.)
- Your collection is damaged, wrinkled, stained, stolen.
- Nags and insults increase.
- Insurance goes up!
- Your car is ruined (because there was never any room in the garage).
- You'll only be busier!
- You'll get all too used to having it around.

3. When You're Dead:

If you don't do it, you stick someone else with the job, and

- You lose your chance to choose the final resting place of your junk.
- You'll be responsible for a lot of fights and animosity in the family.
- The wrong people will benefit from all your efforts.
- The lawyers or the government will get anything of real value.
- Your stuff will be plundered and unappreciated.
- It's guaranteed there'll be a gross invasion of your privacy.
- You'll realize you never did use it!

One nice thing about decluttering now, before you're old and creaky and it's too late, is that you will have a chance to shift into gear and do some of those things you always meant to do. Later they will fade and be wasted; today you can rip into them. It's a simple matter of math—if the years you have left won't even dent that mountain of junk you're dragging around, you need to start dividing instead of multiplying.

CHAPTER 5

A 4-Step Program to Lower Your Clutter Count

A plan guaranteed to lose hundreds of pounds of ugly stash in 90 days or less!

1. Recognize:

That junk is bad!
And you *are* a junker.

2. Repent:

Admit that it's killing you (your energy, pocketbook, relationships).
And wearing the cloak of clutter is confining!

3. Remove:

Perform the actual exercises that take away the pounds. (See Chapters 6-16.)

4. Refrain:

From recluttering yourself.
Take the precautions you need to take to avoid gaining it all back! (See Chapter 17.)
Yes, just four simple steps: **Recognize** you are a junker and have a lot of junk. **Repent**—feel some genuine regret—that junk is keeping you from living fully and being loved and feeling good about yourself. **Remove**—the crux of the matter, and the heart of this book. And **Refrain,** or stay on the wagon afterward.

Planning Your Decluttering Campaign

Finding the Time to Give Your Junk the Knockout Punch

Don't worry about outfoxing the clock or calendar to find a "time" to dejunk. "If I just had the time"—you do have the time, lots of it, all you're ever going to have. The only question is are you going to use it or not? Time is allotted equally to every person on earth. No one gets more or less—and no matter what the other demands on you the secret is seizing all the unused time to sneak in a blow or two at your junk.

> No one really has an excuse not to declutter—it takes no preparation, no license, no practice, no permission or permit, no special place or time, requires no extraordinary coordination. You can dejunk while you are listening, visiting, resting, exercising, or even watching TV.

"Too Busy"

This is too miserable an excuse to even bring up. The reported burden of "busy" only serves notice of superior alternatives. I've seen it happen hundreds of times with busy people—a single sentence of the right words is spoken and they have all the time in the world. Even if you could become unbusy, idle or down time is probably a bad time to dejunk because you have no momentum in your soul. When you're just "hanging around" you tend to hang on to what's there. But when you're buried under problems, assignments, pressures, and demands, you're in a perfect frame of mind to master-map your road to freedom. You won't delay or debate forever because you have to make every move count. You'll get to it and get it over with. (Why do you think they say: "If you want to get something done, ask a busy person"?) Busy time is the *best* time to shed those unwanted shelves of stuff that've been paralyzing your living pattern.

Tell me a better time to toss the trash than when you're painting or doing deep cleaning. Preparing for a trip or move is another perfect time to unleash yourself on the tenants of your ten trunks. When you've just emerged from a relationship or a divorce, what more natural time to clear the slate? And it's when we're most deeply involved in projects and deadlines that we can see what's not really needed and get it out of the way.

Busy is the best time to battle emotional withdrawal pangs, too.

You are never going to put life on hold so you can shape up, then start up again. You don't *find* time, you *make* it.

Most junkers claim they don't have time to comb through and come to terms with their stuff. But they've actually proved otherwise—how did they manage to accumulate it? They obviously had lots of time to shop, look, sort, and store.

Should I Tackle It All at Once, or in Installments?

Take a few pointers from the professional boxers—there have been many different world champions over time and they all had *different* ways of achieving the final victory. Each concentrated on his opponent, but some beat on him aggressively the whole time, some danced around quickly and got in hundreds of little quick short jabs, and some waited and watched for the one big punch.

Whether you face the whole of it and tackle it all in one big, big project or reduce it to little bites is a matter of preference. The important thing is to do *something*. Small consistent grabs, or

Should you tackle it all at once...   *or a little at a time?*

one giant knockout blow—it all works, it all wins; the only real requirement is getting in the ring with it. In other words, the important thing isn't schedule or method, just commitment!

Stretches of time—even of half a day—are often better than "I'll do an hour a day until it's done." If it's only one little item on a long list of to-do's for the day, you can far too easily let it fall by the wayside—there's always something that seems more important and pressing than decluttering. Binge and surge and campaign decluttering will really advance your battle plan, when you can manage it. When you can do it all at once, it's great to get the job over and done with so you can enjoy the benefits without worrying about that drawn-out daily or weekly pecking away. Installment plans get old when the newness of anything wears off. On the other hand, if all you can manage is a little at a time, there's nothing you can't get done that way.

Time You Could Devote to Decluttering

- Weekends
- Long weekends
- Holidays (great for Independence Day and the best imaginable preparation for Thanksgiving, Christmas, or that big milestone birthday)
- Vacation
- Leave of absence or sabbatical
- Any "personal days" you have coming (what's more personal than this?)
- Snow days or rainy days
- While you're between jobs (decluttering helps deal with the depression and release the aggression you often feel then, too).

You could quit your second job for a while. Or drop some sport or hobby or class temporarily. Or do it in time you would otherwise have spent shopping. In fact, you could tell yourself you won't go shopping till you finish coming to terms with all you bought in the past.

And if you do set aside a chunk of time for dejunking, don't fall into the trap of spending most of it *deciding* to do it, instead of doing the actual deed. Decide ahead so you can use all your dejunking time just for dejunking.

Should You Set Up a Very Precise Schedule?

A lawyer I met in the course of my cleaning career was a real precision scheduler. He and his wife scheduled their romance for Tuesday and Friday only, at exactly 10:30 P.M. I see real problems with this philosophy. What if you don't feel like it or have the drive or whatever? Or what if you are lying on a lounge chair on the lawn some hot Sunday afternoon and your fantasies really get fired up? Are you going to suppress the impulse until Tuesday night? It's the same with dejunking. Some days, weeks, hours, or wet three-day weekends, you have the ambition and energy and time—so do it on the spot, right then. Some of the most effective junking is spontaneous, so go with your mood for the day. Don't worry about scheduling it: just do get to it somehow at least twice a week—and that won't be hard once you begin to feel the joy of being unjunked.

Of course, the faster you get the unclutter train rolling, the easier it is to stay aboard. One woman told me, "I sat dejected, looking at it for weeks. I knew it was bad, and I hated it and myself. But when the first load left, a feeling of peace and plenty flooded my body, I felt a great sense of control and power.

Within a week, I had processed a garage, two bedrooms, and a basement. A chronic clothes lover, I was now ready, willing, and able to tackle even Johnny Carson's closet!"

Once you start, I promise you won't have to force and flog yourself to keep going. You'll look forward to it! Remember, the rewards of a junk-free life aren't just emotional release and freedom, but physical release and freedom, too. You'll regain the use of your drawers, closets, cabinets, shelves, spare room, garage, and yard—a whole universe of long-lost space.

Reprieve to Relieve (Stop the World, I Want to Dejunk)

The world won't stop when you start dejunking. Few if any regular events will go on hold while you take the time to toss a few tons of stuff. Meals, meetings, lessons, laundry, programs, and everything else that takes time and makes messes will roll on while you dig in! And once you're engrossed in the de-grossing of your storage, who wants to stop and serve the world? If you hang on to your regular schedule you won't make much progress in your decluttering campaign. Decluttering is deadly serious enough to merit postponement of other activities. Cleaning out drawers and cupboards may mean things like dishes and vacuuming don't get done. It is better that one house suffer dust and cold cereal for a while than that clutter control your life forever. It's well within your rights and wisdom to shelve or shortcut regular chores while you're de-shelving overdue clutter. A little delay in everyday dirt and downtown appointments is part of the dejunking design. Waive dealing with the withering flowers and slightly soiled sheets for a week or so; your family will live! If you tell them you're taking the clutter cure, they may even do some of the stuff you were doing—just don't you do it!

What Should You Tackle First?

"I have some good news and some bad news."

When someone says that to you, which do you want to hear first? Half of us want the bad news so we can get it over with, the other half want the good news so we'll be shored up against the shock of the bad. Neither approach is wrong or crazy. And so it is with junking. Tackling the most troubling things first is the direction some professional dejunkers counsel, but it doesn't necessarily have to be done that way—some people like to get warmed up and rolling with something that just strikes their fancy or is easy to take. I've suggested some starter projects in the pages that follow, but there is no official or absolute order, so start any way you want. Don't hang around waiting for a rule to get started.

Make Your Plan

For starters take an overall tour of all your stuff some weekend—don't do any tossing this trip, just make a general inventory of it.

Decide what your overall objective is.

Is your goal to be completely clutter-free, to bring it under control, or just to make some improvement?

Then list all the areas that need to be dejunked/that you want to dejunk, in the order you want to do them (you may decide to change the order later).

You could go about it room by room, or area by area; by mood; by what bothers you most; by what's most in the way;

The Clutter Hit Parade

Take this 5-minute test to see where you stand!

THE TOP 10		You Wouldn't Believe It	Far More Than Enough	Plenty	More Than I Use	Just What I Need	Score
		1	2	3	4	5	
1. Paper	Junk Mail • Files, etc. • Newspapers • Magazines • Books						
2. Clothes	And accessories such as Gloves • Belts • Shoes						
3. Containers	Boxes • Bags • Cans • Plastic Containers						
4. Useless, outdated, but Sentimental Stuff							
5. Gadgets	Kitchen, workshop, etc. • And all of their attachments						
6. Grooming Junk	Unused or outdated makeup and medicine • Haircare chemicals and appliances						
7. Hobby & Sport Clutter	Unused adult toys of all kinds						
8. Furniture	Wall to wall in the house and waiting somewhere to be repaired						
9. Gifts & Souvenirs							
10. Toys	Bought for the kids by you know who						

TOTAL

How to Score
Write in the number at the top of the column that best describes you, then add all the numbers in all the columns and total them for your score!

1-20
You're almost terminal, you know

20-29
You're a terrible example for the rest of us (although there is a flicker of hope for you)

30-39
You're just an average overjunked American

40-50
Feel good about yourself (but keep one eye open)

by most visible to least visible; easier to harder; big obvious stuff to more detailed.

In this, as in anything, it helps a lot to break your overall goal into specific projects you can tackle one at a time. So make a step-by-step plan, with dates. You can always readjust the dates if they turn out to be unrealistic. But give yourself a concrete schedule for each phase.

Especially if you have a great number of cluttered areas to conquer, you may want to take care of all the surface and general clutter in every area first. Then after you get all your target areas basically dejunked, circle back to the fine tuning, the small pockets and projects that can take a lot of time and emotional input, like decluttering and organizing your photo collection or the files. It'll be a lot easier and even fun to face them, too, once you have the sense of peace and control your progress in decluttering to date will have brought you.

My Dejunking Plan

Phase 1 (The things that bug me the most) —To be finished by March 1st

The kitchen cupboards and drawers
My clothes closet
The desk in the den
The stacks of "To be filed immediately" papers in the den
The shelves in the living room
The linen closet
The hall closet
The medicine cabinet
The closets upstairs
My desk at work

Phase 2 —To be finished by June 1st

The junk room
The attic

The cellar
The garage
The storage shed

Phase 3 —To be finished before Labor Day

The storage bin
The stuff I have at Mom's
The Christmas decorations
The boxes of old papers in the back bedroom
The trunk of old letters and souvenirs
Try to get Paul to dejunk the workshop

How Long Will It Take?

One you're convinced and committed, you'll see instant results. I've seen people lose 200 pounds in one day—now that's real junk loss!

Just don't get *over*optimistic. Remember, it may have taken you twenty or more years to put all this into your life.

Don't Count on Instant Dejunking

Your **split-second** digital clock awakens you to a breakfast of **instant** oatmeal and **minute** orange juice. You get **quick** relief for your headache as soon as you open the medicine cabinet, your Polaroid gives you a picture in a **moment,** you don't have to wait long for that **fast**-drying paint, and you enjoy a **short** course in the stock market while you car is in the **jiffy** lubrication joint. Almost everything in our lives now involves instant response and immediate results, so don't wonder why you get discouraged as you sift through your thirty-year assemblage of goods. Rome wasn't built in a day, and a house isn't going to be emptied that fast either. You're deal-

ing with the results of a lifetime of gathering, stuffing, and packing things into your place. Undoing it isn't a wink of an eye away. If you have a lot it might take a year or more (heaven forbid and weep with you) to accomplish, so don't judge the task by the standard of today's instant everythings.

I do promise, however, that the reward of your eventually clean and organized space will surpass anything you ever did. You'll be FREE!

Make Yourself a Battle Map

Successful coaches, teachers, leaders—all have learned that what you keep visual, you keep vital. Remember how the height marks on the door casing turned you on as your growth was measured, as a child? What you *see*, you *seek*. So use your bulletin board (or even a big piece of poster paper) to help plan and track your clutter-clearing campaign. Seeing it all laid out in front of

you like a map or trail will do a lot to keep the raiding spirit alive. Even a simple sketch or drawing (like war-game objectives drawn in the dust)—the kitchen cupboards and closets, then the basement and storage sheds, etc.—will do wonders. You can even make a thermometer-like progress-and-completion chart. You'll have it all in front of your face for a reminder and reward, and it'll also help put family and friends on notice that dejunking is number one until it's done. You'll have the whole community cheering you on to victory. I've even hung clutter giveaways ("Free to any taker") on the board!

The Biggest Single Reason Dejunking Doesn't Get Done...

...is that something else is always more important, more pressing, more worthy of our attention.

The only way you will even win the clutter war is to *make* dejunking number one and *keep* it number one until it's done. Circumstances will never ensure this—*you* have to do it. To help you remember this; I've provided a little poster for you to hang on your bulletin board, the refrigerator door, the bathroom mirror, or wherever.

Dejunking is Number 1 until it's done!

Dejunking is Number 1 until it's done!

Dejunking is Number 1 until it's done!

Dejunking is Number 1 until it's done!

Dejunking is Number 1 until it's done!

Dejunking is Number 1 until it's done!

PART II

The Solution

CHAPTER 6

Finding and Facing the Clutter Hot Spots

A Remedy for Room-ache

So important is it that you sink your teeth into this—the clutter hot spots—that I must compare it to dejunking of another sort. Yes, to dealing with the teeth in your mouth, as private a place as any of the rooms of your house. Both begin to ache when they get in a junked condition. Tooth decay, like room pollution, doesn't happen overnight—it's gradual, taking years of slow accumulation of plaque (or plaques) and bacteria (or backgammon games). Both teeth and rooms seem to be holding up too, until… you feel a twinge biting or walking through, a slight signal something is wrong. Dejunking and dentist visits are two things we want to avoid at all cost, so we chew on one side or walk on the other side of the room for as long as possible, until the pain is too bad to take.

A tour of our rooms is a lot like a dentist's tour of our mouth, too—we walk into his or her office aware only that the second tooth from the back is hurting; the rest look gleamingly glorious to us. Then the dentist tilts us back on that hard leather chair, flips on the examination light, and looks in. Faint expressions of pain, preaching, surprise, and calculation cross his face as he skims through our oral junk room—oh, wow, tsk, hmmm, he says as he finds (like that junk we keep uncovering at home) ever more broken, rotting, chipped, cracked, worn, loose things. We swallow in fear, knowing the worst is yet to come, the X-ray, the final probe into our personal pit. Gad, just think, the visible junk in every room is bad enough—if there were such a thing as an X-ray for junk, we'd need the equivalent of twenty more appointments! "Bad, pretty bad," he says, then he asks you that question: "Why did you wait so long?" Well, why did you? Mouth and master bedroom junk both have to eventually be faced up to, so why wait until it's a surgical situation? Now is the time to head out after the junk in all of these hot spots. You'll be numb for a few hours or days after, but think of the relief—not more nagging pain, no more chewing or walking on the other side.

The Hot Spot Tour Through the House

The Kitchen

Originally intended as a food preparation center, for many of us now the kitchen is the nerve center of our household operations. The junk drawer is always in the kitchen, as is the phone, with all its trailing clutter, a library of books (cookbooks, schoolbooks, etc.) and appliance pamphlets and the like. The kitchen isn't only the main meeting place and message center of many a home, but also the headquarters of all airborne grease, center for spills and stains, and a gruesome gathering spot for gadgetry. (If only there were still a fire pit here—for clutter!) The worst part about all the clutter here is that this is one place we really **need** the space to operate. There's never much room in the room that needs the most room. My worst clutter nightmare is a "country" kitchen with endless old crockery, pots, utensils, etc., hung from every surface—

although at least here the old, worn, and dirty might be mistaken for decor.

A few tips:

- Get anything allergic to cleaning water out of here—if it's in the kitchen, it'll gather grease and need to be cleaned—often.
- Come down hard on the counter-feits. None of us have enough counter space, yet we tolerate all kinds of useless or almost-useless squatters here, such as pretty but utterly inadequate canister sets, bread-bare breadboxes and never-used cookie jars, top-heavy mug stands, and freestanding towel holders, stacks of mail, newspapers, and magazines waiting to be read.
- Dump out and brutally examine the contents of all those hopelessly crowded drawers. Get rid of all the gadgets that never really worked—peelers, openers, etc.
- Clean off those shelves—the third and higher shelf, too!
- Beware of junk bunkers (that means all those knife blocks, utensil racks and holders, spice racks, drawer dividers, wine stackers, and towel dispensers with built-in cupboards and drawers). See page 171.
- Keep a sharp eye out for excess dishes, glasses, platters, and pans. Saltshakers, trivets, toothpick holders, and unused "for company" stuff. At least 40 percent of what's clogging those shelves and cupboards is waiting for the big company-coming day. How often do *you* entertain? How formally? For how many? Review those shelves, cupboards, and china closets and remove accordingly.
- Divest yourself of accessories that just aren't you (gifts, often, or souvenirs from our forays into Culinary Obsession Shops), such as aprons we never wear, place mats we never use, mushroom-, cauliflower-, or frog-shaped anything, Japanese tea sets full of dust and gnats.
- Root out artifacts of fads that came and went without ever really making it into your menu planning (crockpots, woks, souffle' pans, pasta makers, yogurt culturers, ice-cream machines, radish-rose-and-carrot-crinkle-making kits—plus the special pans and appliances for making Danish round doughnuts or German rosettes).
- Unplug those excess and overspecialized electrics. We'd blow a circuit if we plugged in all the choppers, juicers, openers, poppers, grinders, brewers, toasters, fryers, mixers, kneaders, and zappers at once.
- Can those excess containers. The average kitchen has enough plastic containers to fill six freezers and refrigerators, plus an unlimited number of margarine cartons, pot pie pans, plastic bags or grocery bags, empty mason jars, etc. (see page 102).
- Dejunk under the sink (see page 16).
- Scan the walls for overburdened bulletin boards (see page 68). Clocks that have never kept time. The Christmas wreath over the phone. The long-dead plants still standing in their pots (and the almost-dead plant hanging over the sink). All the parts sitting on the windowsill that you have no idea what they're parts of.
- Don't forget the floor. The floor in a kitchen gets more than its share of clutter fallout: Clutter-stuffed giant crocks; itinerant toolboxes; the incubator that was used to hatch the quail eggs; the plants you were trying to start from seed; the bucket of rotting peaches complete with canning kettle still over in the corner or the box of rotting tomatoes cemented to the floor; anything over six stray pairs of boots/shoes; all the extra pet dishes; the appliance stand for the appliance you no longer have; the broken microwave stacked beneath the working microwave; the no-longer-necessary extension cords; the air conditioner you should have put away in September, the space heater you should have put away in May.

The Refrigerator

The refrigerator is a microcosm of our clutter constitution. Food is a big feature of our lives and food has a shorter life span than most clutter, but it too has its keepables and tossables. Such as Tupperware bowls with unrecognizable innards, multihued cottage cheese, you-know-from-the-carton-in-was-sour-cream, eggnog at least two months old, a looks-like-it's-already-been-eaten-once bowl of something, dried-up beef, Jell-O bricklets, shriveled teenie weinies, vaccine-producing cheese, margarine gone white, macaroni surprise gone macaroni shudder. The refrigerator does so well with food, we toss in films we'll never use and fishing worms we'll forget, as well as fingernail polish and medicine—and did you know vacuum belts and batteries last three times as long if refrigerated?

I don't have to tell you what to toss out of the refrigerator. You know. Just do it.

> "I don't mind throwing things out of the fridge after they get fuzzy. They're really no good before that, and I'm not going to use them, but I wait for the fuzz to give me confirmation."

(Don't forget the **freezer,** either. Contrary to common belief, freezing is *not* a way of preserving things permanently. If you've had it in there for more than ten months, it's probably tasteless and textureless and utterly lacking in nutrition—or you never intended to eat it in the first place.)

The Dining Room

Undoubtedly the least-used room in many a house. No one with any class is ever satisfied until they get a dining room. Do people dine there? Seldom, because it's so nice—carpets that match the $45-a-yard living room rug, a table we wouldn't want to get nicked, etc. So dining rooms are full of seldom-used stuff, including the china we scrimped and saved for. And when our precious children and grandchildren come, do we feed them out of it? Not on your life; the little buggers might break it! The upper shelves are lined with likewise unused crystal, the lower drawers full of stuff to use on the table (if we ever used it), several centerpieces or other arty high-risk items, and some of the most uncomfortable chairs ever designed by man. Personally, I'd saw off the whole room, but you might want to take a hard look at this soft underbelly of clutter and measure it against the social pressure to get and keep all this. Anything that doesn't dine with you, consider moving out.

The Living Room

Rare is the living room not over decorated and overfurnished. Which of course causes extra cleaning effort and constant worry when company brings little ones along. For example:

- Excess pillows—a few is fine, forty is too many.
- Over-the-hill houseplants. It's a nice idea to try

and bring the living room to life, but when the bloom is off the Christmas cactus and the Norfolk pine is nearly naked of needles, this isn't interior landscaping—it's ugly clutter. (Dump those old planters, too, where the only thing left is a snake plant and a faded ribbon.)

- The fireplace and mantel area—a dispersal center for soot, ash, and dust. The less here the better.
- A dozen little pictures that could be condensed into one big impressive framed and glassed display, which would look better and be a *lot* easier to clean!
- Furniture. Hard-to-see-by lamps. Ugly end tables. Leaking beanbag chairs. Hassocks and stools that are never used, only stumbled over.
- Reading matter runover—strewn newspapers, moribund books, a myriad of magazines. Outdated phone books.
- Home entertainment (or should we say clutter) center. Duplicate tapes you bought by mistake, broken tapes, albums for which all you've got is the sleeve/cover. Several dozen plastic cassette cases and several dozen cassettes, no two matching. Half a dozen remote controls. Enough videocassettes to open a small rental shop. Twice as many video cassette boxes as videocassettes.
- Dreadful or down-at-the-mouth decorations, such as the wall hanging you've grown beyond, or badly nicked knickknacks.

The Family Room

This place is just one step above the garage as a general catchall, because it's a public area that invites everything not allowed in other rooms. It has a TV, which means food, for example, and old furniture, which welcomes wrestling. It's already full of beat-up furniture, so tossables are often detained indefinitely here. The first culprits to apprehend are:

- Outdated piled papers, *TV Guides*, newspapers, and wretched old reference books (except the one propping up the broken couch leg).
- Excess or too far gone to save furniture (such as never-sat-on love seats and Aunt Mabel's ottoman). Plus all that flimsy, seedy stuff you picked up at garage sales when you were in college.
- Broken toys and radios; abandoned projects.
- Excess pillows, cushions, throw rugs, afghans.
- Sad-looking fake flower arrangements.
- No-longer-played-on pool or ping-pong tables; games with missing pieces.

The Hall

Even in a no-hope house, a hall is hard to clutter—but most of us manage it. Any clutter in a hall is a special problem—it's easy to trip over, and halls are narrow enough without making them narrower! Some basic sources here are overflow from bedrooms and from cluttered coat and linen closets, both easily cured. Kick that bedroom stuff back to its original owners and see the following and page 55. Check out any coatrack, or hat racks here, too (especially the underlayers) for stuff that's been hanging there so long you've outgrown it. And try to avoid adding any furniture here that's nothing but a junk roost.

The Hall Closet

It's right there on the way to and from everywhere, which makes it perfect for stashing everything from everybody. I wouldn't touch this community clutter cache with a ten-gallon box, but I'll give you one suggestion. Don't even think of it as a closet but as a small separate room just like the bathroom, kitchen, bedroom, etc. Just include it in your regular cleaning schedule—review and reduce the contents regularly—and the hall closet clutter problem will be solved.

The Linen Closet

Usually so crowded you can't find anything and too often a refuge for everything but. First purge all that stuff in the back—and on the top and bottom shelves—that doesn't really belong here, like rusty lunch boxes, old waffle irons, shorted-out electric blankets, forgotten vaporizers, leftover rolls of wallpaper, boxes of old insurance policies, etc. Then move on to the malingerers amidst the linens:

- Fitted sheets for bed sizes you no longer have
- The incredibly unrestful (loud) sheet set someone left behind
- The battered beach towel you found floating downstream
- Excess towels and washcloths
- The table runner you've never used
- Tablecloths and cloth napkins you never want to bother to iron
- Your unworn apron collection
- Nonabsorbent dish towels
- The single tea towel with toucans printed on it
- Disintegrating dishrags
- Disused doilies
- Burned potholders
- Ratty or not-right-for-your-decor rugs
- Shower curtains that were replaced

The Bathroom

A bathroom, in the cleaning business, usually takes longer to clean than a giant living room. That's because per square foot, bathrooms have more dirt and clutter collectors—cabinets, shelves, fixtures, windows, ledges, vanities. There are too many towels, too many magazines, too many decorations—and all of this is bathed constantly in moisture and soap scum.

The Medicine Chest

If there are just two of you using it, each of you usually has your side. Unbelievable, all that's in here to try and make us look and smell better, wake us up, put us to sleep, cure all our ills and imperfections. What if someone you were really trying to impress—say, a new love or a new boss—came and looked in yours right now? Bet their estimation of you would drop 23 degrees instantly. Stuff is stacked three layers high on the shelves, and it doesn't improve with age any more than we do. Bad enough when our face sags; let's not do it to those poor shelves, too. If we got two points every time something dropped out of the overcrowded cabinet, making a dead shot into the sink, we'd win the NBA (National Beastly Assortment) Slam-Dunk Competition hands down.

The first thing you'll find when you force yourself to look behind those toothpaste-spattered mirrors is that at least a quarter of the stuff here really doesn't belong here, such as flashlight, matches, WD-40, Batman night light, high school ring, can of Drano.

Then once the medicine cabinet is stripped of outdated drugs and empty tubes and bottles, you can move on to:

- Nonsticking corn pads
- Rusty razors
- Frizzled toothbrushes
- Toothpaste you'll never use—the one that tastes like bubble gum, the one cousin Frank left behind, and the one you bought when they were out of your brand
- The drug chain's own unsuccessful imitations of several over-the-counter remedies you *do* have confidence in.
- Capsules and tablets you wouldn't dare take, because you're not sure what they are
- The tiny tube or jar of stuff they gave you after your wart-removal operation ten years ago and said to apply for three days afterward
- The two dozen drug samples given to you by as many doctors over the years
- The dregs of the drug that gave you a serious allergic reaction several years ago
- The antique antibiotic ointment that might save your life in a national disaster
- Travel-size everything in addition to regular and economy-size everything

"My memorabilia? It had to be the medicine cabinet."

Sink cabinet junk (on top, underneath, and in the drawers):

- Lipsticks, nail polishes, foundation makeups, shampoos, conditioners, hair colorings, and setting lotions you tried and didn't like
- The denture fixative and cleaner, hemorrhoid remedy, and laxative that didn't work
- The two types of curlers you used before the kind you use now
- At least one nonworking hair dryer, curling iron, electric shaver, or heating pad
- Barrettes, ponytail bands, and every other variety of hair adornment you never use
- Types of makeup you no longer want to be bothered to apply
- The bottle of bubble bath that hasn't been uncapped since you bought it from the Avon lady in 1969
- Sprung cuticle scissors and nonworking tweezers
- Five extra applicators for anything that requires an applicator
- Little odds and ends of soap you are *never* going to melt down into a whole bar, or use
- Aged contraceptive preparations and appliances
- Soap you don't like the smell of and would never use even if you were out of everything (including dish soap)
- Combs or brushes or hair picks of the type you never use

- Hotel junk: miniature soaps, lotions, and moisturizers and wispy shower caps
- Eyebrow pencil stubs, and the still-good brushes from at least twenty previous compacts
- Eight-year-old air freshener

Elsewhere

Once you cleanse the cabinet, the drawers, and all those decorations, don't let the sneaky areas get past you. The tub edge and toilet tank top were made for functional purposes, not for lining with clever wire racks and clutter holders. It's ugly, dangerous, and unsanitary, so flush it. Bet you half of those bottles are empty or full of stuff you hate!

The Laundry Room

This is clutter's no-man's land! Pocket paraphernalia, hopelessly worn clothes, and disintegrating rags all end up here in indecision. Rocks, marbles, business cards, pens, nails, nuts, bolts, matchbooks, lapel pins... the list will never end. And more arrive daily.

Then, of course, there are all manner of soaps, suds, and sprays for before and after treatment of clothes, including the free samples we'll never try, the stuff we tried and didn't like, and at least two boxes or bottles of all the old faithfuls (ones we forgot we had). Empty bleach or fabric softener bottles and snoutless or hopelessly clogged spray starch. Odd socks, mildewed clothespins, and wads of dryer lint. Shrunken and bleach-besmirched clothes. At least one broken clothes basket or nonworking iron. Belts, hats, slippers, and other unwashables, and miscellany that has nowhere else to go. Plus a dusty exercise bike over in the corner, used only to hang freshly washed clothes on.

How far we've progressed from the river rock is astounding, and abounding—piles, piles, piles. Tip those piles

upside down one by one and start from the bottom, with the oldest and most damaged or rotted. You'll be in high gear—and dejunked—by the time you get to the top.

The Bedroom

Maybe it's because they're usually somewhere back and out of the way, but bedrooms quietly accumulate a heap of clutter. Right now how much reading is stacked there, for example, and when is the last time you read any of it? Bedrooms can get cluttered faster than any room in the house because they're private. Usually no one sees them but us; they don't get the clean-up-for-company pressure we get in the kitchen, living room, or family room. When you wake up Saturday morning, just lie there awhile and eyeball the situation. Then grab a pen and note the stuff that can and should go. Then do it!

1. Dresser junk. Two major categories here: (a) Dresser-top junk and (b) dresser drawer detritus.

Dresser tops have the fatal allure of any flat surface (a place to plop stuff), made worse by the fact that this is one "tabletop" we're never forced to clear because we need to use it. Most of what's stacked up here was never intended for permanent display, and makes dusting a weekly impossibility. Scoop it all up and sort it according to who parked it there. Then hand it to them to find a decent home for it or dispose of it (after you've done the same with **your** shoebox full).

Without even looking, I can guarantee you that at least 40 percent of any dresser is occupied by obsolete or never-used stuff. The top drawers are usually the worst (contain the most extraneous junk, from penny collections to empty matchbooks to check stubs dating back to your first account), but all drawers usually contain more than their share of hopelessly shrunken sweatshirts, never-worn gloves, pantyhose with runs, single shoelaces, lingerie lingering from younger days, knots of too-small belts, chokers, chains, and scarves; sequin-shedding, never-used evening bags; cheap plastic shoehorns; mashed velvet bow ties; cheap or not-the-kind-we-ever-use gift wallets; pretty hankies still in the pretty box we got them in twenty years ago; shoulder pads ripped from clothes; and pomanders or cedar balls so old they're utterly scentless.

2. Closet overflow (see pages 53 and 109).

3. The bed itself Fancy effects (bolsters, fancy pillow covers, dust ruffles) that don't serve any real purpose and that we *don't* want to fiddle with every morning.

4. Under the bed. Ever notice that some people's beds are higher than a normal bed? I glanced at one the other day and that baby was almost waist-high. "Orthopedic," I thought, but at a second glance that high bed had nothing to do with health or for that matter sleeping. It was a storage symptom. "Under" is one of the last-resort places to put things when all the closets, shelves, and trunks are full. The lack of visibility here is solid inducement not only to stash stuff but also to avoid even thinking of going back through it. So pull out all that under-bed storage that you shoved under and forgot.

We build all our beds with sturdy drawers underneath, so they can at least become a respectable part of the storage system. This keeps a lots of things from getting lost, and because the drawers go down to the floor, there's no room for dust bunnies to breed, either.

5. Nightstand and headboard-storage junk. Bed-area storage collects everything from broken eyeglasses to empty bottles of nosedrops and tissue boxes to unfinished books—plus non-functioning clock radios, telephones, and night lights.

6. Health, fitness, and vanity clutter. Here we find anti-snore and anti-wrinkle aids that were tried and abandoned and nonfunctional dresser sets (gap-toothed comb, black-spotted mirror, and balding brush, all kept because of their silver, ivory, or handsome wood handles). And don't forget the traction apparatus from your back/neck injury eight years ago.

The Workbench or Fix-It Center

The contents of this generally masculine preserve are rarely questioned by anyone because the man of the house has convinced everyone else that his workshop is the Pentagon of repair. After all, the Pentagon has $2,000 screwdrivers, and the home hobbyist keeps a $10,000 inventory of tools to replace a $2.75 fan belt every six years. The place is utterly unnavigable by anyone but the owner. What *is* all this stuff? Dried-up caulk and glue guns and rigor-mortised paint rollers waiting for the resurrection that will never come. Important fluids in rusty cans without labels, at least four cans of half-used oil, coffee cans full of unidentified objects, rubber parts from missing machines, mixed nuts and bolts by the pound. Appliance parts that have been replaced (if they were successfully replaced, they're trophies!). Wads of wire and twine, every circuit or light switch that's ever shorted out, blackened light bulbs and fluorescent tubes, and dead batteries. All "pick-up sticks" mingled with the good tools. Complete sets of shiny, never-been-touched tools, including a metric set of nut drivers, made to fit snowmobiles made in Korea.

There are always a few worthless attachments to things around the house, but the workbench is a whole National Guard arsenal of attachments, not a few of them to no-longer-owned machines.

If Mr. Fix-It's wife is a crafty lady (or a Campfire leader) and shares the workshop, you can add a few misshapen teddy bears and miniature geese to the pile of sawdust under the jigsaw, brushes stuck to the bottoms of cups of evaporated thinner, armies of pinking shears, electric scissors, and X-acto knives, etc. Plus hollow goose eggs, strings and strands of wire, scattered beads, strips of leather, frayed feathers. And a giant pile of driftwood waiting to turn itself into marvelous character carvings.

Sprinkle this whole setup with some sawdust, spilled cement, torn sandpaper, and broken things waiting to be fixed and you have a clutter banana split supreme. It laps and tracks and spills over into all the other clean and orderly parts of the house and yard. And a lot of these things are fire hazards, as well as being ugly and smelly. Convert the junk bench back to a hobby bench this weekend!

The Sewing Room

Just when I thought clutter was losing in our house, I walked past my wife's sewing room and found a sticker across the door saying, "She who dies with the most fabric wins."

She'll win! I bought her a super deluxe sewing machine (she's an expert seamstress) and then a serger too, and that only inspired her to collect more. (It's always more fun to look at new fabric than sew up the old.) Where is it all? If you run out of fabric in the middle of a quilt, just stop by—we can match anything.

A sewing room is as sacred and necessary as a kitchen in my book, lots of good apparel and personal satisfaction comes out of here. It's the clutter oozing out that we don't cotton to, so stop pulling the wool down over your eyes. You don't need a pattern to dejunk the sewing room: it's your domain and your business. Just remember that all those scraps (who knows how many years worth?) earmarked "to make a quilt someday" need to be dealt with. Not to mention:

- Outdated or incomplete patterns
- The thirty spools of unbelievably cheap thread we bought but aren't willing to use on anything. Ditto all that material bought on sale
- Six inches each of about 132 kinds of lace and trim
- Nine boxes of wool medallions that are somehow going to metamorphose into a lovely lap robe
- Crooked straight pins
- Poorly designed pin cushions
- Anything over three measuring tapes, thirteen thimbles, or six scissors
- Salvaged ugly buttons and buckles
- Stuck zippers
- The sock darning egg that should be moved to the antique shelf
- Sentimental favorites too far gone to be mended, but too precious to throw away

- Fabric scraps, and all the pieces you cut off old clothes, and at least one book on how to use them

> "I purged my excess sewing patterns—I became a nonsmocker!"

The Attic

If you have an attic, chances are you have a lot of old stuff, a couple of hernias, and a higher-than-normal fire-insurance policy. Fortunately for you junk and clutter crammers, most new homes don't have attics, only cramped crawl spaces over the rafters (which the hard cases can still manage to shoehorn some stuff into).

The attic at least has some romance, and anything you want badly enough to lug up here you're probably entitled to keep awhile. Seriously, though, remember that rafters and ceiling joists are made to hold snow load; terrible accidents have happened to people who continually pack, stack, and stuff heavy things up there above the living room. Remember, too, that the attic gets hot, and dries things out, shrinks things up, and warps them. When the attic clutter stops feeling romantic, go for it.

Or wait until fall or winter, then get up there. Start your "sort," "charity," and "junk" piles (see p. 152). And take a friend or kid with you. It'll be fun and much easier to face.

The Basement or Cellar

> "Last year my Aunt Delia finally gave her deceased husband's long out-of-style suits to Goodwill—but only after the heating company looked in her basement and said, 'We can't install a new heating system in here until you clean it out. There's no room to work.'"

I know we think that anything in the cellar is half-buried anyway; so it's not *really* in the way! Those of you who lead a post-cellar life have missed out on the real meaning of damp, mold, and down under. Cellars generally have cracked or crumbling cement or dirt walls with 704 insects per square foot of wall or ceiling. If you have a clutter-packed old cellar, make an effort to clean it up—or at least run a paid tour; there's got to be something pretty exotic to see down there.

Carpenters don't usually enclose the space under the basement stairs and thus junk is packed under there in a pyramid shape, so tight that a piano could be dropped on the stairs and they wouldn't even creak. Smart builders—and owners—locate the water heater under here or build some fake braces in to keep out the clutter—so shame on you if your stairs are stuffed.

If you'll just take the time to actually look at it, you'll find that at least half of what's down here is so rotted, rusted, water-spotted or mildewed you won't even have to debate if you should throw it away.

Nonworking air conditioners and dehumidifiers... old curtains and extra sets of dishes... the mason jars that have been gathering dust and dead spiders since you got the freezer... forgotten winter and summer clothes... old unused fishing or other sports equipment... at least one box of sentimentalia from each family member, present or nonpresent...

Out of the House Isn't *Out!*

Inside we take full responsibility for our things (even if we intend to heave them), but on the porch/patio and beyond into the yard, we have a silent partner—Mother Nature—and most of us just wait for her to act. Or we secretly hope all this stuff will be stolen or that a good-sized dog will drag it off. But let's get real. Stop dreaming and start with the porch.

Porch Clutter

Yes, Virginia, there *is* a halfway house for the old hutch, a life-support location for dying stuff; an asylum for the unburied, a rest stop for stuff "that has to go." It's already left the mainstream of life (the house) and is now on the porch or patio, so we can see if it can survive one more season. The porch or breezeway always reminds me of the strainer in the sink—it's where everything left over ends up. And no matter how clean the house or the sink itself might be, this one highly visible spot will greatly influence the impression made by the whole.

Porch mess—what is it? Battered toys, worn-out sneakers, well-chewed dog bones, and dirty pet dishes. Plus the broken, the old, and whatever we failed to figure out what to do with when we cleaned the house itself. At least in the sink, there's a chance it might go down the drain if we run the water fast enough. But with the porch, no such luck. Stuff just stays there and looks awful.

If you deal with clutter when it first crops up, it won't get shuffled to the porch. And porch mess (generally aged and awful) can't get shuffled back into the house.

The Patio or Deck

This is our outdoor display area for unreliable lawn chairs, rickety tables, splintered wicker, decaying patio umbrellas, leaky rain gauges, rusting plant stands, cracked cement flowerpots, rotted flower boxes, and woebegone wind chimes. I know that first barbecue served you well, but you now have a good gas grill and *that old one is not used anymore.* Someone with no grill at all might really appreciate it.

Under the Deck

You unfortunate folks with elevated decks have undoubtedly found yourselves another clutter cave, and now you have to face all the stuff you shoved

under there, out of sight and mind. Just to jog your memory: remember all those leftover boards and moldings from remodeling, flowerpots complete with dead plants, broken chaise lounges, forgotten barbecue attachments, garden tools that never worked? Then there's the mower or snowmobile that just needs a few parts. Well, they're all still there, plus (unbeknownst to you) your family, neighbors, and friends have stuffed a couple of extra items each in there—not to mention what the dogs and cats have drug under there and buried. And all of this has provided an elaborate playground and breeding ground for bugs, reptiles, and rodents.

Nobody wants to play with a deck this full, so save a little Saturday morning time for this. Have a pickup backed up and ready, and wear heavy gloves. Get rid of all the rotted and bend or break the rusted up into little heaps and get rid of it. The rare savable stuff should be set or stacked across cinder blocks to keep it up off the ground. Do this job alone or with one obedient, non-tattletale kid.

The Garage

One woman's hysterical plea to firemen: "Let the garage burn, then put out the fire!"

The man of the house has generally staked his claim on this territory, so walk softly and carry a big sack.

Other than his stuff, junk in garages isn't quite as sacred as junk in private areas of the house; it's out on the range, so you should be able to take a firm hand to it. There's a lot of stuff just "temporarily stored" here—on, under, and in the way of everything. A lot of this stuff falls on and against the car—which is what causes a lot of those mysterious, maddening nicks and dings. The majority of junk in garages is just lying in wake. Why not get on with the funeral, now, today?

Mr. Carter's Last Stand

Out with:

- Cans of unused paint, hardened cement mix, dried-up spackle and wood putty, etc.
- Old half-finished or never-started projects, and pieces of stuff to build or rejuvenate someday
- Going-to-fix-it-someday junk. Make *this* the day; fix it now or toss it out!
- Bicycle, tricycle, motorcycle junk
- Hanging-from-the-rafters junk
- Vehicle-attachment junk, like bike racks, ski racks, luggage racks, cargo carriers, trailer hitches, etc. (Question: Do you still have the vehicle it attaches to?)
- Aged car-accessory junk, like curdled car wax, hubcaps and wheel rims and snow tires and wipers and touchup paint for cars you no longer own, old license plates, the jack and floor mats to every car you ever owned, open cans of oil and transmission fluid
- Life-threatening ladders
- Broken badminton sets and other sports junk (see page 73)
- Garden junk (see page 74)

The Backyard Storage Shed

The garage's little brother or offspring is the backyard storage shed (often masquerading as a "tool" or "garden" shed).

This little metal shed or bogus wooden barn is a disgrace—often so light and flimsy that it blows over, leaks, gets dented, erodes your neighbor's image of you, and reduces your self-esteem. All for junk.

The suburban shed, like its ancestor the old-time woodshed, gives a junker the unfortunate impression that here there is room to store stuff too rank or questionable even for the cellar or garage. So in addition to holding all the clutter overflow from the garage, the shed ends up full of things like broken windows in rotting frames, superseded storm doors, sagged screens, salvaged

funeral-wreath trappings, rusted curtain rods and old disintegrating shades, ancient stained rugs and burned-out vacuum tubes, old chipped chamber pots and umbrella remains, the rusty broken gate we removed, all of our former mailboxes, every pipe or gutter that was ever replaced and every worn-out mop, rake, and broom.

Get your courage up some bright sunny day and work your way through it from one end to the other. There's a lot of big junk in here, so the weekend before Cleanup Day would be ideal. Otherwise arrange for disposal by one of the means described on page 164. You might want to bury the barn itself afterward.

Outside Junk

Close your eyes for a minute and think of the beautiful grounds of the parks, shrines, nature centers, or visitors' centers you've visited: immaculate grass and flower beds; walks, fences, and planters in perfect repair; no weeds or waste paper anywhere; everything clean and fresh. Now go out into your own yard and open your eyes. If your yard resembles a time-decayed Disneyland (which too many do), it's time to *un*adulterate it. Let Mother Nature be your inspiration. Most synthetic (man-made) stuff looks sleazy outside, and weather only warps it into utter ugliness. Exterior trash is awful to look at, bad for neighborhood relations, and dangerous, too. Dump it! It isn't dealt with by the handful or even the armful. We're talking truckfuls here—you need to have a big dumpster or truck bed available to do a good job. Trying to reduce this stuff to sack size is like trying to pack a quilt into a pillowcase. So say farewell to:

- Shabby hammocks
- Swing-set remains
- Broken outdoor sculpture
- Rusted sundials
- Out-of-favor lawn ornaments
- Beside-the-point-now basketball hoops
- Nonfunctioning fountains
- Never-filled hummingbird feeders
- Falling-apart fences
- Leaning or collapsed sheds
- Leaky water troughs
- Broken cement pieces, parts of cinder blocks, and half-bricks
- Rotted picnic tables
- Weed-filled sandboxes
- Leftover piles of sand, gravel, wood chips, rocks
- Abandoned compost heaps
- Last year's Christmas tree
- Uprooted stumps
- Rotting logs and decayed woodpiles
- Ugly brush piles

> Snow is slippery, cold, and wet, causes accidents, depreciates buildings and roads, and costs money to remove, yet "nothing is as beautiful and quiet and peaceful as snow"—why? Because it covers all the clutter.

Rental Storage Units— Clutter at 75 Cents a Square Foot (or more)!

This is the junk rest home, complete with visiting hours. Most of this stuff is just in a holding pattern until the day we finally get around to disposing of it.

About the only way "the bin" ever enters mind or conversation is in the form of "I've really got to get down there someday and clean it out."

The fact that we put something here, that we don't even need it to be in the same location with us, is a big hint that it's the excess, the-not-quite-needed, the no-longer-wholly-wanted. You could argue that most "storage bins" are nothing more or less than giant emotional withdrawal boxes (see page 152). It would have to be emotional, because if you ever actually added it up, the cost of several years' room and board for ugly old lamps, broken headboards, topless coffee tables, and almost-bald tires sure wouldn't make financial sense.

My friend pays $120 a month for a 10 x 20 unit with a concrete floor and tin walls. He's not even sure what's there. One man even forgot a car he had incubating in his unit. Insurance adjusters tell me in cases of flood or robbery, most people can't account for 50 percent of what they have in storage areas like this without a list. If you have one, better run over right now and take inventory. This will accomplish at least three things: you'll find a few lost things, pre-

Rest in peace...

pare yourself for future insurance claims, and probably add $120 a month to your income (after the storage bin sale).

Cadillac Clutter

If cars had clutter dip sticks, we could just drive into a gas station, unroll the window, and holler out, "Fill 'er up, and would you check the oil and clutter?" But the clutter is unlikely to be a quart low—limousine, mid-size, or compact, our vehicles all hold and haul stuff that was never designed to be slipped under seats or to roll around on the floor. What we don't leave in them, we add on to them, from grimacing Garfields to dangling dice, until we finally have it: the perfect reflection of our personality.

Clutter is worse per square foot in some cars than in the hall closet. I've seen cars with just a cubicle left for the driver to slip into. It's time to declutter your Camry, dejunk your Jeep, detrash your T-Bird, unpile your Porsche, unlitter your Lincoln—today. We especially don't want clutter that will travel

Rest in pieces...

with us to work, to play, or to the great beyond. And remember: car clutter can even cause accidents!

Vacate for Vacation— Motor Homes, Campers, Boats

Motor homes, campers, boats—all clutter closets on wheels. Already cramped and compressed with every corner in use, these things have all too many gadgets already. Before long, we have a mini-mirror image of almost all the clutter in the house: mini-bottles, -boxes, and -tubes, mini-salts-and-peppers, mini-dish-drainers, mini-pots and -coffeemakers, mini-pans, and mini-overcrowded clothes closet.

Everything not quite good enough for the house (and the "old one" of anything new) gets dumped in the camper, too. Odd, mismatched pillows and bedding; bent utensils; ever-so-slightly-melted-by-the-dishwasher plasticware; rusty flashlights, at least two for every year you've owned the RV; foldable, collapsible and inflatable contraptions, from tables and chairs to cups and toothbrushes. Plus the sadly decayed "in case it rains" contingent of cards and games and entertainment items, and a whole battery of boots and slickers and raingear and in-case-of-emergency stuff —duplicates and triplicates even—of which little is in working order.

Every cubbyhole will be full by the third trip; then you start hating the unit. Any extras you add not only won't fit, they'll roll and bounce everywhere. And junk will run the ride.

The only way I finally controlled my vacation home was to relieve it of any junk at every rest/gas stop rather than wait until the end of the trip. (Confucius say he who carry too many fishing poles get hooked!)

CHAPTER 7

Some Fun and Easy Places to Start

There are at least a hundred categories of clutter roaming (and rooming) all over your place, which can be pretty discouraging to think about, let alone deal with. On the ranch where I grew up, we had a herd of Herefords, and when they were all in a milling mass, they were impossible to approach—just like our clutter mounds. But if we simply cut out the nearest calf (or easiest decluttering chore) and squeezed him into a chute, we could dehorn, brand, clip, etc.—take care of it in a minute, with no injurious interference from the other 119 still left to do. I became as good as my father at cutting out cows one at a time, and I've cut some clutter in my day too. Let's start circling your herd.

Carry-Along Clutter

What more logical place to start than with the junk you've got right on you—in your purse, wallet, or handbag? How many of you are still lugging around your old high school lunch ticket with two punches left on it, or have to sit sidesaddle on the chair because your wallet is so thick? I realize the other woman always has the biggest, ugliest purse, but you ought to see to it that whatever is making your own bulge is something that really belongs there. I know you take a certain pride in being able to supply almost anybody with almost anything out of that bag, but unless you live in one of the underdeveloped countries, forget it. It's not worth the sore shoulder you'll eventually get from slinging all that weight around with you. As for you fellows with the fat wallets, forget about competing for Mr. Plastic Fantastic. A man going for the world's largest collection of credit cards had 1,397 by 2001—all different—totalling 1.65 million in credit. He kept them in a 250-foot-long wallet that weighed 38 pounds.

The worst thing about this particular form of clutter is that you don't merely own it, but almost always carry it right along with you! And sitting on a too-heavy wallet (or carrying a too-heavy pocketbook) can actually cause back problems. Oversized, stuffed handbags and wallets wear out clothing, too, and are one of the biggest damagers of doors.

It's time to reduce the clutter in those purses and wallets. Don't wait for that embarrassing moment when you set your purse on the counter or floor to write out a check and passersby begin to throw trash into it.

The Wallet and Purse Winnowing List

Goodbye to:

- Anything over three lucky charms
- Obsolete business cards of your own, or of contacts you no longer want to make, or dog-eared and dirty current business cards
- Expired membership cards, credit cards, insurance cards, registrations, licenses
- Pictures we shouldn't be packing anymore
- Scribbled phone numbers of who knows who
- Makeup we no longer use, melted lipsticks and Chapsticks
- First-aid supplies so old and purse-worn they'd only hasten our demise
- Self-defense equipment we don't know how to use, or would probably injure ourselves with
- Nonworking mini-flashlights
- Keys to extinct vehicles or locks that have been replaced
- Candy with hair, lint, and leather particles stuck to it
- Antique toll and airport parking receipts and old credit card carbons
- Several books of matches with one or two left in each
- Subway tokens for cities you no longer live in
- The piece of material you've carried since 1982, hoping to find a match

- Outdated pocket calendars
- Worn-beyond-belief wallets

And after you get this stuff out, don't go *adding* anything—keep them clean and free.

The Briefcase

A briefcase is generally only "brief" for the first few weeks after purchase. Then it becomes a way to carry around, out of sight, worthless papers (such as used boarding passes, empty manila envelopes, chafed, wrinkled stationery, expired Frequent Flyer cards and deals, old phone messages, last month's must-reads) and an amazing variety of other things, from dull disposable razors to crumpled cigarette packs—all in all, a failure as a portable filing cabinet. Case thinning, as we call the process, is best done while on the road—waiting at an airport, marooned in the motel, when you have dead time and feel too dull to read or write, too tired to be absorbed by anything on TV. Make sure you're adjacent to a garbage can, and then open

your case and sweep right through it. When you get to the bottom and find that elusive collection of lint, crumbs, loose staples, etc., get a damp cloth or paper towel and pick it up. Presto! You'll no longer have to press the lid to close your case and your right arm might even unstretch back to match the other one.

Jewelry Boxes—Another Personal Place to Start

A peek into most of our "jewelry boxes" would sorely disappoint a sneak thief. They may be brimming, but there's a glittering array of junk mixed in with those jewels. We get pierced or stabbed every time we paw through those drawers of gifts not to our taste, plastic rings and pins from the kids, and snarls of shell and nut necklaces. There's usually a random few rare coins and an elk tooth or two. But rest assured: the pins on one of those brooches (tangled with a pendant you haven't worn for at least fifteen years) will prick your consciousness a final time, and you'll decide it's time to dejunk.

Go to it! If you move out those coffee-bean bracelets and sixties peace medallions (shovel them into a box for your favorite subteen), it'll give the good stuff some room to breathe and a chance to shine.

Excess personal ornament is just one more slow choker of our time and room. And the jewelry box is a nice small place to start and build decluttering confidence. Empty the whole thing on top of the table or do it drawer by drawer.

1. Evict any stray nuts and bolts, strayed Easter basket chicks, etc.
2. Gather up all the nonworking watches, mateless earrings and cuff links, unstrung beads, chipped enamel earrings, pins with discolored or worn plating, etc., and either get them fixed or quietly retire them.
3. If you can't bear to part with it, at least move the mere memorabilia out: the circle pin that was so in when you were in junior high, your first-ever steady's school ring, the micro-dot diamond from your first engagement.
4. Pass unused valuables to family.
5. If you love the stone but hate the setting, reset it to your taste or style so you can use it.
6. Sell the stuff you never liked if it's genuine. Sure beats being anxious about it—for nothing, in this case. A trip to somewhere you've yearned to go would add more sparkle to your life!
7. Give all those one-time tie pins and novelty necklaces and earrings that will never grace your neck or ears again (the miniature glass giraffes, the pot-metal pandas, the three-colors-of-feather creations, the earrings made out of avocado pits or miniature fishing lures) to someone to whom they're still a novelty.

The Junk Drawer (a.k.a. Morgue Drawer for the House)

No way would I expect you to cleanse it completely in a day. This thing has a mix of live, dead, and comatose so detailed that a medical examiner couldn't do justice to it. But you can start by picking off the top layers of totally gone stuff: the broken, bent, worn, and obviously worthless tossed in here. Face it, man: that dried-up package of glue is a goner, those burnt-out receptacles and worn faucet parts are in here because they were no good where they were before—and they can't ever go back. Don't pull the whole drawer out (hernia city)—just open it and scoop out some of the worst today: outdated phone books, mangled appliance booklets, overflowing and abused drawer organizers that are now part of the junk, matchbooks with one match, one button off each piece of furniture in the house and from each piece you've ever owned, parts to departed

tools, a half-dozen freebie sewing kits, postage-stamp-size school pictures of your nieces and nephews dating back to the beginning of time. Spend ten minutes a day for the next few days and that valuable drawer might actually reach 75 percent efficiency.

"After reading your first book on clutter I decided to clean out my junk drawer, Now, I always thought I needed a drawer in my kitchen for all the little odds and ends that really didn't fit in any category and just didn't fit into any other drawer. At first I just picked through it, removing things that I hadn't used in years (a blackboard eraser, a pocket knife), but after a few minutes of that I decided to dump the thing and just put things I *really* used back in. I ended up with scissors, a few pens, tape, elastic bands, a deck of cards, a paper punch, a notepad, and a calorie-counter book. I threw out a whole bunch of stuff, and now I don't mind opening the drawer like I did before! And no longer do I have to rifle through everything for five minutes to find what I need. It's there in plain sight!"

Bulletin Board

All clutter isn't crammed, stacked, or hidden; some of it is displayed! Standing in front of our mirror we see an image of ourselves—standing in front of our bulletin board we can see that and a lot more. A bulletin board (at work, home, the shop, and anywhere else we have one) is a public posting of our mental state: what we have there, how it's hung or attached, how old it is, how much there is, how many layers deep (by the way, the record is 207 notes, photos, recipes, and cartoons held onto one refrigerator front with magnets). A cluttered, outdated bulletin board is a clue that we're the same. Attend to this telltale artifact now. Off with the old stale jokes, last semester's school papers, too-late-to-question repair bills, didn't-get-rid-of-an-ounce diets, you-can-be-sure-it's-no-longer-available classified ads. Out with those exceeded estimates, superseded schedules, and ignored reminders. Same with last season's upcoming events and the phone numbers and addresses written at all different heights and seven different angles. Most bulletin boards look about the same as the one at the local laundromat.

Yet used properly, a bulletin board is the perfect way to keep aware of and prepare yourself to face the big stuff right around the corner. See page 45 for how to use your bulletin board to aid your decluttering campaign.

P.S. Taking clutter off the bulletin board and slipping it into a drawer doesn't count!

Notebooks

Well, it seemed like good information at the time…at the class, the conference, the meeting, the presentation, when we were brow deep in that project or proposal. We had no doubt that all these notes would be valuable to us or our organization someday. The sturdy covers or folders that surround them look and feel so valuable, those crisply snapping ring binders and information storage pouches so official.

Most note taking is done in deadly earnest at the time, but the majority of notebooks in this world are reproaches to their owners. Much of what's in them is long dead or no longer necessary, and at least a third of it is indecipherable. Many notebooks are only about a third full, and all those empty aged pages take up a lot of space. The average person has at least three of those two-inch-thick spiral bound jobs packed with outdated pages they never will again need or refer to. It's time to translate or transfer those notes (to the file or list that will put them in action) or else just toss them. Get them all out and gut them—lift/tear out all the good stuff and dump all the chaff. Okay, you can keep the binders or folders. Keeping the good notes in the best binder doubles your pleasure and the room for new notes!

Photos

How could photos be clutter? Easy. Photos have only one value—to be seen! What percent of all you have now is ever seen or appreciated? Probably about 1 or 2 percent. Where are all the rest? Tucked away somewhere, working on that browned, antique look. Why do we stack them in boxes and wait for the basement to flood or the attic heat treatment to destroy them?

There's some pure junk mixed in there, too. Many of us have everything from Instamatics to semiprofessional outfits today, yet we still manage to cut off heads, miss our shootee entirely, or foul up the focus. And what do we do with all this? Keep it, of course; we toss those blurry buggers right in the pile with the others, along with the Polaroids that only half developed, miscellaneous mountains and trees from God's country ('cause only He knows where they were shot), the inside of the car/kitchen/camera bag that Junior snapped, the half-photos that used to contain your ex-spouse(s), photos of people and places we never really wanted a picture of, and pictures handed down to us by people at least equally unsure of who they were of. These days we not only get all of our pictures back almost instantly; we get double prints even of all the things we didn't want in the first place. And right in the box or drawer, too, are those little end strips from the film, totally black or psychedelically off-color shots, aged coupons and brochures for photo cards and enlargements, mailers for never-tried by-mail film-developing companies, and of course the negs. None of which we get rid of at the grand opening of the freshly developed pix—instead we put it *all* back in the envelope to deal with "later." So we end up with a lot of "developed clutter" as well as a lot of super value, all mixed together.

Pictures are not only the first thing people run to save in a fire, they're one of the most effective life enhancers around—if we let them be. They're also one of the easiest clutter clogs to deal with because there are only three categories:

- **Trash and trimmings:** The film ends, brochures you're not interested in, film containers, etc. Toss them right away when you open.
- **Bad shots:** They aren't ever going to improve so toss them unless they're your *only* record of a person, place, or pet past.
- **Good Photos:** You've got lots of them, right? Great! So make good use of them. And in this

department there are two divisions:

Keepers: These are the ones that prompt a sigh, smile, or tear—they're precious indeed, so why have them packed up in a box or stored away? They have absolutely no value if they're not seen. Put them in an album, on the wall, in a scrapbook or family or life history, make use of that amazing eyewitness record, and watch a new spark come into your life.

Givers: These are pictures, old or new, of people, places, or things that others will enjoy a hundred times more than you. Slip them in an envelope and send them as a surprise to your old classmate or former neighbor or army buddy.

As for Negatives: If you toss these in the drawer, too, right along with everything else in there, you'll never make a reprint of *anything* because you'll dread searching through that whole mess so much. As soon as a set of negatives comes back, slip it into an envelope marked with the date and subject(s), and put it in a special area set aside for negatives.

Frozen Projects

A lot can be said for having several fronts to fight on; having a few different projects under way and unfinished gives you some variety to choose from to suit your mood. But most of us have more than a few—including many we've outgrown or lost interest in and just don't want to admit we have. This particular stuff is among the most invisible of all clutter, perhaps because we don't *want* to see such evidence of fickle interests, interrupted ambitions, and failed will. Frozen (in time, and forgotten) projects can be anything from the corduroy jumper we got half cut-out last Christmas Eve to the room addition still unfinished, the tarpaper tacked over the naked framing slowly weathering away.

"The tangled macramé with the ropes all bundled and rubber-banded, the Christmas stocking pieces with sequins and beads still Zip-locked in a plastic bag... a kit to make an advent calendar, a big tree on a red felt background and pockets numbered for each December day—I think I cut out the tree nine years ago... a set of four bibs with Mickey Mouse printed on them that you simply cut out and sew the edging on—they're all pinned together ready to stitch, and I remember them at least once during every friend's pregnancy... bags of goose feathers still waiting to be washed and made into a pillow, the partly completed model Piper Cub, the woodburning kit still in its original box, with half a bald eagle burned out, the assemble-it-yourself radio kit three-quarters done (but now missing parts), that strung-out string art project..."

MY GOSH, HEINRICH, IT LOOKS LIKE AN ANCIENT FROZEN PROJECT.

ANTARCTIC EXPEDITIONS

Today is the day to yank these out of the drawer or closet, spread them out, and review their status in your life at this time. Deep down you know how deep they still go with you. A few judgment factors here:

1. Your enthusiasm for them NOW;
2. The time available to do this, compared with new or other projects you have in the works, or would like to have;
3. Cost: is it really worth finishing?

If you're not going to defrost that frozen project, dispose of the remains—today.

Finished Project Clutter

The little projects we do at home aren't much different from the big hotels or commercial buildings going up downtown. We need tools and supplies and maybe even machinery to help accomplish ours, too. So we set up tables and sawhorses, make patterns or diagrams, we assemble tools, supplies, and materials galore. But too many times we finish the project itself up fine and then forget about all it took to finish it. Here, there, and everywhere, often for months afterward, are little mounds and piles of unfinished project mess—the afterbirth of missions accomplished—that scrapbook, science fair, or painting project. It doesn't just clutter the place up—half of this is dangerous or is stuff we've been looking for ever since we finished. What if builders and contractors left their scaffolding up after the building was finished?

Next project, think of the three "P's": Plan it, Perform it, *Police* it. Don't let the beauty of the building be belittled by a bunch of outgrown support stuff, like:

- Glue bottles and cans of paint
- Dropcloths, old newspapers, masking tape
- Directions and instruction sheets, reference books
- Droplights, extension cords, flashlights
- Cord, string, and measuring tapes
- The packaging and containers the parts and supplies came in
- The tools we used
- The nails, screws, and washers we didn't need
- Clamps, forms, frames, braces
- Solvent-soaked or paint-smeared rags
- Scraps (see below) and piles of sawdust
- Cigarette butts, empty soda cans, cups of moldy coffee
- The portable radio or tape player that helped make the job tolerable

Scraps

The most endearing and enduring clutter of all. Even the purest and most disciplined neatnik has a few (more like a few hundred) of these "pieces of eight" stashed in their garage, cellar, attic, bin, or shed. The very rich and the outright poor are equally guilty of it. There's scarcely an activity that doesn't yield some kind of scrap, and since this stuff has no regular dimensions there's no reasonable or orderly way to store or stack it. We rarely have a real use for it when we seize it, but it's every woman's dream, every man's ambition to weld a bunch of old stuff together into something useful. Never do we hear more pride in the voice, no greater statement of accomplishment is there than "Look, I made this out of scraps."

Scraps! They ensnare us by their very virginity. They're too crisp and clean to commit to curbstone or trash can. They're small, sure, but still *new* and good, those leftover part strips of panelling, tiny 2 x 4 slices, and odd bits of insulation. There must be some way, if we just have enough faith, to render them whole again! Just think of the silly scraps you've clawed and fought to get and keep. Who knows how many brain cells are burned out processing and reprocessing possibilities for these pathetic pieces and for what? We cut it off once because it didn't fit, and it sure doesn't fit now!

Out with stupid scraps:

- The original: tiny strips and scraps of Christmas paper
- Enough-left-to-go-once-around-the-roll shelf paper, wallpaper, or contact paper
- 4-inch-wide rug remnants (a red carpet for a Barbie wedding?)
- 5- or 6-inch lengths of electric cable, dryer vent hose, plastic or metal pipe, wooden molding
- A few leftover half-shingles or pieces of vinyl siding
- Teeny pieces of screening
- Bits and strips of vinyl flooring
- Ten or twenty ceramic or vinyl or acoustic tiles (too many to use for hot plates, too few to make a floor or ceiling)
- Almost-empty cans of roof paint and blacktop sealer
- Odd, small pieces of Formica, Masonite, or sheetrock
- Three or four bricks or cinder blocks
- The 2 or 3 inches you cut off anything you ever hemmed
- Less than a foot of anything, from eyelet to ribbon to bias tape

Keeping stuff like this is legitimate only if you own a farm or furnish dollhouses.

HONEY, I TOLD YOU MY SCRAP BIN WOULD COME IN HANDY. SEE?... I FIXED THE CHAIR.

Bad Sports

The score of much of your sports stuff is now 0. It's lost its greatest fan—you. It's ready to be a free agent. Come on, I dare you. Spread it all out on the playing field and be an umpire willing to call things out. The season or inning's over for:

- The two oars and anchor (no boat, of course)
- The bowling ball drilled to fit whose fingers, you have no idea! (but it's so heavy it must be worth something)
- Shriveled golf gloves and golf aids, and accessories that never were par for the course
- Dry-rotted and rusted ice skates that would pinch your toes even if you were willing to try to stand up in them again
- Unstrung tennis rackets
- Broken badminton nets, beat-up birdies, and unraveled rackets
- The single pool stick or golf club cowering amid the tomato stakes
- Croquet sets for games you'll never play
- Cracked baseball bats
- All that unsafe and out-of-style ski stuff
- Flat footballs and basketballs
- Moldy sleeping bags (you've reached the Holiday Inn stage, anyway)
- Ammunition for no-longer-owned guns
- And all that sports stuff you bought for Show and Tell only.

It may have been Olympic once, but it's limp now! No substitutes, please!

The Tackle Box

If you happen not to fish, you're excused—unless you have one of its identical twins (sewing box, jewelry box, toolbox, etc.).

Don't wait for lakeside to start rummaging through those tangles of "someday salvageable" leaders and "remeltable" sinkers, the reel you hate to use but have carried for years "just in case." Everything you stuffed in last fall will be stiff and attached to everything else when the big fish start biting at the water's edge. So at home, today, out of the wind and cold, open that box and enjoy true fisherman's luck. Arm yourself with a pair of scissors and a container for tossed junk. Then empty the whole box on a tarp or the table, spread it all out, and sort through hooks, spinners, and flies. While it's all out, you'll actually be able to wash the scales and dead bait bits off (mummified worms, minnows and marshmallows, moldy cheese and doughballs) and out of your little chest. Now, instead of when you're standing over those little plastic drawers shivering with a flashlight, you can separate the #8 hooks from the #10's—and even find a little empty box to stash them neatly and safely.

Tackle Box Toss List:

- Broken floats
- Whiskerless and featherless poppers
- Empty packaging
- Rocks and pebbles
- Lures that have never caught anything
- Half rubber worms
- The incredibly beat-up plugs and spoons you found
- The magic lure retriever that didn't
- Torn nets
- Ruined creels
- Dry-rotted or hopelessly holey hip boots/waders

- The ice-fishing tackle you used once six years ago, and will never use again

Gardening Garbage

We got into gardening because we love the natural, but we're somehow quickly surrounded by the man-made. A few fatal clutter-encouraging ingredients here: the need for tools (a good gardening freak will have 10,000 tools to produce six cucumbers and five radishes) and a tendency to dream up/plan more than we can enact. Plus an excuse to ignore at least half of it because it's the wrong season.

Grub out that garden garbage now:

- Broken trellises
- Part bags of seed/fertilizer/chemical you don't recognize
- Broken spreaders and sprinklers
- Holey watering cans and leaky hoses
- Toothless rakes
- Sun-rotted plastic mulch and rain-rotted burlap
- Rusty, rickety hose reels
- Unsuccessful self-watering units
- Clogged soaker hoses
- Bent prong forks
- Poisons that are no longer approved
- Handleless trowels
- The extra half-dozen hand cultivators
- Hardened fertilizer and caked lime
- Tiny pieces of flower-bed edging
- Abandoned Gro-light outfits and start-your-own-from-seed supplies
- Unassembled strawberry pyramids
- Fingerless garden gloves
- Hoes and trowels with broken handles
- Broken flowerpots and crushed peat pots
- Slow grass clippers
- Broken plastic plant labels and snapped plant stakes
- Decomposing flower bulbs and expired seeds
- Nonrunning lawn mowers
- Bottomless bushel baskets
- That rusty sculpture of stuck-together tomato cages
- The little plastic tray from every dozen petunias you ever bought
- The seeds you saved from _____ (?)
- The cactus the cat chewed
- The amaryllis, Easter lily, or poinsettia you will never bother to get to bloom again

Art and Craft Clutter

The urge to create is a worthy one, but it clogs more than its share of cupboards and cubbyholes. The *idea* of doing something arty is so appealing that we run out to get all those supplies. We dive into a project for a while; then we don't get the results we expected, or simply lose interest and move on to other neat-sounding crafts.

Halfhearted or fad hobbies are the worst. We see a clever woodcarver at a mall show or county fair. The whole crowd is oohing and aahing. "Boy, would I like to do that," we say. "It looks so easy." We take the name and address of the knife company, but by the time the 22-piece cased set arrives, the craving for carving has whittled away. Stiffen your resolve—it doesn't take too many of these little purchases to fill a room or a life.

We never get rid of any of this because we're firm in the illusion that we'll take it up again someday, and of course, we don't intend to waste our investment.

Pull all this stuff out, apply the test questions on page 144, and give away whatever flunks before it's no good to anybody.

- Dried up poster paints
- Aged oil paints
- Hardened modeling clay
- Used paraffin
- Unopened latch-hook rug kit or bundles of three-inch leftovers from previous hookings
- Retired rock tumbler
- Rusty lettering pens and evaporated ink
- Coffee-stained illustration board
- Partly done needlepoint project
- Huge wad of leather swatches
- Boxes of pop pull tabs and walnut shell halves
- Three-quarters of a quilt frame
- Abandoned mosaic ashtray
- Half-painted ceramics
- Glitter, glitter, glitter

Music Junk

You have none? If you haven't looked around lately, here are a few sour notes you might find:

- Broken-reed harmonicas
- Old horns with no mouthpieces (or mouthpieces, no horns)
- Headless drum sets
- Cracked guitars and maimed mandolins
- The castanets or maracas somebody brought back from Mexico
- The instrument you thought you might like to play/that someone talked you into taking lessons on/that was popular that year
- Sheet music with two sheets missing
- Warped records

- Tapes or CDs you never liked, or on which you only like one song
- Earphones to missing player
- Spaghettied tapes
- Eight-track tapes (no players around for them since '79)
- Turnless turntables
- Component with the "ponent" gone
- Broken music boxes
- The stereo you no longer use, and the "record player" you used before that
- And don't miss the big one: the piano you got for a mere $150 (the veneer is peeling off and more hammers are missing than present)

Electrical Junk

I pull out an electric cord at my De-junking Seminar, and the spirit of "value" surges through the audience. For some strange reason an electric cord sanctifies and excuses. Anything (no matter how worthless) remains in storage if it has a cord.

I hold up another item: "Five years ago when the electric dishcloth came out, how many of you bought one?" Gasps are heard, brows wrinkle, many reach for their checkbooks. When they come to their senses they realize the cord did it to them, as it does to all of us. Just clip off the cord on that rusty old mixer out there and see what happens to your allegiance to it.

Today, make a little expedition to the kitchen, shop, office, attic, basement, in search of electrical clutter, especially:

- Appliances you already have one or two better of
- Gadgets and machines that come into use far too rarely to deserve the prime space they occupy
- Machines with too limited a function—i.e., the electric olive stuffer
- Broken electric things not worth fixing/they don't make parts for anymore
- Things that do things you still think the manual edition does better

> "One of the best feelings I've ever had was to take the food processor off my counter and put it in my box marked 'garage sale.' I told my husband I felt like I'd lost 50 pounds! That thing had been an albatross in the kitchen for years!"

Gauche Gift Day

Ours is not to reason why, some people bless us with goshawful gifts. We can all look around right now and spot at least a dozen of these white elephants: that set of purple plastic patio ware; the complete set of soap, powder, bath oil, and cologne in a scent we detest; a musical coffee mug; a six-foot-tall stuffed animal; the pictures from old calendars our cousin framed himself; the crocheted doll whose arms encircle the toilet paper roll; the 18-inch owl outdoor thermometer; a little machine for making square hard-boiled eggs; a gaudy plastic "lawn ornament"; the hand-thrown ceramic baseball-cap-shaped ashtray (personalized with our initials).

We can appreciate the love, care, cash, and maybe even hard work that went into these, and how genuinely the giver intended to please us. But we don't have to let stuff like this take up space on our premises forever. If we don't ever intend to use it, don't really want to look at it, and refuse to display it, it's true dead weight. It's not unconscionable to thank the person for it sincerely, let them feel your genuine appreciation of the thought—and then give it away (see page 165). There's someone out there who might actually be delighted by it.

Other People's Possessions (Another Easy Starter)

Just how much of the stuff straining your shelves and clogging your closets isn't yours? My dad taught us to take anything we borrowed back in even better condition than when we got it (cleaned and shined, or with extra parts or nails, as a little act of appreciation and thank-you). If you follow that philosophy faithfully, you'll have little around the house that isn't yours. So I thought! But I found—as you have, too— that I have all kinds of things around I didn't ask for, stuff people just dropped off and forgot or were looking for a place to stash. Or they wanted to share something with me and my family so it ended up at my house.

I thought I had nothing borrowed and only a thing or two parked at my house. Well, guess again, Virginia; I had over seventy pieces of equipment and old projects from my company, at least forty articles my scout troop and various weekend guests had left behind, thirty or forty things each of my children had blessed me with (including and not limited to motors, working and nonworking; cars in the process of restoration;

wedding reception gift arrays; muskrat traps; walking sticks; posters; hammocks; suitcases; cosmetics; etc.).

There's lots of room on a ranch, and I also own several business buildings and properties (which means space)—much of it accessible to the public and thus overjunked. Friends, relatives, and even enemies find storage at my office, warehouse, shop, and sheds, as well as home. I even have stuff from friends of friends!

As for the borrowed stuff, when you really start looking around you may discover that your place is partly furnished with other people's possessions. Most of us even have a church hymnbook or two we somehow picked up and dragged home and keep forgetting to take back.

So, folks—and this is one dejunking act that's fun and easy and little anguish—return all those borrowed and abandoned things today. It'll make a big dent in your assemblage.

Most of this isn't good enough to confiscate—the really good stuff they usually come back and get quick. So get it back to them—or get rid of it—now. The community center will be glad to see those old folding chairs again, and the library thrilled to recover those long-lost volumes.

Just go on an old-fashioned roundup for stray dogies, corral them, read their brands, and call or visit the owners. Always box stuff like this neatly and deliver it crisp and clean and then you're off the hook, not to mention much lighter: "Here, Harry, I thought you'd want these back. Sorry I've had them so long."

Other People's Stuff (They Left It Behind or You Borrowed It)

- Old raincoats, sweaters, overshoes, umbrellas
- Hats, scarves, and gloves
- T-shirts and socks
- Suitcases and trunks
- Eyeglasses and/or glasses cases
- Keys
- Hair-care stuff: shampoo, styling lotion, etc.
- Toothbrushes, mouthwash, shaving cream
- Single earrings and junk jewelry
- Golf clubs, fishing rods, tennis rackets, sleeping bags
- Cassettes, CDs, videotapes
- Books and magazines
- Travel literature and maps
- The plastic container, plate, or casserole they brought their covered dish in
- Punch bowls and oversized coffeepots
- Coolers and thermos bottles
- Tools: saws, hammers, drills, shovels, rakes, posthole diggers, etc., etc.
- Toys from visiting kids
- Whole boxes and half-cellars of junk, broken down motorcycles, and cars, from teenage children now grown and moved

If all else fails, put rigid requirements on any storage on your premises, such as "only in neatly boxed condition." This alone is often enough to make the storer look for another storage spot. Here are some other ways to make the muckers move or at least think twice about entrusting their valuables to you:

Fear: "My house was robbed twice this summer—I don't think they got any of your stuff." "We're hoping to give the whole place a good cleaning out this spring." "Somebody came by last week and moved out a whole pickup load, I hope they got the right stuff." "My eight-year-old's feet are almost big enough to fit those boots you left in the basement."

Or best of all, in my experience: Tell them you can't find it. Say, "Did you take that stuff home? I hope no one tossed it out." Let it ride for a few tortured days and notice the agony and horror in their voice, then tell them one morning you found it. It'll be gone in hours. Works every time.

Workplace Clutter

An uncluttered workplace feels good, looks good, saves us time, makes us more efficient, and is healthier and safer. It also is sure to impress the boss and fellow employees.

A messy workplace is demoralizing and makes every job harder. It also creates security problems and diminishes respect. It even undermines our chances of promotion and advancement—superiors can't help but wonder how we could run a department if we can't even control our immediate area. And what critical company business or long-forgotten correspondence is buried under all that?

Do any of the following sound familiar?

Homefront Hanna

The company told Hanna to feel at home, and she took it literally. Plants, pictures, statuettes, planters, souvenirs, coffeepot, toaster, etc., cover and surround her desk and make a businesslike atmosphere or actual work almost impossible. Her collection is also a temptation for thieves and an invitation for breakage during the cleaning process.

James and Joan Junkdesk

Both had security blankets when young and still have, somewhere in their desk, every letter anyone ever wrote them after they got that new title. They have a graduate degree in piling and have to burrow to find anything. (Don't even *try* to calculate the time lost when they can't find something.) Their desk and area constantly embarrasses the rest of the office, but it doesn't bother them.

Larry Lockerful

Larry has a wife at home who dejunks, straightens, and cleans his closets. She can't get into his locker at work, so it's a chef's salad of clutter (he even left a dead salmon in there once). When the door will no longer close, the overflow rests right on the floor beneath the bent or sprung door.

Junk, as well as good stuff stacked up in high-use or highly visible areas, makes the whole place look bad and cuts everyone's efficiency. Inevitably, this piled material will:

- **Get damaged or broken:** The janitor's floor-stripping water will seep under it, people and machines will run into it, things will get set on it, it will get knocked over, knocked off, or spilled on.
- **Stolen or missing:** Even if it isn't valuable, if something is left out long enough, it will be taken, borrowed, or used by someone else.
- **Multiply:** Just put one piece of junk or clutter on a shelf, desk, floor, or cabinet, and it will soon be joined by scores of others.
- **Cause accidents:** Most office accidents—for example lifting, falling, and fire—are the result of junk.

Getting rid of all this is easy, especially if everybody pitches in (or out)! Declare an Office D-Day (Dejunk Day)—or week!

Rolodex Day

Time to tackle the Rolodex (and all variations of these miniature name-and-address catalogues). Ever try to find things in a four-year-old phone book? That's why they update them yearly, and you should, too. Nothing is static in life or society, and that includes your Rolodex and all of your other address books and listings. Your time is valuable. Who wants to do a hunt or play a guessing game, or to call defunct or wrong

numbers? Think of the new matches and detachments every year (marriages, deaths, divorces); add in moves, bankruptcies, paid-off and new accounts, and all the things that are now *ex.*

This will take less than an hour. Just flip or scan and pull. Bad food? Out goes a restaurant address. Traded the Dodge? Out goes its service center card. Retired? One more contact bites the dust. Stood up three times? Out goes Wonder Buns or Handsome Harry. Then spread all the yanked cards out on a clean table or countertop and quickly review them (just in case you got carried away). Now dump all the defunct ones and you and Rolo can twirl again.

Lockers

Ever wonder what a professional cleaner's most dreaded assignment might be? Unquestionably, lockers. Most lockers are used so intermittently they can easily be piled full and defiled and left behind for another day. All lockers start out like children: innocent, open, positive. Then we convert them slowly to junk banks where we make regular deposits and no withdrawals, until we can barely force the door shut.

Lockers look so innocent that no one would ever guess the long-overdue purge pending within. A wide selection of dried-up half sandwiches and partial candy bars, empty deodorant cans, deformed posters, a complete array of forgotten clothes from old raincoats to athletic supporters, broken sunglasses and wrecked racquetball rackets, last year's top-20 cassette, dead AAA batteries, empty paper cups, old invoices and papers graded F, and at least one abandoned book or notebook. Your locker probably reached the no-more-compression mark months ago.

Take a sturdy box in with you today and scoop out all those foul finds. This move will re-establish you as a good sport to all your neighboring locker mates (and they might even start including you in their social circle again).

The Junk of Your Profession

Just as most doctors were once general practitioners, we all used to be general junkers, with the usual run-of-the-mill stuff. Now we're all specialists as well in the unique junk of our profession—keeping it for parts, for evidence, for research or for the record, or as "a resource." A professional packrat is the most dangerous species!

Some percentage of this does have a valid or even important purpose, but as for the rest of it, why, honestly, are we keeping it? To hand down? Even if our son or daughter is in the business, they either aren't the least bit interested in what we saved or want a newer model, but we are keeping it just in case. It helps create a professional atmosphere, maybe? Most offices or shops would look a lot more professional with at least six layers of this litter gone.

A lot of this professional stuff has so many precious memories and miles on it, evidence of our past accomplishments, that it seems heartless to heave it. But a workplace has only so much space for memorabilia, as opposed to active, needed working gear. So put your work down for a minute and just look at the clutter, lying around here, there, and everywhere. Who else can evaluate it but you?

- Outdated business cards, stationery, brochures, flyers, catalogues, magazines, books, directories
- All the junk you scooped up at those trade shows
- Antique samples, including stuff you collected to study the competition about a decade ago
- No-longer-needed files
- Leftover piles from long-past projects
- Obsolete equipment or machinery
- Superseded uniforms
- Now-unnecessary supplies
- Worn-out or substandard tools

The biggest reason we're half-buried here isn't hard to figure out. The whole thrust of modern enterprise of any kind is Onward! Forward motion! Next steps! New properties! Next month's/year's priorities! The minute one thing is safely delivered/handed in (or long before it is), it's on to the new, the upcoming. All very well and good and possibly profitable, but it sure does encourage skipping or ignoring an important last task on the old.

The last thing we need to do on those old or recently finished projects is dismantle them—put the tools we used on them back, return the files we got out for them, throw out the scraps and leftovers and all those pages of scribbled notes, go through all the papers we assembled for this and put the few that are really worth keeping somewhere they could actually be found if we needed them.

Putting away/breaking camp/disassembling isn't sexy; it may not be fea-

tured on the front page of the *Wall Street Journal* and might even be un-American—but if we don't do it sooner or later we'll be out of business.

The Toolbox

Why, we wonder, is there less and less room for tools here over time? The toolbox that was once a clean-trayed womb of the right wrench and ratchet to squeeze, pound, screw, cut, or tighten any ailing object now has so much extraneous stuff in it that it could more accurately be called a bumble box. Where does every leftover bolt or tack go? Parts almost but not quite dead? Half of a pair of anything? Rusty nails and removed staples, no-lead pencils? We throw empty cartridges, lids, broken blades, spent thermostats, worn-out sandpaper, and crumpled warranties in here, too, and it ends up overflowing the dividers and making the box so heavy it can't be lifted (as a live toolbox needs to be). Then we add the finishing touch by spilling something sticky that will never evaporate in it.

Any fixer who wants to stay in business can't dodge decluttering the toolbox. Get tough with those broken tape measures and chewed-up screwdrivers and ruptured ring clamps today. How long will it take?

- Tot toolbox—five minutes
- Teen toolbox—give it fifteen
- Hardheaded handyperson—a half hour
- The seasoned pro—an hour max
- Middle-aged yuppie or multihobbyist—better set a Saturday aside! Do it!

Sad Suitcases

I've yet to meet a person who doesn't have at least one suitcase with a broken lock or latch, a sprung hinge, or something impaired to the point that they need to rope it together or say a silent prayer for it before each takeoff. When you see that bra or spare roll of toilet paper coming around the carousel, you know whose case it slipped out of. Today pull out the one suitcase that makes you shudder, the one you feel guilty even lending to desperate relatives. Get it fixed or get rid of it!

There are plenty of sad suitcase innards, too—many of us take 300 or 400 percent more than we need on any trip, and it weighs us down, slows us down, and makes us anxious every step of the way.

Some quiet evening or boring afternoon, when you're trapped in the hotel or motel room anyway, edge over to that suitcase on the stand and take a good hard look at what's in it. How much of it have you used this trip, or will you actually use before you head back? Being prepared is one thing; trying to duplicate your entire wardrobe and home arsenal of equipment is another. Most of us are traveling to places where we could run out to the nearest mall and get al-most anything we need, anyway.

Luggage is a good place to do some dejunking. "Lug"—"age." Enough said!

Stuff at Other People's Places

Yes, even we who have tons of other people's stuff stored at our house still have things cluttering up other people's homes or garages. We may have left it there when we moved out, to "come back and get later" (nine years ago now). Or we asked someone to stash the surplus for us when all our worldly possessions wouldn't fit into our new home. Or we picked something up on vacation and left it "to get on our next visit." Bicycles, motorcycles, boats, books, toys, baby tenders, sports stuff, tools—think and grow guilty and then go get it! Or arrange to do so, but dejunk it. Let's be fair about this: Mother could use the room, too! If any of the clutter is aged-out, rotten, or worthless, junk it right on the spot.

A nice excuse for a call or contact today.

Falsie Clutter

It's easy to overlook this very common type of clutter—the stuff we assemble to appear to be something we aren't. The cowboy or cowgirl impulse, for example, can result in a closet full of boots, buckles, bandannas, hats, and spurs, a lot of it with designer labels, no less.

Disguise or pretend is fine if we actually aspire to be that. But wasting a good portion of our available space (not to mention money) on all this should be reviewed if all we do is dust it and shuffle it from one side of the house to the other. So today, take a hard look at all those "trappings" and see if there aren't at least some you'd be willing to admit aren't—and never will be—you. A few examples here to get you started:

- Outdoorsy "roughing it" stuff—everything from climbing boots to hunting coats to survival knives
- Weights and weight-lifting equipment
- Jogging stuff—endless styles of shoes, sweats, and little sun visors
- Skis and ski accessories right down to the fondue pot
- Gourmet cookery and bakery gear, from copper kettles to cannoli molds
- Wine paraphernalia—racks and glasses, all manner of openers, wraps, coolers, buckets, and bags (especially if you'll never know a chateau from a chalet and truthfully don't care)
- Entrepreneurial and investment accoutrements—magazines, newsletters, seminar literature
- Hardback books to appear the intellectual, including any number you've never read
- Highbrow music you never listen to
- Tools you don't know the use of
- Rarely touched hobby stuff so you can say, "Oh, I do a little..."

Adolescent Appropriations

There is a time in life to leave what we lifted. Oh, I know it wasn't *really* stealing—it was just freshman filch, sophomore seizure, junior pillage, senior swipe—but some way, somehow, it sort of accidentally or innocently got mixed in with our stuff. Thus we end up with a government goodie such as a road sign (No Trucks Over 10 Tons), litter basket, or "caution cone," a few restaurant ashtrays, or an ice bucket from the Hyatt.

Stuff like this may serve well for a while to decorate our room, to display our nerve and satisfy the urge to appropriate something that doesn't really belong to us. But in the end it's real double-burden junk. It takes up room and that mental space called guilt, too. Once we're rid of it, our sentence is served and we're a free man or woman.

So just pack it up and send it back—anonymously, if you prefer. If that's just

FALSIE CLUTTER

not possible or practical, I'd give it to a kid decorating their first room, or just dump it. I doubt the original owner still has an all-points bulletin out on it.

Today's the day to surrender all and any Jesse James Junk: stop signs, statues, towels with someone else's name on them, silverware or salt shakers from Fisherman's Wharf, pilfered pitchers—yes, even that "Do Not Cross Police Line" sawhorse and the charming old can opener you snitched from the state park cabin.

Trophies/Awards

"But I never won anything in my life," you say. Hey, man, these days losers get equal certification. If you're merely alive you're bound to accumulate an abundance of recognitions and keep every single one of them to prove you performed, chaired the committee, or rode the river raft. Trophies and awards are kind of like saving smoke after you've known fire; most of them are really just tangible thank-yous, and after the moment has gone, so has their impact. Except for the nameplate or line with our name on it, few of these are works of art or built for the ages, and they can really pile up if you're a veteran golfer, bowler, shooter, elkhound breeder, etc. Few of us have that much shelf, wall, or mantel space. I found out by removing an award from the frame and glass it's a lot easier to keep and store (and then you have a nice frame for a favorite photo). You can take a picture of yourself with all your outgrown awards and then dispose of them. At least give the broken or tarnished ones to the kids to play with!

Samples

What's a senior citizen going to do with one pantie shield? A middle-aged couple with a couple of aluminum siding pieces or a keychain of Formica chips? A thirty-year-old with two dozen different tiny bars of acne soap and scrub? *Nothing*. These things are all samples given or taken for a cause that is now long past. The possibilities of collecting enough shingles to cover the roof are pretty remote, and any sample of anything you've had around now for more than six months is highly questionable. Its only purpose was to prod us into buying something—and we either did or didn't, so either way the sample is long spent. The very cuteness of those tiny jars, bottles, and tubes only assures that we'll never use them: more samples succomb to frayed packaging (from being transferred from drawer to drawer, cabinet to cabinet) than anything else. Get a bucket or laundry basket out today and make a sample raid—don't let the kids see it, they'll think it's toys—then dump it.

Holiday Hangovers

Not the food or drink we've overconsumed, but all those decorations that have seen better days. No matter how far gone they are, we take them back down, tape or splint them together, and tuck them back into the box. They won't improve any in storage, no matter how well we wrap or pack them. A lot of this was never meant to hold up for more than a couple of months anyway, so look at the stuff as short-term trimmings. When the party's over, part with it. (It makes some of the prettiest color flames in the fireplace!)

Christmas is the big collector here. Most of us have boxes somewhere filled with flattened bows and broken Christmas balls, wads of hopelessly entangled ornament hooks, nonworking strings of Christmas lights and burned-out bulbs (which forces us to retest all over again next year); tinsel garlands with big stretches reduced to bare string, the two tree stands we bought before the one that finally held the tree up, crushed pinecone wreaths, a rusty clogged can of spray snow, the ceramic village or candlestick set that was supposed to light up, half-burned Santa candles, and mangy manger sets.

But New Year's (with that cache of stained crepe paper, leftover confetti, mashed paper hats, and honkless horns from every New Year's Eve party in the past two decades) and Easter (sun-bleached flock Easter bunnies, all the egg-decorating kits you bought and forgot, enough used Easter grass to turf the Colosseum, and mummified candies that "were too cute to eat") aren't far behind. And so on through the year, right up through the haggard door decorations, scorched plastic pumpkins, and coming-apart costumes of Halloween and the battered centerpieces and cracked turkey platters of Thanksgiving.

Dejunk! Do it the morning (or at least the week) after. Have faith, the holiday decorations people will come out next year with a newer, nicer version of almost anything you've got.

It's Your Birthday

The perfect day, coming only once a year, to lighten the weight of the years by ridding yourself of the stuff that's still in labor and is never going to deliver. Like crafts, projects, or collections you never did like, that you kept for a rainy day, for sometime when you were down or sick or bored enough to finish them. A birthday is a day for new hopes and goals and plans, not to be bowed under the burdens of the old ones. So when you blow out the candle, blow out the year's (or the decade's) residue of refuse… and it will be an above-average birthday!

- Cashier clothes that don't suit who you are now— are outgrown, too teenagerish, too matronly, whatever.
- Bag birthday presents you never liked or used.
- At least *thin* that collection of all the birthday cards you ever got.
- Single out some room or area that's closely linked to your self-esteem and give yourself a big lift—declutter it.
- Take a trip or day trip somewhere without all the usual clutter.
- Spend a few minutes meditating: What life goals did you have that have long been lost in—or obscured by—clutter? Now's your chance to re-focus on them as well.

Wedding Whatzits

This is something we intend to do only once, so we do it right with all the trimmings. After all, it's the climax of the whole romantic quest, a chance to build a real monument to the moment.

So weddings mean keepsakes—color-coordinated, of course: invitations, programs, matchbooks, swizzle sticks, and napkins imprinted with the newlyweds' names, champagne glasses, favors, the cake knife, the ceremonial garter, every discolored proof of the wedding pictures. Everything is dated to this special day and most of it (such as the charming little cut-glass saltcellars and sweet little swan nut cups we carry away from every wedding we attend) has no real practical use, but we keep it. We even sneak several of those icing roses and the remains of the bouquet home and put them in cold storage, so they can be kept indefinitely.

The wedding gifts that come rolling in don't do anything to aid the situation: at least two-thirds of them are duplicates of things we already have or carefully chosen to be "fancy" (which almost guarantees they will rarely or never be used): walnut napkin rings, sterling-silver pastry tongs and calling card trays, filigreed platters and bonbon dishes, expensive decorative bowls of uncertain purpose. China, crystal, all the "collectibles." And as for the wedding dress, as well as bridesmaid dresses complete with net headdress: If I told you how many of these we pro cleaners have pulled out of thirty-year-old boxes in attics and basements—wrinkled, flattened, yellowed, mildewed, stained—you wouldn't keep yours two hours after the last photograph.

The only "must" keepable here is that license signed by yourselves and the witnesses. The rest is up to your sentimental thermometer. If you only intend to get hitched once, I can understand your wanting to keep everything, including the motel key. But if you've still got the person, you may no longer need all that proof. And if you redo the job, you definitely will want to review those wedding whatevers.

Anniversary Clutter

A friend of mine worked for a major greeting-card and gift manufacturer, and when he told me how many people there were hard at work thinking up ideas for every imaginable anniversary, I was too stunned to even try to imagine all the other manufacturers also hiring professionals to come up with yet more anniversary inspirations. Add to that the 270 million Americans all marking their own calendars with days that celebrate time elapsed since something or other.

Anniversaries accelerate as we get older—first it's a simple birthday, then school anniversaries, work anniversaries, marriages, and marriage milestones. Unfortunately, the vast majority of stuff conjured up to commemorate all these occasions is perilously close to a perfect example of C-L-U-T-T-E-R.

My advice is to hold it in your heart, not your hand, shelf, or drawer. If you can't wear it, eat it, or sleep on it, do you really want it? Another anniversary is sure to come along better than the one you just celebrated.

Crib Clutter

Just watching a child can heal us of almost anything, and even the meanest miser's callused countenance cracks when a baby's face lights up in a smile. So why do we hook our little ones up to the clutter cord the minute the umbilical is unhooked? Most of us start out having a pile of things even before we're born, so it's no wonder that by the time we're adults, things have gotten out of hand.

It all starts with the cascade of kid clutter called the "shower"—seldom useful things that would really assist the new parents, like a month from a diaper service; usually things like crocheted dresses that snag little fingers and absorb burp stains like mad, or tiny barrettes for a bald baby (we keep them like amulets to coax those first little hairs along) or shoes. (Babies hate shoes but goo-gooing grandmas and upwardly mobile aunts get them nice $25 Nikes, tiny cowboy boots, and even those steel-stiff patent leather things.) Baby shoes have about a fourteen-day life span before they're outgrown, but once a footsie went into one, it can only be dropped into the drawer of sacred shoes waiting to be bronzed. After the shower come those precious first birthdays, and all the stuff *we* buy because it's cute, it's the rage, or we can't do without it.

The useful life of baby stuff passes swiftly—a matter of months at best and then you're stuck with a shelf full of apple juice jars (the kind that come with a nipple already installed). The span from your kids to your grandkids is about twenty years—a long time to keep sagging swings, slow strollers, and faded, wilted nursing bras. Make this **Baby Day**. Once you know you've made your last visit to the maternity ward, pass all those child accessories on. If you're sure it's good stuff, then put it to good use: Make an unexpected gift to an expectant mom.

- **Baby clothes** are one of the few genuinely appreciated hand-me-downs, because kids outgrow clothes fast, before they're even broken in. Other parents are thankful even for garments they can use as play clothes because then they can afford some nice ones and keep them nice.

- **Toys.** Many of the toys we get for kids are things we secretly wanted ourselves. If the baby doesn't play with it, get rid of it; they know what they like.

- **Baptism clothes** are more of a blessing treated as one-shots. Use that lovely outfit once, or for all *your* kids, get all the pictures you need, and then let it go. Save the next generation the feeling that they're duty-bound to slip their little one into a musty, yellowed "heirloom."

- **Mini-remedies.** All those half bottles of cough medicines, mini-aspirin, etc., left over when baby was cured that you were saving for another bout with the flu. Okay, but now that the "baby" is five I'd go for a fresher flask. And keeping old medicines around is dangerous!

- **Furniture.** Everything from mini-chairs to high chairs to potty chairs, cribs to playpens, strollers to rocking horses to swings. When it's obsolete, it's obsolete, and this stuff takes up a lot of ROOM.

Natural Junk

How could any of Mother Nature's offspring be clutter? Be it pine cone, rosy rock, abandoned hornet's nest, or dramatic piece of driftwood, it isn't only pretty and educational, but glory be, it's free! Mother Nature would never attempt to store any of these beautifully constructed wares of the wilderness, but we mere mortals will gather them up and try to pack them in—somewhere. Where we found it, it's elegant and blends right in; inside or in our yard, even colored sand or conch shells seem to clash with everything else. Natural things are all too likely to return to nature (i.e., rot and disintegrate!), too, and attract natural little beasties (bugs, beetles, mice, etc.) to devour them. And how do you like dusting those bird nests you collected? Take a look around for natural junk today:

- Overdried gourds and gap-toothed Indian corn
- Raunchy old raccoon, rattlesnake, or deer hides
- Half sets of antlers and miscellaneous skulls and bones
- Moth-eaten hunting trophies
- Ancient, dusty dried arrangements dropping fuzz, leaves, and seeds all over
- That natural wall hanging that now looks like a natural disaster
- The crumbling pods you picked two years ago
- The ornamental grass you draped over the top of the fridge and forgot
- The hickory nuts and black walnuts you collected but couldn't quite bring yourself to shell
- Tired tumbleweeds and shedding bittersweet
- The set of mud chunks you saved from the pond excavation
- No-longer-iridescent dead butterflies and moths
- Dried-to-powdery-husks garlands of garlic or red peppers

(And while we're at it, the remains of that bouquet of flowers you got last Mother's Day and those overripe pussy willows that have littered half the living room with pollen.)

Medical and Dental Junk

Sick of it, right? I know that bite impression for that tooth cap cost you $600 before you were through, but the old incisor is gone and new one's doing fine. Why keep that chunk of refined concrete and all its relatives—old, yellowed teeth, retainers from long-ago braces, broken bridges, obsolete dentures? Or all that stuff you hauled home from the hospital (removed casts, pins, and braces, pans, jugs, masks, bottles of leftover pills, etc.)? No first-aid kit needs more than six Ace bandages, no attic more than one set of crutches. I guarantee your next trip they'll make you buy all new stuff, and there's no trade-in, so you might just as well gather it all up in that gown that ties in the back and get rid of it today. It's a sad sight and grim reminder anyway. Toss that umbilicus, trash the jar of tonsils, get rid of those gallstones. Being an organ donor is in.

P.S. Why not part with any old prescription eyeglasses you can no longer see out of, too? Organizations like the local life squad or Easter Seals will be happy to get still-functioning medical equipment.

Pet Clutter

How could these unassuming creatures, who have never carried a shopping bag out of a pet boutique or wheeled a cart past the pet section of the supermarket, accumulate so much? Kids may begin to make their own little additions to the clutter pile by a certain age, but in this case we really do have to take the whole rap.

Our furry, scaled, and feathered friends do call for some special equipment, to be sure, but here, too, the mania for multiplying and the temptation to upgrade the trappings rear their heads. Many folks, and families, too, go through stages of pet ownership; those stages rarely reverse themselves, yet we keep everything from the pets we used to have plus everything for the new. Fads in pets come and go but leave a clear set of tracks of what we used to be wild about—in garage, attic, and basement.

- Old bird cage/complete aquarium setup (no storage area complete without one or the other)
- Abandoned rabbit cages, and gerbil or hamster "habitats" (complete with water bottles, etc.)
- Boxes of half-used food (after the pet is long gone) or foods that our pets refuse to eat
- Outdated pet medicines (a miniature of our own medicine chest)
- Old rusty leashes/half-rotted collars
- Leftover white-dog-only shampoo
- The harness you could never get the cat to wear
- Moldy tack and spoiled hay (from the horse you used to have)
- Fancy pet beds they refuse to use

- Unsuccessful self-watering and -feeding devices
- Poop-scooping equipment for the pooch you will never have again
- The two bags of fur you were saving to spin into sweaters
- Disused doghouses
- Flown coops
- The too large, too small, or Fluffy-doesn't-like-to-use-it bowl
- Sweater from a long-deceased chihuahua
- At least four brushes/combs for every animal that could conceivably be brushed
- Toys that never got a tumble/are more than half eaten

Love Anchor Junk

It always existed, but now it flourishes—because man/woman relationships are so much more versatile than in the old days of meet and marry. You form a relationship and at first it looks as though it will last forever, so infatuation overrides good sense. The two of you exchange commodities. (There's something about each of you having something valuable that belongs to the other that seems to really put the seal on your togetherness.) Sometimes it's done very consciously and solemnly and sometimes just by accident—some of your stuff ends up there because you spend so much time there. However it happens, she ends up with the nine iron (out of your $700 set), and you have two leatherbound volumes from her set of Great Books. Then the relationship fails, suddenly or slowly, and you both have the other's clutter, which does neither of you much good. But you'd both rather keep the stuff than see that "ex" again, very possibly in the company of his or her new flame. You won't throw it out because maybe it's valuable and maybe your ex will want it. There are rare cases of keeping for revenge, of course, but for the

most part the stuff just clutters up the premises and makes you grind your teeth whenever you happen to run across it.

Cut the chagrin today: Send all such stuff back with a self-addressed and stamped box so there can be no excuse for not throwing yours in and shipping it back. (If it doesn't come, you'll know it was given to the new boyfriend or girlfriend.) If the item in question is too bulky to be treated this way, and the person doesn't live too many states away, you could enlist a sympathetic friend to go pick it up for you and even arrange the pickup, if you're *really* chicken.

If all else fails, here is a form letter:

Exchanging things in person might be a little awkward / inconvenient for both of us, but I'm sure you've missed this. Enclosed is a self-addressed label / envelope / jiffy bag. Could you just slip my_____ in it and drop it in the mail?

(You can enclose a check for additional postage if you think it's going to be more than what it cost to send theirs back.)

And Now That Mental Clutter

When someone says "clutter" we immediately visualize a pile of stuff—but let's dig deeper. As a certified doctor of dirt and maven of mess for more than thirty years now, I believe that the worst clutter problem is not in the garage, basement, or rental unit. The greatest battle with clutter of all is in the mind— what we carry in our head and heart. Long after the closet is decluttered, many of us suffer on, because we didn't hold a mental garage sale too. As Richard Lovelace said so many years ago:

If I… in my soul am free,
Angels alone that soar above
Enjoy such liberty.

Unnecessary **anxiety** drags us down and robs our ambition and energy. **Unpaid debt** is dead weight unmatched by forty old appliances, and **old envy** is greener and ranker than the mold on anything in the refrigerator. **Lust** or **coveting** burns up more ambition than tending ten storage units.

Physical clutter is easy to see, reach, and deal with; mental clutter is the real killer. Stored jealousies and resentments will litter your life far more than a few excess bags and boxes.

> **Mental clutter can affect our character**, slowly, silently, but surely, and do a lot more harm than a collection of old hats and heat coils.

Mental clutter is tough to conquer, but it helps to go after the physical stuff first. Go after the gullies of garbage around the house, yard, and office first and watch what happens in the old head—a great surge of motivation and momentum. *Everyone* tells me, "Once the stuff went, my mental struggles were much less, the cobwebs seemed to clear out of my brain." What an incentive to *unload*! Do it!

Double-Reward or Chain-Reaction Decluttering

Have you ever lined up a bunch of dominos, knocked over the leader, then sat back to enjoy the show and watch him mow down all the rest? You can do this with clutter, too. Old Jed, for example, had a pile of tires in his backyard. He kept them all, bald and dry-rotted, because he thought they must be worth something. Nobody liked Jed's tires, and someone finally convinced him to take them all in on the town's "old tire collection day." Jed had pushed the lead domino, and suddenly his wife became affectionate, his neighbors started talking to him again, the mosquito problem vanished, rats stopped appearing in the yard, the city quit sending threatening certified letters. And he had a garden spot again! All of this and he only did one thing—toss the tires!

Yes, *one* act of dejunking can create a chain reaction, can iron out twenty other things. And you get all kinds of neat byproducts: respect, space, clear conscience, safety, even charity. For instance, if you:

- **Stop smoking:** You'll breathe and run better; you'll have no more holes in the upholstery or sticky yellow walls and windows, and you save money.

- **Stop drinking:** Your head will no longer hurt in the morning, your liver will last longer, you'll have fewer nasty arguments, enjoy your guests more, and save money.

- **Stop garage sailing:** You'll save gas, save money, have more room for your own clutter, and

no longer be tortured by all those second thoughts, or the feeling that you need to find the time to do all that fixing and refinishing.

Conversational Clutter

This is tougher to blame on others than our other clutter—it comes right out of our mouths and minds. Well-thought-out words can master almost any situation; the reverse, junk talk, reveals a fool—not us, of course, the other guy—at work, at school, or across the street.

Consider the conversations you've participated in recently—say, just the last two days of talking and listening. How much was muttering, making excuses, arguing, criticizing, complaining, and gossiping? Some of it may have been unavoidable, but most wasn't worth the effort either to absorb or to pass on. It's cluttering your life as much as your crammed closets or grubby glove compartment. The more junk in your talk, the less likely it is that you'll say something important—so the less people really listen to you.

Endless repetition is one kind of conversation clutter. Do you have twenty conversations a day—or the same old conversation twenty times? How often have you left a place, a group, a friend, a relative, or a business meeting and then realized, "Boy, we've talked about that same thing a dozen times, heard the same arguments about the same things, come to the same conclusions every time." If you find this happening a lot, you need some dejunking—you're wasting your most valuable commodity: time.

Or take complaining, for another example. Why snarl and snipe, groan or gripe about a lousy deal, a disappointing place or person? Complaining won't change what's past and is only too likely to distract us from making any constructive moves in the present or future.

Criticism, too, is largely clutter—not because criticism is bad but because it's seldom said to the one who will benefit from it. Criticism can be an act of love—if gently, intelligently, and personally delivered to the deservant, but seldom is that so. If you spend a lot of time listening to or parroting criticism, try turning all that negativism into some positive thoughts and actions. If you're unhappy about something or somebody, face up to it or them, and correct it.

Profanity isn't worth the effort, either. Why accumulate and store a lot of words and phrases you can only safely use part of the time and in some places? You have to stop and sort and filter and worry about whether you can or should say it—it sure makes you inefficient. Who needs it?

Jargon can be verbal junk, too—we all know people who use these magic words, acronyms, and abbreviations in every other sentence so you'll know they're up on the latest books, trends, and theories. Too often the wielder of such words is in danger of becoming as slick and remote as his vocabulary.

Language is our precious way to *communicate*—share our thoughts and experiences with our fellows. Anything that stands in the way of that is clutter, no matter how many syllables it has.

Social Calendar Clutter

Can't we all name people we've collected in the course of our life, who, like some of our clutter, we no longer find compatible or enjoyable in our life's pattern now? Yet we are stuck with them—those we no longer have (and perhaps never had) much in common with, folks so negative or destructive they poison everyone and everything around them, people so emotionally draining that just hearing them come through the door wears us down. Or old drinking buddies, members of cliques we no longer aspire to, idle and unmotivated folks trying to kill time. A less polite name might be hangers-on. They call, come over, invite themselves, and invite us to things we then feel obliged to attend. We care about them as we would any fellow human being, but spending so much of our time tending them is eating our life away with little or no benefit. We all believe in being kind and helpful, even tolerating an obnoxious relative or overzealous fanatic or two, but if not controlled, character clutter will undo you. Other clutter may crowd your space, but "junk on the hoof" invades it. Ever think about narrowing your social circle to the people you really want to be around? Meditate on it, and I promise you'll have more time to meditate.

CHAPTER 8

The Dirty Dozen That Often Do in Dejunkers

There are some categories of clutter I know—from all the cards, letters, and calls I've gotten, and for that matter my own experience—that are hard for all of us. These are the things we're tempted to leave till last, or maybe dodge entirely, because they're the most emotionally charged, or the most endless, depressing, and perplexing. Or they're so entrenched by time, tradition, or habit they're actually invisible to us.

I know how demoralizing these can be, so I want to give you a guided tour here through the toughies. And a little inspiration, too. Decluttering is a lot like mining, and when you dig for gold (as they do in my home state of Idaho), you end up with great piles and mounds of "tailings"—the first stuff that's separated out and disposed of. But once the easy stuff is gone, the gold is still mixed in with other, heavier, and more deceptive minerals that have to go, too, if you want to end up with only the high-grade ore. This last batch of debris that surrounds the real treasure is the hardest to get out, because—like the Dirty Dozen types of junk that follow—it often looks and feels, at least at first glance or fondle, a lot like the real thing.

But what if after all the sorting, sifting, and slogging that went before, the miner gave up or slacked off when he or she reached that last sorely needed separation? Well, the history of the West—not to mention all the rest of us—would be poorer. You, too, will never strike it rich—or rid yourself of clutter—until you pull out these last impostors!

The Restoration of Some Real Estate

The excited voice broke through the static, a call from deep in the Egyptian desert! The *National Geographic* crew, after years of arduous digging, had hit pay dirt. They found a new room in King Glutramekin's tomb and were minutes from removing the capstone and opening a fabulous new chapter of archaeological insight. The suspense was electric—in previous months they'd found the kitchen, bath, bedroom, living room, even the treasure room of the pharaoh's palace, and were now wildly speculating on the nature of the additional room. The call was fed into the national network so many could experience this unique moment in history. The door was opened for the first time in 6,000 years! A dozen lights flooded the chasm, the cameras were rolling.

But what's this strange stuff? A bed with a missing leg? Boxes of broken stone tablets and smashed pottery, first-draft papyrus scrolls, frayed fans, obsolete oxen yokes, pictures of an unpopular aunt, a bunch of empty anointing oil jars, snarled hippopotamus snares—the place was loaded with thousands of things! All junk and clutter—the whole roomful. What had they discovered? A phenomenon all too familiar to all of us—the Junk Room!

The junk room has existed since the beginning of human civilization like an ugly wart on the nose of decency. It's been an unmistakable part of our profile despite its clever disguises or aliases: all-purpose room, storage room, spare bedroom, sewing room, project room, hobby room, pool room, everything room.

The junk room, like a malignant growth, invades and chokes the life out of rooms intended for other purposes. Junk takes a room from you more efficiently than any repossession specialist around; if you don't do something about it, it soon owns the room, and you can't use it anymore. When you finally realize you have junk-room cancer, it's too late to operate, because it's all through the place.

The junk room is the only room in the house legitimately excused from cleaning, because we know deep down inside that the contents are all worthless. All this stuff is just lying in wake...

waiting to be buried or cremated. The junk room is a decision reliever, the perfect place for procrastinative pieces of stuff, a safe place to deposit our junk for later evaluation. It delays the pain of departure more effectively than if the space had been used for an opium den. The junk room isn't just *there*; it cunningly coaxes us to keep garbage, to delay decisions, and to stockpile stuff... not only to fall over but to argue and fight over.

Why pay for all that space—mortgage, heating, and taxes—just to house junk and clutter? Even if there were something worthwhile in there, it would be impossible to find it if you needed it.

Will a future archaeological expedition find your tomb room just as they did the Pharaoh's? Not mine; I dejunked it and made a grandkid's paradise out of it (you might be more interested in making a pet playhouse or a *real* guest room or a greenhouse/atrium out of yours).

Need some space? No need to remodel or add on—just clean out the junk room!

> "Someday, just someday, I'd love to have a bedroom that is just that; not a library, or tool warehouse, or sewing room."

Invisible Clutter

Almost all professional organizers (see page 172) tell me that the biggest aid they are to their clients is in helping them find the hidden stuff—the clutter they couldn't or wouldn't see, even when it was right in the very same room with them. We've all known people who can live with dirt and mess and total chaos and look up blinking innocently to say, "Mess? What mess? I don't see any mess!" Anything that stays around long enough becomes so familiar it disappears.

Let's head out after that invisible clutter, armed with our junk boxes. It's unquestionably your enemy; you've been in a cold war with it for years. You're anxious to get rid of it now, but be warned: junk can be harder to see than an enemy sniper. Here's the lowdown on how it's disguised and where it's hiding.

Top Of

Somehow we expect all the no-good stuff to be somewhere down low, if not on the floor. When things, no matter how awful, are elevated, raised, or on a perch, we mostly don't notice them. And even if we do, somehow "up" often justifies or excuses their existence. A lot of this particular junk, too, just gets parked there and then forgotten, because it's out of our line of vision. Take a quick tour of all your tops and above-eye-level ledges:

- Refrigerator
- File cabinets
- Mantels
- Windowsills
- Ledges of any kind
- Bookcases
- Wardrobes
- China closets
- Whatnots
- Doors

The Third Shelf and Above

Generally holds the untouchables and unusables, mainly because for most of us, it's unreachable! Get up on a good sturdy stool, look at all of the third and higher shelves right now, and pull down the clutter you don't need, don't want, and never use. As a bonus, you'll also find the good stuff you'll never use as long as it's way up there.

Hanging

Hanging is one of the least noticed spots—if someone went to the trouble to hang it, maybe even frame it, it must be worthwhile, no? A hook or hanger is like sanctified wire to a lot of us. You could hand some people a sack of garbage on a designer hanger and they'd store it in their closet forever. Depressing pictures, ugly light fixtures, terrible antiques and trinkets are all hung inside and out on the walls, ceilings, rafters, soffits, stairwells, door frames, siding, porch, and even fences and trees.

Raise your sights and run a cold eye over those plaques, hanging plates, and posters. Check out the long-forgotten or never-used garments on those hooks, racks, and pegs. Tear down all those shedding wreaths, nonworking thermometers, grease-collecting aspic molds, faded and dilapidated wall "decorations" of any kind, the macramé whose intricate cobwebbing overshadows any weaving talents you ever had, the three-tiered vegetable hanger with various vegetables in various states of decay, etc.

Behind or Between

No self-respecting junker would leave perfectly good cracks and crevices unfilled, so keep a sharp eye out for behind and between junk. This particular species of clutter, once we're sensitized to it, at least is easy to identify: it's *flat* (either originally or by the time we get it out of there):

- Pictures that look just as good faced against the wall
- Sad, battered folding tables and chairs
- Poster paper left over from when the kids still had school projects
- Wadded paper bags
- Shopping bags from your last thirty-four department or specialty-store visits
- Flattened cardboard boxes
- Forgotten cookie pans
- Posters you collected but didn't like well enough to hang
- Unused bread boards
- Outdated portfolios
- Mirrors we couldn't find anywhere to hang
- Mops, brooms, and handles to things
- Screens from departed projectors
- Glued-together jigsaw puzzles

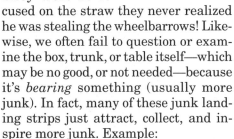

Bearing

Remember the guy who was wheeling out straw every night from the factory and the security guards kept searching the straw because they *just* knew the fellow had to be hiding something in the straw? They were so focused on the straw they never realized he was stealing the wheelbarrows! Likewise, we often fail to question or examine the box, trunk, or table itself—which may be no good, or not needed—because it's *bearing* something (usually more junk). In fact, many of these junk landing strips just attract, collect, and inspire more junk. Example:

- Tinny, rickety, rusting appliance stands or carts
- Shelves that serve no function except to make

us feel obligated to fill them with junk
- Mini-tables designed to do nothing at all but take up wall or hall space (and hold a few select pieces of junk)
- Five-foot-high "baker's racks," wicker shelves, and ateliers that seem like such a neat idea (but don't turn out to be a convenient place to put the stuff we really use)

Buried

We Americans all have so much, so many, there's always something down under or at the bottom of the pile that we never see, though we often pass by it (or even unearth it) when we're digging and hunting for something else. Buried junk has a way of staying buried. For example:

- Threadbare or ripped sheets
- Cat-bed quality blankets
- Worn out, junky, or broken garden tools
- Not-all-there patterns

Blended In

Or mingled with the herd. Shoes do that. As in a snake pit, the shoes with broken shanks or hopelessly stained satin pumps curl up cozily with the two or three good pairs in the pile. Your library, too, will have hopelessly outdated, bound volumes—utterly uninteresting junk—snuggled right next to the thesaurus or the encyclopedia. Keep a keen eye out for blended or mingled junk such as:

- Worn-out socks or gloves

- Socks, gloves, or scarves we never actually wear
- Belts to outfits we no longer own
- No-account knives nestled down amidst the Chicago Cutlery
- Keys to locks and vehicles you no longer have (surely there are several on your key ring)
- The McDonald's toys among the curios
- Empty tins and shakers taking up more than half the room in your spice cupboard
- Old leisure-suit jackets lurking in the coat closet

Mobile

If it moves or travels with us, it must be live and functional, right? Maybe yes and maybe no. There's an extra trap here because if something puts in travel time with us we're loath to toss it. An old briefcase can be completely worthless, with handle and lock broken and leather worn down to suede, but we keep it, strictly because of the mileage we've shared. Old suitcases, too, with too-many-times-strained hinges and failing catches and skinned sides always seem to beg for a travel tenure stay of execution.

Check out your vehicles and purse and pockets for mobile clutter.

Big Invisible Junk

We often wage our junk war so ferociously on the fine detail and little things that we don't see the big stuff. I still remember when my college roommate's classic Hudson was stolen. The police launched a three-state search for it that lasted three months. No luck. One day a sixteen-year-old walked up to the desk sergeant and asked how much they wanted for the blue Hudson parked in the number-six spot fifty feet from the front door of the police station (in their very own parking lot). On a trip to New York once, too, I panicked as I suddenly remembered I hadn't seen my motor home for a month or two. After several hysterical calls to the office, then home, my wife assured me it was parked right in our yard, as it had been all spring. I had gotten so used to seeing it that it had become invisible.

You might have unused furniture (the most common hidden junk), such as a never-played-on piano or Ping-Pong or pool table, obsolete or broken appliances or machinery, unfinished unfinished furniture, a junk vehicle or I'm-bored-with-it boat, a passé wading pool or no-longer-functioning fountain, even a junk building or two.

Sentimental Clutter (Isn't It All?)

HARRY WAS CUSTODIAN IN THE ELEPHANT HOUSE AT THE ZOO.

Most people think sentimental clutter is just those old special cards, trinkets, or mementos that wrap themselves around and tug at our heartstrings. But as the song says, "It ain't necessarily so." A broken garden hoe and a rabbit cage can be sentimental clutter if you're keeping the cage to remember the departed bunny or the hoe was run over in your driveway by Elvis Presley's father-in-law when he stopped to ask directions once. Well-qualified junkers can edge 80

The stubs from your first Broadway show... every brochure, postcard, snapshot, and napkin from your senior tour of the East Coast, neatly tucked in a Saks Fifth Avenue bag... love letters rubber-banded in bundles by boyfriend... the remains of the bouquet your best friend sent you when you had your tonsils out... every greeting card you ever got from every friend and cousin... the autographed-to-you board your sophomore boyfriend broke in a karate tournament... the dried dropping from the favorite horse you had at camp the summer you were thirteen... the faded and wilted peacock-feather pen from the guest book at your wedding reception, still in the box it came in, with the stand, and it still writes...

percent of their stuff in under the definition of sentimental.

We often attack junk and clutter with a physical offensive and lose—because attachment to junk is *emotional*. It's emotions we're afraid we're casting out. We confuse the object (rabbit's foot, teddy bear, lock of hair) with the experience, when it actually was only a tiny appendage to the occasion or event. But gradually the locket becomes the love and tossing it or giving it away is giving up the love.

Worse yet, most sentimental clutter is singular, not plural. There's no one on this earth (or elsewhere) who can tell us what we should do with it—not even a professional organizer or a loving spouse. Sentiment is the most personal feeling in the world, and it's a good healthy one. But have you heard of sentiment overload? It's a disease common among clutterers who have so much stuff they run out of sentimental juices so it all begins to haunt instead of help them. Remember: the feelings are in *you*, not in your mementos.

So What Do I Do with It?

I've collected some ideas here, from some of the world's outstanding sentimentalists, to mull through your mind as you circle that pile of sentimental clutter lying in state (or several states, as the case may be).

I had a $1.50 pen once, for example, from which inspiration seemed to flow when I wrote. I did the best part of a major book with that pen, truly a user-friendly tool! When it ran out of ink, it couldn't be refilled, but I couldn't just chuck that wonder pen that had bled blue for me; I owed it a better fate. One afternoon I laid it in the still-wet cement floor of a toolshed I was building—and boy, did that feel good! My pen was preserved forever—yet gone, too. I'm not suggesting you hold a ceremony or service for 6,000 pieces of stuff, but selecting a place you feel good about for the really special things to go makes parting not only possible but even a sweet experience.

Sentimental Clutter

It's worthless, outdated memorabilia from the past that we've packed around and boxed and reboxed for years. Yet every time we have it poised over the junk bin, we're seized by a warm wave of sentimentality, and we hear ourselves fondly saying, "But this is the skirt I was wearing the very first day Jerry asked me out!" (Thirteen years and four sizes ago!)

"But Junior brought this back to me from his trip to the Grand Tetons when he was ten." (Junior is now 28.)

"But these World War II Navy uniforms are pure wool. They just don't make them like this nowadays." (Size 28 waist, too!)

"But these high school wrestling trophies might look neat on the mantel in the family room." (If we ever build a family room.)

"But my little girls will probably enjoy playing dress-up in these old ballerina tutus of mine." (So far we have four boys.)

So we give in to this fleeting wave of sentimentality and the result of all these weak moments is our having to shuffle, dust, rearrange, feel guilty over, and hassle with all these boxes and jammed storage area for several more years—until the process is repeated.

Possible Solutions for Sentimental Clutter

Your choice here may depend on whether it's something useless that inspires fond feelings, or something you hate given to you by someone you love. Having more than one route to go is always better when it comes to anything sentimental, because whatever you decide, having alternatives makes you feel the move was a carefully considered one, not just a toss-'em-in-the-turf undertaking.

❑ Make it into a collage/montage/sculpture/scrapbook.
❑ Old clothes clutter: can be made into a quilt.
❑ Frame it and put it on display (even an old doily can be framed attractively).
❑ Give it as a gift to someone who admires and will cherish it.
❑ Put it into active use, or convert it into something useful.
❑ Recycle the best part of it.
❑ Give it a new job. I've used a rock as a doorstop, a cruet as a vase, a pretty flowerpot as a toilet-brush holder, an orphaned saucer as a candy dish, a class reunion mug as a pencil holder, a quilt as a wall hanging.
❑ Create a memory room—decorate a spare room, den, or study for a favorite activity—like writing, sewing, or crafts—with all old sentimental things.
❑ If you can afford it, devote a whole room or floor of your house or a little shed to it—then at least it will be out of the way of the living areas and active storage.
❑ Give it to your offspring (as soon as they say they want it, before they change their mind).
❑ Tactfully give it back to whoever gave it to you (they may really want it back

but be too shy to ask).

- ❑ Give it to a local museum and go there every so often to see it.
- ❑ Keep a small part or piece of it to remember it by and get rid of the rest— i.e., miniaturize it.
- ❑ Take a picture of it, or of you with it— then you can get rid of the object and keep the picture.
- ❑ Leave it within toddler or puppy range; soon all you'll have to do is throw the pieces away.
- ❑ Burn it and keep no more than an ounce of the ashes (at least it'll be smaller and less of an eyesore).
- ❑ List it all (with romantic adjectives, if necessary) in a special memorial notebook and then get rid of the item itself.
- ❑ Write a poem or essay about it and then get rid of it.
- ❑ Leave it on someone's doorstep with a soulful note.

- ❑ Sneak it into the back room of a museum.
- ❑ Sell it and use it to buy a very special something you want and need NOW.
- ❑ Sell it and use the proceeds to do a secret good deed.
- ❑ If you have a big enough place, give it a decent burial (run it through a compactor or make it into a time capsule first, if necessary).
- ❑ Put it in a safe deposit box at least a county away and don't bother to pay the rent next year.
- ❑ Melt it down (you'll still have a lump, but less of a lump in the throat to deal with).
- ❑ Check it out with antique-shop owners or flea-market dealers. Sentiment can sometimes be overcome by cash.
- ❑ Pick out the best of it and pack it into a box under the stairs; label it carefully and keep it until the basement floods and you can throw it out.

"A great idea! Condense the memories. I will ritually write down what I am folding into my thrift-shop bag, and as I write, I will pause and think about what it means to me.

"My son's blue grade school blazer. In the pocket is a ticket stub from the Volksoper in Vienna. We had hot chocolate *mit Schlag* in our hotel room afterwards. Proof that he had an acceptably happy childhood. Proof that I loved being his mother.

"Two men's polo shirts. Proof that I once loved everything about a man, the way he looked and smelled and dressed. Proof that once we spent lovely weekends together, and it went wrong.

"Four yards of purple gingham, saved in case I ever had a country house. Proof that I always wanted the country house I now have. Proof that I am no longer someone who would consider purple gingham.

There. That is a start. Off it goes. Memory, possibility, and nostalgia reduced to one page of notes, an orderly record of the past. I would have been simpler to prove my own existence to myself if I had kept a diary. But I can do that now if I want to. I can do a lot of things in this new space. Throwing out seems to be not a final but a first act."

—Jane O'Reilly, from an article originally published in *House and Garden.*

Deep-Dark-Secret Junk

If all the scandals over public figures' "sins exposed" haven't made you deep-six your deep-dark-secret junk, you've been asleep. Ministers, senators, bank and college presidents, even Miss America have all had the ugly experience of someone finding their deep-dark-secret stuff and displaying it for the whole world to see. There has been some gory in every life along with the glory, and if you have any bad stuff you're hanging on to. I assure you it isn't buried deep enough. No sliding panel is secret enough, no vault secure enough to guarantee that the kids, a partner, a lawyer, an investigator or enemy or auditor won't find it—especially when you're not around! Our world today has a marvelous ability to keep records on us and to find ones we've lost or forgotten, so there's no sense keeping them on ourselves. It's one more good reason to de-junk our lives—not merely for fear of getting caught, but to prevent the invasion of our personal life and the hurt and cost it could be to others. Revealed at the wrong time to the wrong people, even stuff that isn't bad or wrong can set us back a notch or two. Not only you but your family, your company, friends, and community all can suffer when some of your intensely private stuff is suddenly revealed. There are no secrets when there are cameras or copies or hard evidence.

Deep-Dark-Secret Debris

You'll have no doubt what it is when:
- Your spouse finds in your purse or pocket a "flir-tation note" you recently got (and were saving for egomania).
- Your grandma helps you sort the children's books and comes across the gag gift you got a few years ago at the company Christmas party.
- You realize those explicit college love letters should've been burned, not trashed.
- Someone unearths that booklet on cures for impotence, or the body paints you got as a wedding shower gift.
- Your kids inflate the life-size doll you got at your bachelor party, or pop that racy cassette into the VCR.

Sure, personal privacy is a right granted by the Constitution, and you can have it in your mind and thoughts, but trying to keep "stuff" a secret is more than risky: it's an undertaking bound to end in discovery. The bottom drawer, the back of the closet, the very bottom of a trunk full of junk—all will come to light again and *never* when you intended!

Some aids to recognize it:
- Anything you've been saving to get even someday.
- Little communications from a secret lover.
- Photographs that incriminate rather than edify.
- Anything you come by illegally.
- Drugs or pills you once got hooked on.
- Records from a rebellious past.
- Souvenirs of earlier sweethearts that you didn't ditch when you found the one and only.
- Letters you wrote that you weren't proud of later.
- Personal diaries and journals that could undo your employment or domestic harmony.

Now, don't just run and look to see if "it" is still there, and then spend the day or week trying to come up with a better hiding place. Deep-dark-secret junk and clutter is just like cheating in anything else. You usually get caught, but even if you don't, you worry about it so much you lose either way.

Containers—
Boxes, Bottles, Cans

I am a whiz with boxes
I pile them two miles high
Lord help the person who gets
   them...
After I should die.
             —Ginny Kent

Containers (spelled contagious). You modern-day plastic-container accumulators would weep like wounded woodchucks if you could get your paws on an old-time box. Now those were the days! It's easy to see why you'd want to keep an orange crate, dynamite box, cheese box, or cigar box—they were solid wood (sometimes even tongue-and-groove construction), better made than some of our furniture now. They really could be used and reused to store all kinds of things away from rain and snow and rodents for years. Then, too, there were stout wooden barrels and sturdy tin containers. All of this must have sired our passion for saving containers of any kind. The very fact that it held something seems to give us a secret signal to hold on to it! And after all, to get to the bottom line, a container can *hold* other clutter. So we save all and any containers, whether we have a use for them or not. We snatch up every coffee can, shipping bag, and shoebox. We keep "the original box" to everything. We never get around to recycling them, and we rarely haul groceries back to the store, but we keep those crinkled sacks by the stacks. We even use some sacks to put other sacks inside—sack incest, no less!

"Boxes and containers seem to double the pleasure of possession," as one junker pointed out.

Hard-core container clutchers exchange tips on how to store containers inside each other so they can keep more containers.

The proof is in the pudding container. Even I, the viewer of many clutter caches in my capacity as a professional cleaner, have been surprised to find containers, sacks, boxes, and packages (that includes freezer cartons, too) in sturdy third place in the sheer-quantity-of-junk sweepstakes. Sixty years ago packaging was sparse; now you don't get out of a grocery store without at least four of those noisy plastic sacks, and anything strong enough to hold heavy cans and quarts of milk is a sure keeper. And then there's all their relatives—aunt TV dinner tray and pie tin, cousin pickle jar, brother box, grandma gunny sack, stepchild cottage cheese and Cool-Whip container (counted only in lots and dozens). Trouble is none of these relatives are ever removed.

Bet you have more empty jars than full ones right now!

At a Farm Progress Show a while ago I saw plastic bags 12 feet by 120 feet that held 150 tons of feed—heaven help us if they ever come to the attention of packaging rats!

> The perfect present for a packaging rat—a tote bag to tote kept bags!

An alert packaging rat can amass the packing materials that come in packages, too, thus stockpiles of Styrofoam "peanuts," wood shavings, shredded paper, wadded paper, and bubble-pack packaging—more than even the real rats nesting in the storage area could ever use—are not unknown.

I'll admit that sometimes the container is prettier than the contents (and sometimes more valuable), but the sheer mass of packing materials around today won't allow us to be passive about this. If we don't take action, we'll be buried

in boxes and containers, beautiful as they might be.

There's actually only one box we get to take with us—that final pine or bronze-plated one. All the others you've collected will be left behind. Sure, some of them are perfectly good and the inner conviction that they can hold something is hard to shake. But if you keep them they'll only tempt you to fill them with junk. And getting rid of them (or at least the excess) is easier than you think:

- Scan your flock and pick off the flimsy, stained, ripped, half-crushed ones. Even the most container-crazed of us can manage to expel these.
- Pick out the best of the herd and use them to repack your good stuff as you unearth it in the process of dejunking (and trash the junkier, less nostalgic boxes your stuff is in now).
- Recycle whenever you can. Hit your box collection every time a friend's about to move or you need to ship something.
- Break down (flatten) the boxes you think you really can and will reuse, for easier storage. Why waste all that precious space on plain old air? You can easier tape them back into thrilling three-dimensional life as you need to.
- Get rid of the ones that can't reasonably be re-

used, or that you will never be WILLING to actually use (most of us just don't have the space to store a lot of empty containers). Admit it—have you ever found a use for an empty film container or the box the chocolate golf balls came in?

"When Sears delivered a damaged washer (a big dent and gouge in it), I was overcome with joy—because they'd have to redeliver, and I'd get another giant box!"

"One day I realized my collection of empty boxes that I saved to 'wrap Christmas presents in' dated back more than two dozen years. I hadn't been able to part with a single empty!"

Souvenirs

Not long ago I was given a genuine tail of the barbecued pig at a luau in Fiji. I was really looking forward to taking that home to show the unbelieving, but I left it outside a second and a couple of wild jungle dogs ran off with it into the night. Boy, was I burned—my souvenir!

A souvenir can be the perfect seasoning for an experience. But it is not the main course. I've watched people at the Grand Canyon so busy collecting junk at souvenir stands, so absorbed in pawing through and comparing the postcards, that they never took the time to actually look at that awesome chasm, to see all the subtle colors and spectacular lighting effects, all those layers of history exposed. They might as well have stayed home and looked at a picture of it in an encyclopedia.

Don't let souvenirs steal the show. And once a souvenir has done its job, run its course, *it's time to let it pass along.* Most souvenirs are so inexpensively made that if left alone they'll usually self-destruct under all the handling they receive. But we seem to think our trip to the Big Apple will be retroactively revoked if the Statue of Liberty Centennial ashtray falls to the floor. Souvenirs are a great part of the taste of life's undisputed special experiences, but once those are digested, the souvenirs from same are just the pits and peelings of the experience. We'd never keep the peel from a $3 pineapple (I hope not, anyway), but a $3 crepe-paper lei that thrilled us when they draped it over our neck at the airport in Maui—we'll keep draped over the corner of a mirror forever. I say hooray for those Mardi Gras moments in our life when a small foolish thing can elevate our being, a relic can rouse emotion, a token or a trophy can bring a tear to our eye. Go for it! Inexpensive souvenirs beat overpriced, unwanted gifts anytime, and it can be fun to get carried away and carry home a few trinkets as gifts. Just don't carry them away with you forever.

According to a United Airlines in-flight magazine, the average overseas visitor spends about a quarter of his money on gifts and souvenirs. What a paradox! We go on vacation to get away from junk and clutter and 90 percent of what we buy is... **you guessed it!**

LOOKS LIKE THE JONES' ARE BACK FROM THEIR GERMAN VACATION.

I'd say that for at least 855 out of a thousand souvenirs that the glue has been releasing on, hair shedding from, ribbons and bows getting bedraggled on, eyeballs dropping off of, cornhusks crumbling from, arms breaking off of, colors fading on, it's time to go! Recycle or dump them—they're short-range products and that's all they were ever intended to be.

If you like (in fact, insist on) long-range souvenirs, pass up the dinosaur egg enclosed in an acrylic globe paperweight from the La Brea Tar Pits and instead get something *you already need*—just buy it while in some exotic locale. It may cost a little more, but seek out a set of well-made teacups, or a hand-thrown pottery mixing bowl or a room divider or screen that you aren't going to put on a shelf or in storage somewhere, but will actually use. It'll last a long time and remind you every day, as you use it, of interesting places you've been a part of for at least a little while. (Or just have your favorite photograph of your trip enlarged and framed and hang it immediately.)

The all-time best way to deal with souvenirs is with the Art of Pre-dejunking: Yes, getting rid of it before you get it. During that initial surge of want, ask yourself: Do I *really* want this? What will I do with it later? Where will I keep, store, display it? Dispose of it?

P.S. Watch those *paper* souvenirs, too. Sure it's "the trip of a lifetime"—but we all make any number of these and rarely do we go for a repeat. Yet we fill drawers and file cabinets with maps and brochures and quickly outdated tourist booklets from sixteen tour companies and eighteen states we'll never visit again. If you keep just the 800 numbers, you can have updated editions of all this when and if you need it. (Besides, a lot of new routes and roads have been added to Iowa since 1959.)

Collections

If it qualifies as a collection (that's anything over two of anything), we have to be careful. Be it stamps, coins, shells, rocks, or butterflies, model planes or model T's, "collection" is the sacred cow of the clutter congregation. Collections can be educational and edifying, a pleasure to amass and behold. Many of them even have some cash value. Five good reasons to hang on—*as long as the collection is active*. If it's just tucked away (answer honestly, now, is it?), it's nothing but a burden to you.

If there was one thing I learned growing up on a 3,000-acre place, it was that collecting the cattle (rounding them up) was about ten times easier and more romantic than caring for them once they were gathered. (Then it was two feedings a day, and watering them, bedding them down, calming them down, doctoring them, cleaning up after them, keeping them in the corral, etc.) As I observe collection additions, it impresses me that they follow this exact pattern—quick and easy and exciting to get, but once they're corralled in our drawers or closets, collecting is neither free, nor carefree.

Help keep America beautiful by renewing or recycling your collection. Then you can take that ugly label of clutter off it in good conscience.

Curing Collection Clutter

- **Start it up again**, the thing that once turned your crank. Could be good medicine. Get it out of the box or storage bin and learn even more about it; take up a new branch of it or give yourself a new and better collecting den. You could even start to lecture or write on it.

- **Put it on proper display**. Few collections have had the benefit of this. Edit it down to the best specimens, make labels or captions if necessary, lay it out attractively, hang it up or mount it or encase it in glass, whatever—but get it out there for everyone else to see.

- **Sell it**. Its value was probably one of the reasons you got into it. If you sell it, both parties will benefit (and anyone who wants it enough to buy it will give it a good home).

- **Give it**. To someone as a gift. As Mr. Emerson said, the finest gift is a portion of thyself and a collection is certainly that. Give your hard-gathered collection to a family member or a friend who's shown real interest in it. The feeling of satisfaction you get and the gratitude they will feel will be second to none.

- **Donate it**. To a school, library, museum, etc. Good collections are generally welcome, and your name will be carried along with it to be thanked by thousands who will get to enjoy it as much as you did.

- **Photograph it**. If you're having a hard time parting with it—it's beautiful but you're bored with it now, or it's just so space-consuming it has to go—take a portrait (or a whole roll of photos, if necessary) of it and slip it into a file or album so you'll always have a vivid reminder of it.

Gifts

"But they gave it to me!" is one of the biggest, if not *the* biggest excuse for hanging on to junk. Gift disposal definitely hasn't undergone the technical advances toxic waste disposal has. The story is an old one. An occasion crops up where we really should give a gift. What?… Well, if we didn't think of it well ahead of time, it's too late to get something good, so we debate the matter for days, trying to think of the right thing. When we can't come up with anything, we turn to the last resort—shopping, a process in which we wander anxiously through the assemblage at the mind-boggling malls, eye-balling, evaluating, and feeding all sizes, shapes, and costs into our computer. And what… what is this? We've found it, by Jove. The perfect gift for the Joneses: three intertwined imitation gold hands with little clamps to hold notes by the phone. It was $39.95, but it's marked down to $1.12. So we buy it and actually have the nerve to lay something like this on our friends and loved ones (it would even be a dirty trick to pull on an enemy).

Worse yet, we begin taking our kids with us so they can learn the skill, too. True, it's better to give than to receive, but when someone is giving, someone is receiving and wondering, "What do I do with this?" Unless they've learned to give things that do the job and then disappear. This, again, is the best dejunking—*pre-dejunking*—and it works better than any process of remedial junk-ridding.

Twenty years ago a wise and widely revered man happened to be passing through my area, and he told me something about giving and gifts I never forgot: "If you really want to show love and appreciation to someone, there are two gifts that always work:

1. *Visit them when they're sick or in need. You don't have to bring anything; just visit them.*

2. *Give them pictures or photos of themselves, their family, their place, or their pets."*

This advice sounded pretty basic (not to mention simple and easy), so I followed it. And it worked. People didn't respond any better or more genuinely when I was the bearer of an expensive gift or a bonus check. People do forget trinkets and even money, but never concern. And the pictures—what an idea! They're inexpensive and last so long; they give forever for a few dollars.

About five years ago, for example, we needed badly to give our neighbors something to say thanks for all their help during the year. We'd made signs for everyone one year and baked cookies and all of that the next, so we needed something different. Suddenly I remembered that my son had flown over our farm in a little plane in the spring and taken a couple of rolls of film. Things were so green and pretty he'd photographed all the neighbors' farms as well. We pulled the slides and had them blown into 8 x 10 color prints ($3 each). Years later now we still get comments and thanks for those photos, all done in a few minutes and for a total of $45.

Start out with the two I mentioned. Visit the sick, the needy, the injured, the aged, and the lonely. If you want to do something that will change your life as well as theirs, do it, just do it—it doesn't take long, it costs nothing, it lasts forever, it's the finest possible gift and creates zero junk to deal with later.

Then, as for photos: Start today, or some quiet afternoon, to go through all of your photos and slides (yes, dig them out of the drawers and boxes) and sort out the pictures of friends and family you really don't want or need. Either send the picture itself or have it reprinted or even enlarged and send it. For a special occasion you can even have it nicely framed before you drop it in the mail. I promise you the next time you meet that person they'll weep upon your neck in gratitude and love. I used to take my camera on all Scout trips and shoot a $4 or $5 roll of film; then, when parent night came around, I'd spread the photos out on the back table and allow the parents to go back and take and keep any of their boy. I had 100 percent attendance at most of these occasions, something seldom achieved otherwise. It was the pictures!

We all have birthdays, anniversaries, holidays, and forty other occasions to get or give gifts. The potential for getting stuff is enormous, unless you write a book about dejunking and teach it in seminars, which puts you in an entirely different light. I've become the acid test for gifts that are not junk yet do the job.

My mother, for example, is a gifted gift giver. For my birthday several years ago she gave me a tape with all my favorite violin concertos on it, and I've used and enjoyed it daily since. The next year she gave me a nice pair of leather gloves for stonework, which I use thankfully and will wear out and they'll be gone.

Several years ago on my birthday my daughter put fourteen pints of home canned raspberries on my desk (I'd sell my birthright for raspberries). I lined them up on my library shelf like little soldiers and once every three weeks in great sensual ceremony ate one of them (then, of course, I gave her the jar back for next year). This year on a hot afternoon she left a quart of ice-cold hand-squeezed orange juice and some whole-wheat cookies—the best gift ever! A loaf of freshly baked bread will be remembered longer than a $75 pair of cuff links.

Not long ago, my son gave me a receipt for a hundred cinder blocks for the new fence I was building. Now that was a gift. I picked up a truckload all paid for, took them home, and in a couple of evenings laid them up into a fence that will last forever. Someday you might even sit on it.

The nice thing is that once you start giving this kind of gift to people, it puts a little pressure on them to give you the same kind back, so you have a double-edged sword to help cut clutter in half! Start today to give new tires, plane tickets, or gift certificates (this at least lets them pick their own clutter!). If you give money, and the person buys something they really want or need, you may avoid committing clutter entirely.

Here are some other guidelines that might help both shopping worries and the war against clutter:

A Few Good Nonjunk Gift Ideas

- Anything edible—a gift that warms the tummy warms the heart as well. Every Christmas my production manager gets five pounds of cashews from her dad and she savors and shares that gift longer than any other. (Just try to steer clear of consumables that come in decorative tins, baskets, containers, or decanters, include tiny cutting boards, etc.)
- Flowers (as long as they're not artificial, and do not come in a vase or pot the recipient will feel obliged to keep). And you might want to strip the bouquet of all bows and ribbons, plastic hearts, or bunnies on sticks before delivery.
- An offer of a certain number of hours or days of help (with any chore or errand they'd like help with). Even baby-sitting, pet-sitting, or plant-sitting.
- Some little home-improvement you know they

really need—one double-glazed window or an arrangement to have a local handyman do a certain number of hours work on the repair of their choice.
- A gift certificate for long-distance phone calls, or a call from you on that special day.
- A scrapbook or memory book made just for them (we all love these but so rarely GET AROUND to it).
- Tickets to an event or entertainment you know they'd be delighted by.
- A trip somewhere. Or have everyone in the family put the money they would have overspent on gifts together and take an extra little midyear family vacation.
- Membership in an auto emergency assistance program such as AAA, car emergency equipment, or a car polishing by yourself or the pros.
- Give up a habit you know that person hates (and probably isn't all that good for you anyway).
- Give a hair styling or ear-piercing appointment, or scuba diving, racquetball, or community college lessons. (Something you know they've always wanted to do but haven't quite had the cash or courage for.)

"If you happen to have an old family home with basement or attic jammed with 'treasure,' you might consider having a treasure hunt for the youngsters on your shopping list. One grandfather tells us that his grandchildren come over just before Christmas, go through the attic, and select one item to take home with them (a World War II army shirt, one of grandmother's outfits from the 1940s, etc.). The children then get some fruitcake and punch at a little party. According to this gentleman, everybody enjoys the event, and his wife particularly likes the idea because it forces him to clean up the attic when the children depart!"

Let me end here by acquainting you with one of the more interesting organizations in the world:

SCROOGE: Society to Curtail Ridiculous, Outrageous and Ostentatious Gift Exchanges, 1447 Westwood Road, Charlottesville, VA 22903; Phone: 804-977-4645. Founded: 1979. Interested persons in the U.S. and overseas united in lighthearted effort to de-emphasize the commercial aspects of Christmas by supporting those who want to (or must) reduce the exchange of expensive and often useless gifts. Suggestions include: limiting the buying of gifts to small presents for children and giving inexpensive gifts that require thought and originality. Discourages use of credit in purchasing Christmas gifts; advocates self-control in gift exchanges. Publications: *Scrooge Report*, annual.

Clothes Closets

"Sir, you'll have to dejunk; my company can work wonders, but not miracles!"—Allen and Mary Search, California Closet Company, Boise, ID

Clothes closets are even more prone than other closets to chronic congestion. I've seen closets packed so tight they didn't even need hangers, the clothes were just suspended by pressure. Just about all of us have clothes so old and long unworn we don't even remember them, but they're still corpsing in the closet, stiff and brittle.

Clothes decluttering is among the toughest, so don't save it till the end of a session. You need physical strength and energy for all that trying on, and emotional stamina, too—there's as much sentimental clutter crammed in here as in any curio cabinet. It won't hurt if it's one of those days you're feeling a little ugly, though—it'll enable you to make quick work of that big pile of maybes.

As for what to get rid of, use intelligence, not the old saying, "If I haven't worn this in a year, it's no good." Time alone doesn't always determine value. If you have three winter coats, get rid of the one you hate, but keep that big fluffy six-inch thick one in case you have an extra-chilly winter. Keep it, but place it in such a way that you don't have to paw past it every time you need a white shirt or skirt.

Here are some sleepers we found in our clothes closet. They definitely aren't there anymore!

- Liners to long-gone coats and raincoats
- Ugly suspenders
- Single gloves
- Suits with no skirt or pants, or worn or faded pants
- Period pieces trimmed with fur or vinyl
- Tap shoes
- Bell-bottoms
- Fringed jackets and bags
- Beat-up pocketbooks
- Belts to long-gone outfits
- Terrible ties
- Hats that have never seen the top of your head
- Leotards you haven't worn in the last fifteen years (and those were the more likely fifteen)
- Antique ultraformal wear
- Men's underwear with hearts, cupids, or reindeer on it
- The thing you had altered twice and still can't bear to wear
- The outfit piece that's still nearly new because you never wear that part (vest to suit, shawl that came with dress)

Clothes-Chucking Checklist

- ❏ You like the color/material but you hate the style.
- ❏ You like the style but hate the color/material.
- ❏ You never wear skirts/dresses/shorts that length anymore.
- ❏ It looks great on the hanger but not on you.
- ❏ It's too see-through/not see-through enough.
- ❏ It's a style that always makes you look too fat/too thin.
- ❏ It's (plaid/a loud print/whatever) and you've never liked those.
- ❏ It has a feature (it has spaghetti straps, is sleeveless, double-breasted, or whatever) that never does anything for you.
- ❏ It's scratchy or otherwise uncomfortable.
- ❏ It has elastic in unfortunate places.
- ❏ The lapels/legs are the wrong width.
- ❏ You'll never have the guts to wear it/____ will never let you wear it.
- ❏ You're still waiting for it to come back in style.
- ❏ It's damaged (motheaten, stained, scorched) and, face it, is never going to look the same.
- ❏ It's too tight and was *always* too tight.
- ❏ It's nice and practical but…
- ❏ You've always liked the idea of wearing it better than wearing it.

"What is it with us bathing-suit savers? We not only keep hopelessly out-of-style suits of our own but also anyone else's that ever fell into our hands. How many of those in the drawer are faded, stained, or shrunk, or have rusty snaps or buckles or sagging or disintegrating foam rubber? And how many would we actually want to be seen in again?"

"I cleaned out my side of the closet! I'm proud of myself for actually doing it. And my fewer clothes actually seem like more."

"I can actually pull out anything I want and wear it without first having to drag out the iron and ironing board because it has been jammed in with my accumulation of clothes for the past century."

"I'd swear I heard the closet sigh with relief when I finished dejunking it!"

Drawers (Now You See It, Now You Don't)

Drawers are the easiest place to dispose of something—a squeak, a slam, and it disappears. "What should I do with this?" "Aw, just stick it in the drawer." For this reason, drawer impaction can be difficult to detect; it usually starts with one and spreads to the top drawer, middle drawer, bottom drawer, under drawer, file drawer, junk drawer, chests of drawers, and the secret drawer —all efficient incubators for any and all stuff stocked and stuffed therein. Drawers promise privacy, too—until they're overloaded and can't be shut all the way, or the handle or back or bottom gives out trying to bear the overload.

The golden rule of Don's Drawer Manners—the only one: Always run (operate) on three-quarters of a tank. No drawer was designed to function when 100 percent full, so only fill a drawer, even with the purely useful, three-quarters full.

Desks

Most of us have not one desk but two or more. I have one at home, one at my cleaning company headquarters, and one at my writing and publishing center. And my wife has a couple. Even those who have never seen the inside of an office have at least a mini-desk at home. It's all your business; you can keep it just the way you want it. And you sure don't want it to be a four-legged advertisement of your disorganization.

Don't even attempt to argue that cluttered desks are "creative." I once read a six-page article arguing the finer points of having a disheveled desk:

"Well, look at Tom; he's a slob but leads the company."

That's about equivalent of "Well, look at Grandpa. He drank like a fish, smoked, overate, never exercised, and lived to be 110."

Play the percentages; don't keep looking for the rare exceptions—90 percent of the time, messy-desk people are not only less efficient and less in control, but less respected (including by us cleaners).

Everyone has to dejunk his own desk, but here is a checklist for reality:

- Obsolete files
- Old letters
- Envelopes sealed by humidity

- Pencil stubs and nonworking pens
- Ossified erasers
- Dried-up correction fluid
- Congealed rolls of tape
- Rusted paper clips (or anything over 1,600 paper clips)
- All the types of paper clips and clamps you never use
- Ineffective letter openers
- Neat things you never use (such as fancy pen sets, paperweights, exotic drafting devices, grease pencils, fountain pens, or fancy bookmarks)
- Cassettes, cartridges, refills, etc., to recorders, pens, etc. you no longer have
- The leftover tabs and label inserts to at least ten past boxes of hanging files
- Old cracked typewriter covers
- Plaques and paperweights immortalizing the company president's favorite mottos of the past four years
- Rubber stamps, labels, and stationery engraved with obsolete addresses
- Drawers crammed with coffee mugs, sugar/sweetener, stirrers, plastic spoons and forks, salt, pepper, napkins, and aged packets of catsup and mustard from takeout orders
- Anything over six phone message pads
- Anything over two staplers, staple removers, scissors, rulers, desk calendars, aspirin bottles
- Anything over zero used scratch pads, crumpled tissues, outdated phone books, candy wrappers, safely-got-there Fed Ex receipts
- (Mostly empty): Holders, holders, holders—pen, disk, paper clip, Post-It note, business card, Kleenex, etc.

Desk-cleaning can be rewarding as well as revealing—you might, for instance, find a check you thought was a bill and shoved aside. You don't ever really finish dejunking a desk. Twice a year I go through mine, sometime when my mind is tired of more strenuous pursuits. It's even kind of fun.

NO, MISS FRIP, I CAN'T FIND IT. ARE YOU SURE YOU GAVE IT TO ME?

Magazines

A mention of the word "magazine" will always get a moan or groan from a junker—but never a commitment to dump. Why the printed page has such a hammerlock on human emotion is a mystery we can't unravel here, but in general the brittler it gets, the tighter we cling.

As for *National Geographic* (undoubtedly one of the least pitchable pieces of printing around), if you're thinking of out-collecting anyone, forget it. Dr. Lew Begley, a retired physician of Mesquite, Texas, went for the gold (or at least bright yellow) and has over 400,000 of them in *his* magazine mound. I think there's some kind of potion incorporated into those slick pages; when your thumb makes contact with it, it's absorbed into your bloodstream and you become not only loyal but addicted. It never helps that the very day you're planning to finally part with the backlog of the past fourteen years, a beautiful mailer comes from *National Geographic* headquarters offering handsome slipcases, complete with map cases. Talk about incentive—with just a simple stroke of the pen you can stay the execution of all those wonderful volumes. Just purchase a bona fide junk bunker (see page 171).

I often ask my audiences: "How many of you have old magazines lying around?" (Talk about an unnecessary question!) Everyone has stacks and bales of magazines, as 100 percent of my audiences prove with waving hands.

"Do you realize, readers, that 70 percent of a magazine is... (they finish my sentence) *ads*, and ads are

updated every month? So that means 70 percent of that big pile behind the curtain, beside the couch, under the bed, in the basement is junk—totally worthless! You can read the worthwhile third of a magazine in minutes. If you see something keepable, like 'How Tom Selleck Adjusts His Microphone' or 'How to Take a Bath,' you can just remove it and then get rid of the rest of the magazine by ripping it in two."

Shrieks of horror are heard. I point to the source of the loudest one: "You want to save the rest for what?"

"A recipe!" Twenty voices tune in.

"How many cookbooks do you have?" "Tons." "Lots." "Shelves/boxes full." "You wouldn't believe it, Don!"

The average person has at least 25 cookbooks. At one home I was in recently the couple *claimed* ten, but I counted 69. An apartment dweller I know said, "I have a few—like 149!"

"How many recipes do you use out of each book?" I ask next.

"A few," "One" "None" greets my question. So not only why have all those cook-

SHE'S DETERMINED TO READ THEM ALL BY THE TIME THE TRASHMAN COMES TOMORROW

books, but why keep old magazines to get more recipes?

If you can't face those stacks now, how do you expect to face them ten years from now? Will you have any more interest in them after they're warped and water-spotted, covered with mouse manure, and tied up with strings?

"During my working years, I was spread very thin and found I simply did not have time—or couldn't stay awake when I did have time—to read each month's issue of the religious magazine I subscribed to faithfully. So the ones that were neglected got put in the end table. Well, fourteen years went by and I had quite a little stack. Every time I opened the doors of the table I felt guilty. Every time I moved the table it was too heavy. Then after I stopped working I tried to catch up on reading those magazines. I read quite a few and disposed of them, but I wasn't making much headway, really; and the time I was spending reading them was robbing me of time to be attentive to my elderly friends and those who needed me.

"After reading your book, I decided that stack of magazines was junk. Not their contents, but what they were doing to me. Each month I always read the magazine and I studied the scriptures daily. And during those ten difficult years, I was *living* the gospel. I just didn't have time to read it. Out to the garbage they went. Now I can move the end table easily. The guilt feelings went with the garbage truck, and I can spend the time I was using to read all those back issues to cheer some lonely soul."

How to Save Time and Minimize Magazine Clutter

When browsing through a magazine for the first time, tear out the articles you'd be interested in reading and staple them together and throw the rest of the magazine away. If you haven't dealt with those torn-out articles in six weeks, throw *them* away.

If you have recent magazines you don't want, call the library—you may be able to fill in their collection. Libraries often appreciate fill-in help, such as *Good Housekeeping*, which always disappears at Christmastime.

If you have a mess of magazines to go through, scanning the cover and contents page is the best and fastest way. If you browse the magazine itself, you'll be lost for an hour or more.

As for saving clippings to show or send to everyone and his brother, who ever told you you had to be a librarian for your friends? You don't have to save every article, even for yourself. Even librarians go to libraries. The information is all there in an easily reachable form and it's there for you! If instead you rely on your files, then you have to deal with all those files and all the old outdated stuff in them, plus the stuff that never gets filed. Clip only the most compelling and consult the rest at the library—when and *if* you ever need it.

If you're intimidated by libraries, remember that most libraries have a reference librarian who will be only too happy to help you. They also have all kinds of indexes and reader's guides to subject matter and other references such as online terminals for tracking down the topic you're entranced by. Libraries and librarians can find almost anything for you, so why not use them? (Rather than clip and stash and cause a fire hazard in your home.)

Books

You knew I'd get around to something intellectual sooner or later. I guarantee you can go through your library right now and dump at least a third of it as worthless. I know you're gasping now because somewhere back in the "little house on the prairie" days or earlier we were really bedazzled by the word "book." It's in the *book;* we're gonna do it by the *book;* we're gonna throw the *book* atcha. No wonder they have such an aura about them. Why, if we damaged a book when we were growing up, we'd get a knuckle crushed by the stern-browed schoolmarm. So now we rarely stop to consider just what is *in* a book; the very fact that it is a book must make it worthwhile. My favorite question at my dejunking seminar is "Do we have any accountants in here?" Three or four hands always go up. Then I ask them, "How much is a big beautiful hardbound tax book from last year worth?" "Nothing," they say in unison. Then I ask them why they are keeping it. The accountants roll their eyes nervously: "Don't know…." Well, I know, it's because it's a *book*. The same is true of those almanacs so old they've become history books, those outdated directories, the books on your shelves in languages you can't read, and the books you salvaged from someone else's discard pile. A book isn't automatically valuable; it's just a way of binding sheets of paper together to make them easier to read. The question to ask when scanning the contents of those shelves is: Is this anything I want to read, or will ever read?

Tricks and Seductions Magazines and Books Use on You

- **Color**: If it's in color, it's worth more. In the old days it was true, but today color is so common that the local paper prints acres of ads and wishes you Happy New Year with it!

- **Hardback**: Means hard to dispose of. Paperbacks are tough enough to toss, but when we get to hardbacks, we're talking hefty and expensive, and surely lasting value and virtue. Wrong; today's hard covers are just thicker cardboard covered with paper, and whether a book is hardcover or not is just a publisher's gamble he can get a couple more dollars out of you that way. A lot of older hardbacks are just obsolete pages between stiff covers.

- **Free issue**: You didn't want any issue and wouldn't have paid for it, but a free one is pushed into your hands and starts a collection.

- **Book clubs**: A sure way for procrastinators to pile up unwanted books.

- **Trial subscription**: A less expensive way to start a new pile beside the couch.

- **Commemorative Issue**: One that will take you at least six times longer to throw away or realize you don't want or need.

- **Boxed set**: A copy of the one the publisher hasn't been able to unload, along with the one you really want.

- **Series**: Why get just a book or two on the subjects you're really interested in—why not be nagged by the feeling that you really should have all the others?

- **Slipcased or deluxe edition**: A good way to guarantee that you'll never actually read it.

THERE GOES THE NEIGHBORHOOD

CURRENT USED CAR PRICES 1956

> "To get rid of books, I take them first of all to a shop that specializes in collector's books (they're listed right in the Yellow Pages). What they reject I take to a regular secondhand bookstore. What they reject I take to Goodwill—all the same day, while I'm tired and want to get it over with."

Paper
The Paper Tiger... Has Mighty Big Litters

After emptying thousands of people's closets (as a cleaner, not a burglar), I'd have bet my lifetime-guaranteed brass squeegee that nothing could edge clothes out as the No. 1 clutter. But I was wrong! The real leader is paper, and if we don't find a way to deal with it, future generations will read about us rather than Pompei. Most of us are buried beyond the neck now, and there's no sign of a slowup in the flow! Paper trails don't exist anymore, they're paper highways. And paper is a physical, not merely intellectual, problem. A single sheet in the form of a memo or a message may seem innocent enough, but the sheer mass of paper that accumulates! And as you read this, every other country in the world is inventing new machines to copy, collate, file, and bind more of it.

In case you have any doubt that you have a paper problem, let me ask you the same thing I did many of my coworkers, family, and clients not long ago: "How many sheets of paper do you deal with a day?"

The thoughtful answer: "Er, ah, well, let me see, I'd say about twenty-five."

Wrong.

I asked my business partner as we left for the airport and Atlanta, about 11 A.M. one day: "Arlo, how many sheets of paper do you deal with in a day?"

He thought and gave me a little more accurate answer: "Oh, about eighty!"

Remember this was 11 A.M. (only a third of the day gone), and I'd already seen him handle, read, or sign more than forty-four pieces of paper. I continued to watch him from noon until bedtime, as we rode, visited, etc. He read (then kept) the 120-page in-flight magazine, read 72 pages of corporate reports and a booklet from BSCA, wrote six pages of letters, read a 28-page newspaper, had four pages of tickets and boarding passes, and crumpled up three wrappers. When he got home that night he'd received four pieces of junk mail, two invitations, and four bills, plus other miscellany—are you counting? Over *250* sheets of paper he dealt with, just his!

I get at least thirteen professional magazines and six newsletters each month. This alone averages almost 50 pages a day, and this is less than a tenth of my personal and business paper flow!

Now it's your turn. I want you convinced, before I give opinions and advice on what to do with it. So you won't miss anything, I've made a little outline for you (at left), so just fill in the blanks quickly (don't bother to hand count).

Okay, now (just to give us the idea here; don't worry about exactness) add up all the sheets, multiply them by 365, and you have a rough estimate of how much paper you deal with in a year. Time-and-motion experts tell us we spend eight months of our life just opening junk mail. Can you imagine sorting, moving, storing, and working around and through all that paper? Bet it takes years off your life.

A paper-flow expert at a convention told me there were 5 million secretaries in the United States who generated one million documents per minute and that was B.F. (Before Fax). My wife and I had as dinner guest one Sunday, an engineer who said his company was on a push to cut down paper use, since their 1,000 employees added up to a $75,000-per-year paper bill. (That's $750 each annually for the raw paper alone.) Many of us these days spend most of our time working with paper.

Magazines (if it's a monthly, just take the number of pages in the last issue and divide by 30)
Newspapers _____
Newsletters _____
School papers _____
Brochures _____
Catalogues _____
Notices _____
Announcements _____
Invitations _____
Cards _____
Advertising flyers _____
Schedules _____
Instructions _____
Letters in _____
Letters out _____
Memos _____
Reports _____
Questionnaires/surveys _____
Policies _____
File folders _____
Tickets _____
Shopping lists _____
Coupons _____
Other lists _____
Bills _____
Receipts _____
Checks _____
Claim checks _____
Notes _____
Memos _____
Photos _____
Pieces of junk mail _____

When I started up my cleaning company, the specifications to clean a large building were at most three pages. Now with copies and coverage of every "what if" and "might be," there can easily be hundreds of pages to document and bid an average building.

How much of all this paper do you keep? For how long? Where do you keep it? These are big questions that come to bear on this most congesting of clutter problems.

No matter how well you dodge or reduce the paper flow, there is still enough that everyone in this decade has to devise a plan to process it pronto—like the same day as delivery—or we'll have no chance of survival.

Boil It Down...

The paper passion has not only stimulated production of an unimaginable number of forms and documents, but a whole shelf of books on how to organize, store, save, pile, and file it. Let me give you an easier, better, and saner way out. Start using the word "reduce" instead of "organize." When you condense something, you save storage space, shuffling and hunting through stuff, etc. The cry of the century has always been to generate more, but *reduction* is the key to most success.

> "I am making your book required reading for my girlfriend, who keeps three-year-old notices from the phone company stating their intention to increase rates."

The secret, the goal of it all, is to reduce the 100 percent of papers that cross your path to the 10 percent of pure gold. If you keep the dross and low-grade ore right in with the gold, the gold will be of no or limited value. What good is having and not being able to find or use? When we cut things down, we cut confusion and the time needed to find things.

When I come home from a book promotion tour, my desk can scarcely hold all the mail, magazines, and messages. The first thing I do is strip it down. That means throwing out the envelopes, the packaging, and all the junk mail. A lot of mail can be quickly scanned and then disposed of right after I open it by the waste can. Then I'm down to two big boxes of mail that need some form of attention. Much of this is stuff that needs to be passed along to my partners, associates, or assistants to answer, so I divvy it up. By now it's down to a third of a box, so I take it home and read it and end up with a boiled-down half-handful of stuff to save from several weeks' worth (and I get a lot of mail).

I have a big briefcase and I carry many of the things that do need some action from me right along with me until I deal with them. Then they're gone.

Be hard on that stuff when you're going through it—far better to eliminate things *before* they get into the system (filing cabinet, in-box) than to try to find the time to go through it all and thin it out later. Too many files, for example, are just a neat way to store clutter vertically. Walk over to any of your "To Be Filed" piles now and see if a third (or more) of it couldn't be just thrown away.

If you don't have all that stuff, you won't have to burn up any brain cells remembering where it is or what your rationale was for keeping it. Just ask the good old question "What's the worst that can happen if I throw this out or give it away?" You'll find very few, if any, bad consequences for doing what's smart. I've even lost titles, deeds, transcripts, and receipts in floods and fires. And guess what? Replacing them was inexpensive and easy. Even if you lose your entire tax return, for example, you can get a copy of it from the IRS. The IRS will even mail you a copy of your account free of charge.

> "We heat with wood. Having a wood stove is the snappiest way to deal with paper trash ever. I keep a brown paper bag in my office in the basement. All the burnable trash goes into the bag, particularly the debris left whenever I clean a file folder or finish editing a draft. When the bag is full, it goes upstairs and gets turned into heat. No muss, no fuss, and darn little waste. No second thoughts, either. When it hits the flames, it's gone for good."

Don't forget: with paper there is no "later," only more!

The biggest plug in the paper sewer pipe is the one called: **"To sort or organize later."** But with paper there is no later—only more, and more. Paper never lets up; we have to sort it, handle it daily, or we're doomed. Never stack paper—to *stack is to stay!*

You need to sort that paper now, when it's in hand. Once you set it down, it's so thin, so innocent, so easily buried and never found. And paper has no value at all unless it's seen and read.

It's not hard to sort daily; almost every day there are times when we're too tired or wrung out to do anything clever or ambitious or even carry on a good conversation. Most paper handling doesn't call for a marathon of mental concentration; enough two-minute handling fragments during a day and you'll not have a sheet out of place! Use your half-wit time—at least 75 percent of paper processing (things like reading corporate minutes) can be done with the space between the right and left brain. I always carry all my paperwork—brochures, ads, and letters—with me when I leave the office at 6 A.M. to head for the airport, and just using my spare minutes and waiting time I have it all consumed and digested before the plane is over Nebraska.

Don't "piece" any paper, letter, card, or magazine. Save it for some time when you can sit down at the table or desk and consume it at a single sitting. If you piece at it, it will dog you for days, and what should be a five-minute session can easily stretch to twenty. The words "half-read" and "maybe later" are just pre-burial bargains you make with yourself.

Try to limit yourself to two or at most three options as you go through, rather than a half dozen (like save, store, reread, trade, study/consider further, trash). When you're fresh and focused on it, you know what you want or don't want—right then. If I don't want something I always rip it in half. It's a clean kill, total commitment, and much easier to dispose of. If it's to be passed on (to other family members or staff, etc.), I write OK/DA in a box in the upper corner of it, which means I have no further claim on it. It works well. If I want to keep an address, I clip it and tape it into my blank-page address book right away.

Want to reduce the stack of "to do some day"? Read through it all and schedule it or scuttle it.

Speed Paper Sorting

What weighs on us above all, often, is the backlog of third-, fourth-, and fifth-rate stuff. We go through it all once, initially, pick off all the really important things and actionables, and leave the rest "to go back through some day." If piles or boxes of paper of this type have been sitting somewhere for quite a while, chances are good that you don't need anything in there, so just flip through quickly to see if there are any important documents or buried bills. If necessary, enlist the aid of an intelligent non-nosy employee, friend, or relative. Just have them set anything that looks important, legal, or controversial aside for you to check out.

If stuff like this is really aged—like a couple of years or more—and you have been through it once, you could consider just throwing it all in the trash. I'll bet that all the important stuff with a real live purpose or message will resurrect itself, or resurface (on *fresh* paper!).

Remember, you need to handle paper daily, or even hourly! The secret is *never pile it*. Drop it into the right file, NOW-don't pile it.

Okay, now where does the 10 percent go?

That's a matter of personal taste. I have a file or drawer for every area of interest, and each morning or evening before breakfast or before bed, I take only two or three minutes to distribute each of my saved bits of paper into the right drawer or file and that's it.

Then, when I'm ready to speak or give a Scout program on knots or lifesaving, the files with all the information on those subjects are right there. And it's actually easier to assemble my notes from the rough form than if I had taken the time to recopy everything in there and type it up perfectly. I'm working on more than forty new books now (no lie), and although I've spent little or no straight time on them, the information gathering on them all is well under way. When I'm ready to go on one, I'll just assemble the ideas in the file, create some chapter titles, and write some bridges. Most of the research and ideas are there, put there over a three- or ten-year period of time—with no pain, no strain, and no big frenzy of paper handling.

Watch Those Copies!

Thirty years ago it was one carbon. If you were rich and a good typist, you might go for two, and that took care of that page. Then one day a temperamental copy machine was available. It made messy but readable copies—costly, but they beat carbon. Today we've perfected the copy machine. Photocopies are

119

clearer, cheaper, and neater than the original. One push of a computerized button and we can get as many as we want, any size, any color, even collated, so we make plenty of extras (Just in case). Now it takes seven or eight copies to do what somehow one carbon once accomplished. *Watch those copies!*

As for the sentimental stuff:

"I always had trouble deciding what to do with cards, letters, newspaper clippings, special magazine articles, etc. I didn't want to throw them out, but they didn't do me much good piled in a desk drawer, filing cabinet, or shoe box. From your first book I got the idea to make notebooks—and I have been creating notebooks ever since. I fill up about three 3-ring binders per year. I use monthly dividers and everything I wish to save gets put in here in the proper date order. I keep a daily diary on my computer and put the monthly printout at the beginning of each month. I also put snapshots in non-glare plastic sheet protectors in the appropriate month. I am creating a history of my life along with a terrific walk-down-memory-lane for me."

I get lots of lovely thank-you cards and precious notes from my kids and grandkids, and no way do I chuck them. I snip off the part with the message and stick it in one of my books. Then I toss the sheared bulk. Coming across one of these later is fun and gives a new glow every time.

"All my papers to save were being stored in a large container in my bedroom. I was planning to spend several days of my vacation sorting and creating scrapbooks. Then one day a new cleaning woman came from the cleaning service I use. She thought the container was a wastebasket and she emptied it all into the garbage. By the time I discovered the error, the garbage had been picked up and was long gone. At first I was devastated. There were some special letters and mememtos from family and close friends. When I got over being upset, I was surprised to feel a great sense of relief. I didn't have that project looming over me anymore. More free time!"

Dam the Flow

You do have some say in paper matters, you know. When circulars, junk mail, and the rest are finally running over the banks of your reading abilities, you can ask to be removed from the list. You can write directly to a specific company or send a stamped, self-addressed envelope to the Association of Direct Marketing Agencies (PO Box 3139, New York, NY 10163-3139, phone 212-6440-8085, fax 212-644-0296), and request their free "mail preference" form, which will enable you to have your name removed from any and all lists. You can also use this form to get on selected lists by checking your particular areas of interest, but why am I telling you *that?*

You don't have to keep all those magazine subscriptions, either, or read every newspaper that ever arrives. It's possible to spend so much time reading the news that you don't have time to make any!

You do have one last option—become famous and people will fight for your papers.

Miscellaneous Clutter
Tough Cases

- **Plastic knives and forks:** Another one of those things that multiply, since we've all saved them from box and picnic lunches and takeout orders from the beginning of time. They're preserved even with one prong gone. We wash them off carefully, so we can reuse them—then buy a new box of them right before the next picnic.

- **Heating pads:** Amazing! They quit working but still get warm! It's your imagination.

- **Inferior tape measures:** Broken or stuck or starting at four inches, if there is any caressible calibration at all, we keep it.

- **Candles and candle-related clutter:** Few of us burn the things, or even like them. We've heard horror stories of houses in flames, too, yet most of us have at least three styles of candle snuggled somewhere in a closet, plus several shaped-like-something-else candles we'll *never* use.

- **Wheels:** We keep wheels that come off anything from buses to casters; even when the unit they belong to is long gone, the wheels are ours, somewhere.

- **Fortune cookie fortunes:** These little morsels never taste like much, but we order or serve them up from time to time so a preprinted message can add some excitement to our lives (and tiny pieces of clutter to keep forever).

- **Those little plastic swords,** crepe-paper umbrellas, tassled toothpicks they put on cocktails: They're of no real use even at the time—yet we keep them! At least swizzle sticks (six or eight from your collection of sixty or eighty, from all the neat or well-known places you've ever been) *could* be used, though they never will be. "Oh, pardon me while I run and get my swizzler from ____ to stir this Black Russian for you."

- And my favorite: **Leftover bouquets of flowers.** Almost every event or activity features a vase or bouquet or corsage of flowers. And they can add a lot to brighten our spirits as well as the room. But as the event draws to a close, disposing of any yet-unwilted flowers is always a major decision. So even before sustaining the corporate officers or addressing the $8-million budget, some fair way to dispose of the centerpiece is devised (and someone 3,000 miles from home, over packed to the max already, wins it). They tenderly transport the fast dying flowers and foliage home so they can... *what?* I've cleared out more mummified arrangements from cars and houses that you would believe. "We just had to keep them." Yes, and not only them but the foam they were stuck in, the plastic stalk that held the card, the little plastic cupids it was decorated with, and the cheap ugly vase it came in. Silk or plastic bouquets are even worse; they give us an *excuse* to keep them (to collect dust) forever.

CHAPTER 9

The Basic Technique of Dejunking

Okay, It's Time!

This is the final hour, what you've waited a lifetime for. Your prison term is over. You're getting out! Quit thinking of it as some kind of kamikaze sacrifice or exotic torture. This is freedom in the form of a Boston Tea Party of stuff you really don't want, will never use, and all of your friends and family are snickering at you for owning. This is the revolution, the release of the imprisoned soul that's been cowering in your consciousness for years, decades, centuries even for some of you. You're not only going to live through this, but you're actually going to start living for the first time.

You've traveled lots of miles for this moment, so savor it to the max. You won't be bidding a sad farewell to faithful friends today, you'll be saying, "Thank you, it's been a pleasure, but the visit's over" to some things that helped make life fun once, in the past.

Pre-conditioning warm-up before launching into the game

1. Lifting and carrying a box-shaped weight around

2. Reach—1 2 3, reach—1 2 3

3. Fingertip toughening and flexibility exercises (for pawing through stuff)

4. Tromping and flattening foot-stomp

5. Paper crumpling (rumored to be a bust developer)

6. Head scratching (for all those times you'll ask, "Why did I ever keep this?")

7. Walking to put away

8. Trash-can-toss accuracy trials

9. Trash can heave-and-dump

10. Jumping for joy when it's gone!

Overcoming the Final Obstacles

Other People

You're a believer. You've conquered all excuses, even sentimentality and lack of enough good sturdy boxes to haul it all away. Why do so many of us reach this front line of the clutter charge and then fail to push forward? There's a good reason! We didn't clear all the obstacles, including the one called Other People! They've got some much more pressing project they'd like to see you tackle first. You think *you* protected your junk! Wait till you try to throw it out. They shield it like a wounded soldier, pricking you with charge-dampening questions like, "Are you sure, Gloria, real sure you want to part with this?" "Oh, oh, oh, this was grandma's favorite. If you'll keep it around awhile I'll put it in my new house someday." Or "You can get at least $50 for that from _____."

The second they make you give it a second thought, it's going to get a second chance. I've seen spouses whine, moan, and threaten their mate to get rid of something, and then when they go for it, the exterminator becomes a last-ditch defender. Every other family member is an antiques expert and/or knows someone who made a million off an old cream separator.

If you want to get right to work, dispose of the kibitzers first. What they don't know won't haunt them.

The Actual Act of Dejunking Chicken-Out

"When all is said and done, more is said than done."

An odd thing often happens when a would-be dejunker, like a hunter, faces the real thing. Up till then the hunt is fun: excitement rises, the equipment is purchased, guns are cleaned, provisions are assembled. The dejunker, like the hunter, arrives at the site determined to bag something. Suddenly, out from behind the bushes (or the curtain) is the object of the hunt, the specimen they've sought and schemed to get. They're face to face with it—and in this very moment they're struck with something called buck fever or junk fever. Many, many hunters have experienced it: they freeze up and can't pull the trigger. Who knows what causes it—compassion, indecision, fear, overexcitement—but junkers do it, too. They've sworn on a stack of unused Bibles to declutter, yet when the moment arrives and the objects are at hand, they freeze. And their quarry gallops back into the closet or under the stairs or behind the furnace. Our bravery when we talk about it and plan something is impressive, but when the moment to act comes, it's often another matter.

Starting the ridding process is tough, no doubt about it. It's coming to terms with the past, and you have to do it, have to face it all and sort it. Because only you know the truth about yourself, who you are now versus who you were. It's like the present assimilating the past, or a goodbye kiss. But I promise that you'll become bold when the time is here. Don't lie in bed on perfectly good junking days and agonize over it. Remember, it's now or never. As you lie there your junk is reproducing itself. And friends and relatives are lying in bed too, planning to dump more of their stuff on you (because junk attracts junk). They know you'll hoard and keep it for them. Get up and beat them to the punch. When they see the garbagemen pallbearing your stuff to the burial site, it'll instantly cut you off as a possible dumping ground.

When you deliver all that clutter to the dump or to the Salvation Army downtown, or a relative actually anxious to accept it, the real delivery will be you.

Nothing ventured, nothing decluttered.

Rigged for Rubble! The Dejunking Kit

When you invade your inventory you won't need a clutterproof vest, but there are a few tools that will make handling all those sackfuls of stuff more efficient.

1. Knife to cut open, cut loose, cut off, or dissect as necessary

2. Scissors

3. A good supply of sturdy boxes—not bags! Bags are hard to open, hard to hold open, hard to judge the weight of, stack, see what's in, etc. And they're easy to poke holes in. Bags can break and strew clutter everywhere, too. A box, on the other hand, is an inviting bin—easy to fill, haul, or store!

4. Marker—a black permanent marking pen to identify or assign

5. Tape—good strong sealing tape to seal and reseal boxes, etc.

6. Paper and pencil or pen—you get more ideas, inspirations, and disposal brainstorms while dejunking than anytime in your life. Make sure you've got a pen to write them down!

7. Plenty of good roomy garbage cans

If your hoard seems to call for it, you might also want:

- Labels (if you prefer that style of identification—see page 137)
- Hand protection, such as leather or rubber gloves
- Hand truck, utility cart, or wheelbarrow
- Dust mask (if you're allergy-prone and/or faced with some incredibly dusty old dungeon to do)

The First Dejunking Secret: Divide and Conquer

You one day decide that now is the hour—it's dejunk or die! Then you actually behold the mass of clutter to be combed through and it overwhelms you. Why in a straight decade of decluttering you couldn't make a dent in it. What's the use? So instead of starting you slam the door shut and wait for a miracle. Maybe the miracle is simply learning to reduce it to bite-size—the old "an-elephant-is-easy-to-eat-if-you-eat-him-one-piece-at-a-time" approach.

A dump truck, for example, left 12 cubic yards of gravel on my driveway once, then went back for another load. He suggested I hire a dozer to flatten it. When he returned 45 minutes later, the pile was all leveled out, and I did it all with one little garden shovel. It even surprised me; I'd expected it to take half a day. You won't believe how much you can do one shovelful at a time.

When we were teenagers my brother and I would create huge haystacks in a matter of days with only one team of horses. Some days we'd haul a thousand bales and stack them up by hand (no machine) one bale at a time. It's amazing to think of it now.

Junk is a trial, by the mile!
And even by the yard, it's hard
But by the inch, it's a cinch!

You'd be amazed what can be done in bits and snatches. Bits and snatches add up, and they get the job done surprisingly fast. Wars are won, yes, with an overall plan, but ultimately by many short skirmishes and little victories all added up. It's the same with junk.

The Emotional Exhaustion of Dejunking

Another reason to take it a little at a time.

A few things about those old western movies bothered a lot of us—such as the fact that their six-shooters easily shot thirty-six times without reloading, and a movie horse could run for twenty miles without even getting winded, even with two chubby cowboys on its back.

The process of dejunking can be as physically tiring and emotionally draining as the longest round or toughest race. And we human beings in the clutter-casting campaign do run out of bullets, though we always think we can go on forever. If you feel like folding after two or three hours of hard dejunking, it's only normal. That stuff you've spent years growing attached to, even old feather-light plumed hats and about-to-crumble corsages, can weigh more than any barbell. And dropping stuff like this in the dumpster jolts you as hard as a punch to the solar plexus. When you're decluttering you're facing up to the past, pricing and appraising the heart. Article after article causes a dream, a project, or a plan to resurface, carries a huge emotional message, or is bare-faced evidence of something you never did anything with or about. It can be kind of like admitting failure over and over and over again. And this stuff is all boxed and packed and jumbled together. Junk judgment day is more traumatic than your first solo flight or solo in the choir, so expect to last three or four hours or less at a stretch. I've done eight-minute national TV shows that tired me more than eighteen hours of construction or farm work. Don't worry if you can't set aside days to settle your clutter accounts; short sessions may even be more effective.

"Secret to getting started? Set a very short time to work. Ten minutes, fifteen maximum, and work like fury during this time. Haul the street-side garbage can up to where you're working. I give up when I think the task seems endless. For fifteen minutes, anyone can maintain his or her concentration. Put on some loud, fast music while you do it."

Clutter got there in bits and snatches, so what could be more logical than getting it out the same way?

You can be a superman or superwoman declutterer without leaping tall buildings in a single bound. You can get anywhere you need to go one step at a time.

Some things or areas you can dejunk without ever quite focusing on them. For example every time you go through the garage, or pass the paint shelf, snatch an almost-empty can or worthless board scrap and send it on its way to refuse heaven. After a while, though it's still overcrowded, the spot will start looking a little bare to you. Don't go bother to launch into a reorganization yet; just keep slowly stripping the shelf, drawer, closet or whatever—it's really kind of fun, like not counting your money till the end of the day and being pleasantly sur-

prised. Just keep taking more and more, and bingo! Before you know it the shelf will be *almost self-organized*. Elimination does its own reorganization.

"I employ a program of straightening and discarding a half hour per day. I don't enjoy this activity per se but have managed to make this the most pleasant half hour of the day. I listen to my favorite music, enjoy a special snack, and credit my recreation budget with a penny for every bit of trash or clutter discarded. Most important, I allow myself to relax and enjoy the process rather that being concerned about results. (Almost any activity becomes bearable, even palatable, if the pace is slowed sufficiently.) My cleaning/discarding actually becomes a kind of meditation that helps me unwind after the workday."

"If you're a rebelling or stubborn, perverse soul, a little reverse psychology can work wonders. Give yourself a time limit—okay, you only have an hour, max, to sift your stash. How much can you dig through in that time? Soon you'll be planning and scheming to gutter that junk and clutter."

In the Mood

Mood isn't a moot point here—in fact, it's the spark plug of the decluttering engine. Moods give us more incentive to get into or after something than any form of logic or persuasion. And mood is free, too!

When you're in the right mood or frame of mind, you can unquestionably do better. Anger, for example, lends us unbelievable strength (and can inspire some bad decisions), while sadness can slow our pace and quickly sap us. Melancholy only encourages clinging and collection, as we say, "What have I got but this?" And a vengeful mood can mutilate even the best of things.

Here's a little mood chart to assist you in exorcising your junk. When you reach the condition on the left, attack the items on the right.

When you're feeling	Tackle
Happy	All that outdated old sentimental stuff
Sad	Something simple and physical like moving stuff out of the way, or hauling it away
Spiritual	Plain-brown-wrapper junk, stuff you were saving to nurse a grudge
Angry	Any dejunking that involves flattening, smashing, dissembling, or breaking up
Revengeful	Old gifts you always hated
Urge to kill	Old papers can be sheared through very quickly in this state
Depressed	Anything out of style or ugly, or any dejunking that involves a lot of cleaning (cleaning always gives us a lift)
Broke	Anything/everything that could be sold
Energetic	Anything that involves a lot of sorting and shifting and putting away
Bored/restless	A good time to go after yard junk
Lighthearted/playful	Games and puzzles with missing pieces, your collection of aged party clutter
Racy	Old clothes that would leave you at the gate
Nostalgic/sentimental	Sorting through for expired coupons might be safe
Adventurous	The attic, the basement, or the garage
Rebellious	Outdated school or government clutter, tags on mattresses and pillows
Fed up	The field is yours

Mood can enable us to move mountains, including those man-made clutter peaks.

We often wait weeks, months, or years to get the nerve to confront our caverns of stuff, then one day or hour, triggered perhaps by one too many nags, a stumble over some exposed clutter, or a collapsed shelf, we snap. A binge results, an orgy of reorganization, a jag on our junk—and in an hour we make more headway than we have in years of polite pecking away at it. *Good, good, good!* Once you're on a frenzied fling like this, don't stop for lunch, a break, or because it gets dark—stay on that unfettering frequency as long as it lasts. Make it a marathon!

Give Yourself Some Elbow Room

You can't clean mud off your shoes standing in the mud. Trying to declutter while ankle-, knee-, or waist-deep in clutter is fruitless and frustrating—you have to have some elbow room, some operating room. Emptying a trunk of treasure onto an already littered floor or crammed corner is mighty unmotivating. But when you dump it onto a clean, clear tabletop or stretch of carpet, instead—Behold! it's ten times easier to handle, mentally and physically.

Always carry or drag that drawer to a clearing. Don't fight it on its own home court—you'll lose. A clearing means *light—room—speed.* Decluttering in a cubbyhole is un"hole"some! Anywhere you can create a clearing, do it—then use it! It will be your happy hunting grounds.

Deep in the Heap!

Look at it this way—it's an adventure! When you're unburying, drilling deep through the crust of unexplored clutter, you'll always hit a gusher of great stuff, stuff you haven't seen since P.M. (pre-marriage), B.C. (before college), or A.B. (after baby). It beats volunteering to go help excavate in Ecuador because you'll feel the thrill of the treasure much more personally. There are not only scintillating glimpses of your former selves but also veins of top-grade keepable ore amidst those piles and boxes and bundles. I'd get up and get at it right now—some of that stuff was buried alive and is long overdue for rescue. There's probably a junk thrill in every hill. Start digging now before someone plunders it when you aren't around.

The Three-Stage Strategy

There are times when a flood or a fire or remodeling requires that something be cleared out from end to end immediately. But I like to make three trips or passes instead of one big onslaught:

1. **The obvious.** Some stuff is pure junk and you know it; it's so ridiculous it even makes you grin. So just grab it and toss it. It goes fast and easy and makes you feel so good that there's no risk or regrets. I like to walk by and around a number of areas for several days and snatch off the obvious things one at a time, every day tossing stuff

in the garbage or giving it away. This is sort of like chopping down the wild trees that have grown up in a forgotten garden before starting to pull the dandelions. You'll be amazed how the picture will brighten and the practice and habit of tossing junk will strengthen you, so that the tough stuff you passed over in March will be an easy kill in April.

Just remember you're only doing a rough cut—never at this point attempt any detailed or refined dejunking. Your aim is to reduce the mass, knock off the big/easy, long-dead stuff, give yourself a running start and some room to maneuver. It's like picking the big stones off a new lawn before you try to get up all the little rocks and rake it. Once this stuff is gone you ll have some room to turn, sort, carry, or wheel stuff around, as well as a little relief from the threat of avalanche and somewhat of a path to squeeze through.

Easy-kill stuff is like old insulation—things you can eliminate with no hesitation and no remorse. Stick with the easy clear-cut kills. Don't get bogged down reading love letters or caught in conflicts, which will change your mood for the worse. One box of valentines could take all morning. Other slowdowns are: "I wonder if these batteries work?" "Do we still have the grill this frank fryer fits?" "Whose is this?" "Was this the air mattress that had a leak?"

2. **One of a kind swoop.** Tackling too many different kinds of things at once is a sure way to exhaust your energy and enthusiasm. When you're still trying to reduce things down to less discouraging, take it one subject at a time. For example: first trip, all old tires (that should make a dent in the old heap); next all misplaced tools; then all empty bottles, followed by all burnables or stuff destined for the dump, and finally all old newspapers. Just weed out things that have a clear-cut destination. Collecting a bunch of stuff headed for the same place will also save you steps.

3. **The hard or hidden.** Once the first two stages have mustered some momentum, you can face the junk and clutter you really have to work for—the kind you have to sweat to dig out and sift through, and the emotional-morass stuff. Now that the obvious garbage and easy category junk is gone, you've stripped off the topsoil to display the real bedrock junk underneath.

Now and only now will you find things you haven't seen for years. The first wave of feeling will be elation—to know it wasn't lost for good or that no one stole it. Later, when you really look it over, you may no longer think it's so nice.

Change Foxholes and Keep Fighting!

After you've been immersed in it for hours, some area of clutter will befuddle you, begin to bog you down. It won't be long before you're spinning your wheels or grinding to a dead halt. Whenever interest and enthusiasm wane, watch out—you're about to junk out. Move to another, fresh front. It's like switching arms when you're carrying a heavy suitcase; you can keep going if you just make a little change.

When you've tried on as many ten-year-old clothes as you can tolerate, break open those boxes of spare dishes or the trunk of extra camping gear. I often work on three or four decluttering projects at once, so I can switch when I start losing steam. The smarties among us learn to fight life on many fronts, to sustain speed, interest, and effectiveness.

What Went in Will Come Out

Have you ever witnessed how much an experienced junker can pack into a single closet, cubbyhole, bureau, or wardrobe? They can easily stuff five cubic feet of stuff into two cubic feet of space. We can thus greatly underestimate the full scope (and scatter potential) of a clutter mission, as we go to pull out just a few things and end up with a bite too big to chew.

No wonder we have:

The Torn-Apart Problem

Or the condition the place often gets in during the process of dejunking—everything laid out and stacked up and strung around. It looks as if your house or room or garage has just had a head-on collision of some kind. It looks awful and generates lots of comments from household members and friends (who should be home tending to their own overjunked places). We tear into a closet and discover we can't do it all in a day. We end up not only aggravated, but with a bunch of stuff all over, or the part we didn't have time to finish dealing with still spread around. So we stuff it all back in a hurry and end up with a worse mess than we started with. Or we leave it all out indefinitely in everybody's way till we "have a chance to get back to it."

To prevent this:

- If the area in question (or any part of it) is portable, take it somewhere less central to dissect.
- Don't take on more than one area (a high-traffic area, especially) at once.
- Even if it's just a single deeply cluttered closet or credenza, don't pull the whole thing apart. Do it area by area—shelves, clothes, rod, floor, top to bottom, whatever—till you have it beat. There'll be less out and in the way, less pressure on you, and a pleasing sense of progress all the way through.
- If an all-too-visible area for some reason has to be done all at once, get help!

It's been a part of you for a long time, but you're going to be surprised, as you get lighter, how good it feels to shed all these old burdens. Self-confidence, self-assurance, and self-esteem will ebb into your being as those old belongings bug out. You thought they gave you security, helped make you whole, but all the time they were just holding you down.

How to Clean Up as You Clean Out

The process of decluttering is a dirty deal. We face accumulated grime, rot, rust, mildew, spills, and stains on every side. There's always a mess when we're down or up or under there dejunking—dust and dead bugs and dropped parts and ruined (leaked on, crushed, shattered) things, blackened and dirtied boxes, barrels, cartons, and crates. Then, too, often we need to clean what we intend to keep—or give away.

It got this way because 99 percent of us never clean our junk or clutter corners—it's just junk; nobody sees it; so we sweep around it. For years it lies there gathering dust and dirt, simmering, fermenting—and we all know that in exhuming, most surprises are bad. Fear of the filth we'll have to face is in fact one of the biggest deterrents to dejunking. Sifting old stuff is bad enough, but seasoned with who knows what, it can inspire in us an intense desire to let sleeping piles lie. Having to clean as you dejunk seems to add insult to injury.

But you can easily disarm all the dirt you've been dreading if you just call in the decluttering cavalry:

- **A canister or wet/dry vac.** Forget the whisk broom and dustpan bit. The vac will get it before it gets all over. It will also slurp up those mouse nests and all those insects and beetles, dead or alive, without even a burp, and without the need to ever touch them. Point that vac nozzle at it and zap—it's up and out of your life.

- **A hand-held vac** is handy, too, for picking up pesky problems like spilled sand and fly wings. Run the snout along the inside of drawers to remove those stubborn last little fragments of stuff that usually mean emptying the drawer, taking it out, and beating it on the back. You'll be glad

you have that little vac, too, when that ancient plantless pot tips over on the top shelf and scatters loam and vermiculite everywhere.

- **A lambswool duster.** A large puff of natural or synthetic lambswool on a long handle attracts and holds dust like crazy through a combination of static electricity and the natural oils in the wool. You can easily reach all the hard-to-reach places with this, too, from under the bed to behind the dresser and even up under the rafters. Use your lambswool duster to swipe away cobwebs, dust, and dirt collected in the corners from ceiling to floor, and even under the eaves.

- **A disposable dust cloth** such as the Masslinn (available at janitorial-supply stores and The Cleaning Center 800-451-2402) to clean the insides of drawers and cabinets before you close them. As you lift "keepers" with your left hand, you can wipe them with the cloth in your right hand to remove dust and debris, and also quickly wipe the surface they were resting on. If you do this as you go, you'll only have to handle each item once.

- **A broom**, to clear quick pathways through the junk and clutter and help you redefine the floor once you've found it. Use a big commercial nylon angle-cut broom from a janitorial-supply store.

- **A trigger-spray bottle of disinfectant cleaner** or all-purpose cleaner and some one-time-use rags or paper towels, for the keepable clutter or the structure that has housed it—to remove whatever the vacuum won't whisk away. Spray the surface or object lightly, wait a few seconds for the solution to soften the crud, and wipe dry, and it'll not only be clean but less likely to bloom back into mold, mildew, and the like.

- You might want a bottle of **ammonia-based glass cleaner**, too, and a little denatured alcohol will make short work of flyspecks when you run across them.

- **Cleaning cloth:** a nice strong absorbent piece of terrycloth is the better way to do any damp wiping and buff drying you need to do.

- A plastic maid basket, or **"cleaning caddy,"** is a handy way to keep your spray bottles, dustcloth, cleaning cloths, etc., at your side as you go.

- **A garbage box!** A box, not a bag! One with a wide mouth and stout sides and sturdy bottom so when ruined, broken, rotted, disintegrated stuff shows up, or when you set it aside to dispose of it later (as most of us do), it won't get spilled and spread all over when the bag bursts or collapses. Sharp stuff like wire and broken glass won't tear a hole in a box, either.

And don't shake, blow, whisk, or dump stuff onto the floor or into the air; it only spreads throughout the dejunking zone (and house). Let debris fall into your garbage box, not onto you or the floor, as you go!

You might want to line your garbage box (and cans) with a sturdy plastic bag whenever you know a lot of wet, leaky stuff will be going in.

Watch Where You Pile It

We often toss the discarded or doubtful in a pile by the door in plain view, forgetting that there's nothing more inviting to passersby than a pile of something someone just tossed. To be the first vulture is a prime American aspiration, and thus the rank and rusty residue of decluttering is recycled back through the house. Make sure boxes, bags, etc., of discards are snoop-proof, too, for this same reason.

When Dejunking "Bugs" You

Your mounds might enjoy privacy from your friends and family, even your in-laws, but not from insects. There isn't a storage place yet that seals out everything, and much to our horror a three-inch spider, a colossal cockroach, or a far-from-wimpy wasp comes out with the whatchamacallits. Sow bugs scuttle out from that crack in the concrete floor and silverfish venture forth from that old book binding. And even if nothing live springs on you, you can count on coming across some dried mouse manure, dead flies, termite tailings, or wasp-made miniature mud huts. It's all part of the package and punishment of stashing stuff. Keep a canister vacuum with a naked hose (no attachment) at your side. A flick of the switch solves all fear and fights with the undesirables—the riffraff—of the rafters.

"As I dug deeper into the box and realized I had emptied two small bags of trash, I was actually excited. Reaching the bottom of the box, I was ecstatic—I had actually finished what I started; I wouldn't have to dig through this useless paraphernalia whenever I needed something, and most important, it's a pleasure to work at my desk and I know I'm one step closer to being a more organized person!"

Ambush!

As you blaze a trail through your fortress of fine old artifacts, you're fair game. At least a dozen detours lurk in your litter, and they've derailed many a dejunker. And nothing—after you spent

months getting the guts to go for it—is worse than getting waylaid in your first canyon of clutter. You're just digging in, diligently dejunking and suddenly:

- You find something really neat amid the rubble— your high school yearbook, for example, or that flattering sketch of you done by your old flame, the quartz crystals you chipped out yourself. Should you go show the neighbors or your nearest and dearest? Nope—don't. Not now. Move on!

- You run across something broken and want to stop to fix it, dismantle it, remantle it, or glue it together. Don't! Set it aside and move on; you can fix it during a TV commercial sometime— never during valuable dejunking time!

- You spill something (coffee, cola, custard) all over what you're sorting. That's just a little assistance with your decision to heave-ho. Move on!

- You run across something half finished. Remember: if it wasn't worth finishing when you stored it, it probably isn't now. In any case don't let it break your stride now—dodge that bullet, then move on!

- Packrat pains! You run across something that suddenly saddens or angers you (mouse munches on a book, a moth hole in one of your sweaters). Don't lose your cool over an aged catastrophe—you weren't using it anyway. Ride faster!

- Injury! You break a fingernail, get a splinter, bump your skin, or strain a brain cell while pawing through the pile. Remember—real heroes keep marching to victory even when wounded. Don't stop for anything short of a skull fracture or wrenched back.

- Paranoia of the pile. You suddenly suspect you threw something valuable away. (Was there a hundred-dollar bill tucked in that old textbook? Could the lump in that old glove have been a diamond ring?) Don't stop, it's a mirage! You're hallucinating, or getting junk fever. If you can't get the seizure under control without it, tell yourself firmly that you'll go groping back through those sixteen neatly stacked garbage bags later—*after* today's solid installment of further dejunking is done.

- Or you're really rolling and run across something that makes you remember something you haven't seen for a spell. (Your good wrench: where is it, did someone borrow it, steal it?) Forget it. If it's still alive in your life, you'll run into it again, so work faster. Even if it was gone, you'd only be adding insult—lost time—to injury by looking for it now and sacrificing a good head of decluttering steam.

- Detail, detail. We start cutting the ragged edges off all the recipes we ripped out, or pasting old pictures into an album. Focusing on tiny time-consuming tasks like this is guaranteed to make you grind to a halt. Go for bulk and don't do any fine tuning, meritorious though it may be, on the first attack. Slow your horse up at all and you're an easy target.

- Interference! An ambushing outlaw can appear in the form of friend, neighbor, or relative who has nothing to do but ask, "Why are you doing this?" "Are you sure you want to part with that?" If they don't ambush you, they'll head you down the wrong trail. ("By the way, the fish are biting, right below the dam.") They're often just jealous of your ambition, so dejunk faster and really give them a jab, or give them some money and send them to the movies.

- False security or illusions of grandeur! You reach a milestone, finish one big pile or room or area, and get a sense of accomplishment, so you lay off for a while. It's a trap. Keep at it—there's nothing better than dejunking on a high.

- You just cave in. Nonsense. Go back to plan A. (Or any plan. If you have a plan you won't cave in.)

Take a Rejuvenating Junk Break

You're bound to need a break as you eat your way through that casserole of clutter. You can only chew up and digest so much at a time. But the wrong kind of break—like flopping on the couch, or too much junk food or drink—can smother the spark of invading the spoils. So do something that will not only get you up but turn you on (remember a change is usually better than a rest):

- **Salvage something.** Get the tool you need (screwdriver, knife, hammer) and "caster-ate" that otherwise useless chair, snip off that zipper, rescue that cushion. Reclaiming something genuinely useful from an otherwise discarded carcass will give you a sense of progress and accomplishment as well as a mental rest.

- **Pretty up and prepare to divest.** Clean up that piece you're going to pass on to a fortunate friend. You might even want to gift wrap it, too. Write the last love note for that piece of clutter you've kept for a lifetime and stick it in the package. You'll be getting rid of it and doing something thoughtful, too. Gifting people (as long as you're giving them something they'll actually cherish) is a renewal of mind, body, and spirit.

Weather Guide to Dejunking

Don't try to do paper outside.

Don't try to carry stuff outside when it rains, or if there's ice or snow on the ground.

Listen to the weather report before you gut the garage.

No yard junk at night.

Forget attics in summer.

Don't try to sort small stuff in cold unheated places

A great time to dejunk that cool basement is when it's sweltering outside.

And vice versa—when it's freezing out, light a warm and toasty fire and tear into those boxes or photos or whatever.

- **Leave the scene of the slime.** Don't take a break on the front lines. Instead, go to a place already dejunked to sit down and read another chapter of this book and sip a cold grapefruit juice. You'll savor that exhilarating junk-free atmosphere and be raring to launch another offensive.

- **Chase paper.** Stay on the dejunking channel, just switch to the paper pile. Paper is physically and psychologically different from other junk, because of its essentially disposable nature. This break is kind of like when you've been digging, fighting hardpan, straining and groaning with each scoop. Then you switch to loose dirt, and it goes so easily, with so little effort that it's a real contrast to the other. It's better than a rest—it's practically a reward.

How to Stop and Start Again!

How we all hate to have our momentum interrupted by a phone call, kid call, nature call, or nightfall…because once we stop, we get stiff, sore, lazy, distracted, delayed, etc. Then it's like returning from vacation: getting back in the groove is a grind. And clutter is one thing that doesn't heal itself—how you leave the battle is how you'll find it on your return.

The big secret is not to retreat. Once it's out and in process (being sorted, etc.), don't bundle clutter back into the box or onto the shelf. Leave it out—exposed, testifying by its very presence that it must be completed. If it's ugly, or too tempting to kids or kittens (which it generally is), toss or hang a blanket or dropcloth over it while you do the morning chores, then hit it hard. The longer you wait to get back to it, the worse things get.

If you keep it out so it can be seen, you can grab it and get back to work on it. Nothing is worse than a project that takes two hours to get out and set up for 15 minutes of work on it.

Regroup for the Next Attack

Okay, you've done a great job on the first pass, even if it did take you a couple of weeks—or months. You have 160 boxes of common clutter down to 16 boxes of hard-core clutter or superconcentrated clutter. What now? I'd leave the 16 boxes, pile them neatly and cover with a tarp if necessary for a few weeks, and enjoy all the freedom from clutter you've accomplished. You'll be surprised how quickly you'll get the urge to circle back and attack the last battalions of junk and whip them!

A Couple of Sorting Secrets

Why do we dread sorting? It's the mildest sort of nudge we can give our clutter, a fine chance to dig it out and spend some time with it, so we needn't get our feathers ruffled. Sorting is a skill we practice all our lives, so we should be good at it. At a very young age we start to sort the things on our plate (the peas-under-the-table trick). And now we sort while shopping, washing, and working at the office; our entire day is spent sorting in some way. We even sort for entertainment—what channel to watch on TV, what restaurant to eat at. We do have to sort a lot to declutter, but it shouldn't pose any special challenge.

If you run into some sorting uncertainty, handle it the way we did on the farm when it came time to choose the pigs for feeding or market. We'd bunch them all and then make a pick of the litter. Alone, most pigs and most junk are keepables. The only way to get a fair pick was to herd them all together. Sorting is the art of comparison, weighing one choice against another. So get all six of your umbrellas, or all eight paring knives or pairs of scissors or raincoats, side by side and *sort* for the best!

Sorting methods beyond that can be left to your personality and inclinations. Just in case you're tempted to dodge sorting for another decade, however:

- Dig right in, don't nibble at it. Spread it out. Empty the whole box or drawer. String it out all over in plain view. The pure trash will be embarrassingly apparent and can be tossed immediately, the rest can be rough-graded right afterward.
- There are at least two kinds of sorting—quick sorting (such as when you separate the curtains from the old clock radios) and down-to-the-last-doohickey sorting—and the two are best done at different times. When you're just/still trying to get the attic floor cleared, one shoe box full of salvaged buttons could stop you cold. In your first pass you just have to determine if it's type A or 0, positive or negative. No cutting or stitches. You're just doing a quick scan of the stuff to maybe store it with its species.
- When you're looking for one thing you always find another, so put this principle to good use. Never sort for only one kind of thing at once—always start at least half a dozen little piles and keep adding to them.
- Don't bother to put anything back or away till you've gathered a goodly amount of it. Why make all those separate trips, or flips through all the file tabs?
- Don't fail to do two-handed sorting when you can.
- You can talk while sorting, so why not invite a friend or neighbor (better yet, several) over to catch up on the latest (and help sort) while you separate the six boxes of mixed nuts and bolts your mom passed on to you.
- If you get most of it done, if you get 85 to 90 percent of it back into circulation, don't worry about that last little coffee can in which every single screw, washer, and tack is different. Set the can aside, and go through it only when you've

been through the whole hardware chest and still haven't found the little Phillips-head you need.

P.S. Just because it sorts doesn't mean it's worth keeping. Finding better ways to store our junk is just like consolidating all our debts and loans into one big one. It gives the illusion that they're reduced or gone. Not so! The payment still comes due.

Mixed Junk Is About the Worst

Drawers full of the same thing such as old socks by the score are a little boring but not so bad because at least you know there are only socks in there. Eighty different kinds of objects jumbled together is total time-taking, indecisive confusion.

This "mixed junk" (like the old cigar box filled with nuts, bolts, keys, and tangled necklace chains) can really bog us down. It's a junk pothole or whirlpool, and a professional cleaner hits them at least four or five times a day. I learned fast that you can't let one snag hang you up or put you out of commission. I don't work on close deadlines for this very reason. When I draw a blank or hit a bad spot or get muddled, when I can't come up with an answer for something I'm writing about or trying to decide what to do with, I leave it, put it aside—it isn't going to rule or derail me. Let it go for a while. How long? Well, if you've had it all this time, another four hours, forty hours, or even forty days shouldn't make that much difference. *Don't forget about it or let it off the hook,* but at another hour or from another angle it can look entirely doable.

Branding Time

When we put our dejunked boxes and containers back out on the range (onto the shelf or into storage), we need to brand them unless we want to risk rustlers or straying. Two seconds of branding can save two hours of agony and maybe two tons of good stuff that survived the clutter cut. Mark at least two sides with what's in the box—and notice I said *sides* not top, because the top is almost always covered with *another* box. This will prevent you from having to heave and/or open pile upon pile of boxes to find the one the Christmas stuff is in.

As for what to mark with, there are at least two schools of thought here. I, for example, think a broad-tip black permanent marker is best—easy to read, even at a distance or in the semidark. (I even draw pictures on the boxes sometimes—it's fast.) On the other hand, if you find yourself doing a lot of repacking, or you've got a sturdy box only too likely to be reused for something else someday, writing on a self-adhesive white label might be better, because when you fill it with something else all you have to do is slap a new label over the old.

In any case, try to avoid labeling a lot of boxes merely "Misc." That's a lot to open and paw through and repack when you do need to find out what's in there. It takes a little patience, but you'll be glad you did make a quick list of at least the main ingredients of "Misc." right there on the label.

Do your labeling early, rather than late, in a decluttering session. The will to label wears down as the day wears on.

Take a good hard look at each label after you write it out, before you stick it on the box. If it says something like "curtains the former occupants left behind," maybe you should be eliminating it, not labeling it.

Dig to Display!

The process of dejunking isn't done until the useful is used!

We too often think of dejunking only in terms of tossing it, giving it away, selling it, or repacking it for another decade. There's some good stuff stuffed away here and there, and at the time you buried it in that chest or closet you had a reason, maybe a vision of it playing a very special part in your life someday. So when you come across it during an uncluttering surge, act on it—get it out of the closet and into use, out of mothballs and onto the hall wall. Frame it, mount it, display it, enjoy it. "I'm saving it for later" is about the saddest excuse going.

Why hobble through a second-rate life with your first-rate stuff in storage? It won't mean much to others when you go, so why not activate it now? Breathe life (or new life) into it—don't commit an unintentional mercy killing by smothering it under or in a corner of one of your cobwebbed cabinets!

If those are the good dishes, what does that make these? Get out your good tablecloth, your good silver, your good jewelry, and the good crystal. Do you honestly think your great-granddaughter (yet to be born) is going to appreciate those things more than you do? Appreciate them and enjoy them now—in this lifetime. Don't just be a dusty storehouse for all the good stuff.

"I finally got down my beautiful quilts and put them on the beds. I took the embroidered dish towels and put them in the kitchen drawer to use. I put the silver-plated candlesticks on the mantel above the fireplace, and I put the afghan my sister made me on the couch."

Down-at-the-Mouth Resuscitation Chart

The common ailments of your clutter as you pull it from storage:

RUSTED

ROTTED

WRINKLED

BAKED/FROZEN

DATED

ALSO KNOWN AS...
FIGHTING A LOST CAUSE,
BEATING A DEAD HORSE,
THROWING GOOD MONEY
AFTER BAD

BROKEN

CHIPPED

STAINED

FADED

WET/DAMP/MILDEWED

BLACK LAGOON

RODENTIZED

ELVIS

MOTH-EATEN

SCRATCHED OR GOUGED

IS
RESTORATION
(If you ever get around to it)
WORTH IT?

The Magic of the Move

If you're an average American, you'll have fourteen chances at this, the primo of all jabs at your junk—*a move*. It's the granddaddy of all dejunking opportunities, a rare time of total inventory, the moment of truth for all accumulators, so don't miss it. Doubtful stuff gathering dust in your second- and third-string storage areas is one thing, but taking the time to pack all this up and then pay someone to move it somewhere is something else again. Here's where the cost of clutter moves from merely ten or so times what you paid for it to the sky's the limit. Depending on how far you have to go—a couple of hundred miles or across the country—it costs from 50¢ to a dollar a pound to move things, and it doesn't matter whether it's the crown jewels or worthless clutter! DEJUNK, DE-JUNK, DEJUNK! You want to do it anyway, and doing it now will save cold cash as well as your sanity.

> A lot of the value of stuff lies in *where* it is—why bring crab traps to Ohio?

Be sure to get started as far ahead of time as you can—six months, or even a year if possible. Even before you get formal news of a move, there are often some early warning signs, like lately a bad look in the boss's eye, a bulldozer parked right in front of your aging apartment, your spouse pricing Eddie Bauer's Premier Polar parkas, etc. Act on any sign of moving right then—even if there's a fifty-fifty chance it's just a fire drill. If you start dejunking when you first get word, you'll never have a breakdown (of your strength and will or of the garbage truck axle) by the last week.

If you need a little help here, the minute "the move" has been decided upon—before calling movers or buying boxes or panicking about how to prepare it all for the haul—announce it to everyone. (A dirty trick, but all's fair in love and the war on junk.) The first thought that springs into the mind of friends, neighbors, and relatives, even the most intelligent, will be, "Gads, it's my last chance to get some." If they don't immediately join that line in front of your garage, say something like, "I'd just love to keep this, but I'm not sure I can take it." (It's too heavy, the new house is too small, it's sure to corrode in that climate, etc.) Give them an incentive to grab it. This can even prompt cash offers; pickups will quickly materialize to haul it away.

Your mind will play tricks on you by the end of any move. You'll find yourself wondering if it's worth going on, you'll be ready to throw the baby *and* the rubber duck out with the bathwater. So be prepared for this moment of doubt and overdevout discarding, and pack your stuff by order of value. Make sure you get everything that's really useful and valuable first and never mix good and bad (or doubtful) together. When the boxes are packed and piled up, grade them like eggs—1–2–3—and cull so when you run out of room or will, you'll find it easy to say, "Just leave that old vacuum for the vultures!"

After you arrive at your new location, unpack all the necessities, put them in place, and enjoy that unusually spacious homescape for a while. Then think hard about whether you (ever) want to unpack and re-place all the rest of the cluttery little stuff that fills the whole place up and makes it almost impossible to move around or clean.

"...Three weeks later, when the second 24-foot move-it-yourself van rolled into the yard of our new home and started turning around to back up to the house and be unloaded, I had a great urge to bury the whole thing just as it was, to make a permanent sealed crypt of it—all that stuff we'd gotten along fine without up to now and didn't really want to be bothered to find a place for."

"After her latest move one of my friends discovered that she still had a stack of unpacked boxes though her new home was completely filled. She hadn't marked the boxes and couldn't remember what she'd packed into them. She didn't want to know. She knew if she did open them she wouldn't be able to throw them out. So she took the boxes out in the backyard, set them on fire, and burned them! She never missed one thing in those boxes and to this day has no idea what was in them."

CHAPTER 10

Judging Junk:

How to Figure Out What to Throw Out

We've had enough pacifiers—"transferring" junk, adjusting it, moving it, reboxing it, shifting its position. It's time for a shakedown, a shape-up, a sifting to separate, a culling to cast and keep!

It's time to play ball, to get in the game and go for it. And guess what? With decluttering, there's no team, no umpires, no jury, no committee to judge——you are umpire, manager, and commissioner all in one. All the calls—strike, foul, offsides, safe, fair, clipping, and finally yer out, have to be called by you. You have to be like the home-plate ump and call it—ball or strike. If it passes through an important part of your being, it's a winner! If it sails low or high, loops or curves—if it doesn't enhance your living—it's a

loser. Get it out of your game (and be a real umpire: don't change your mind!).

Anything in your life that suffocates you is junk. Anything that crowds the life out of you is junk. That which restricts our living, loving, thinking, and feeling is junk, be it a thing, habit, person, place, or position. Anything that builds, edifies, enriches our spirit—that makes us truly happy, regardless of how worthless it may be in cash terms—ain't junk.

It only takes a second to toss something—deciding is the hard part. But it's worth it, because when you weed out something old or bad or unneeded, you're making room for other things to grow.

Let's look at some things now that might help speed up those decisions.

You're Fired!

Not a one of us has ever been excused from facing up to our responsibilities to home, self, or job.

"Why did you do that?" Our parents started asking as soon as we could talk—and we had to answer.

"Well, because" never got us very far. When we didn't have a good answer, we got punished or asked again, and even now our boss or others we answer to are still making us accountable. The bottom line—from our coach, our customer, or our employer—is always if you aren't doing the job, you have no value and you have to go! Terminated! Vamoose! Leave! Scram! Get out! And so the pressure to produce and perform is pretty real to us.

But have you ever thought about pulling on your junk what people have been pulling on you? What is the job of your junk and clutter? It must have one or you wouldn't keep it. You must have at least originally had an intention for every piece of it. Surely you do expect something out of it, such as:

- To give you power and prestige (I have 89 stuffed dogs, the most in town)
- To give you good feelings and companionship (I love to snuggle with them)
- To hold the past into today (my favorite is still the felt beagle I got when I was four)
- To make you money (I intend to sell them all—except my beagle—at the big flea market in the fall)

Your reason has to be one or more of these because you've spent lots of time and money and emotion getting all that stuff and stashing it.

What if you find out that a piece of junk is lying down on the job, not doing what it's supposed to? Or that you got fooled, were cheated by it?

It's time to fire, unload, dismiss any clutter that just isn't doing its job!

The question isn't whether it's any good or not; it's goodness or badness doesn't count as much as its usefulness to *you*. Good stuff can be clutter if you don't need or use it. Sure it's good, sure it's useful, but to *you?* How much use would a fully functional surfboard be to you?

You don't want to end up with a bunch of neatly labeled and shelved stuff you still don't use.

Something could have been useful to you once, but it isn't now. When you got it, it was legitimate, it had a real purpose, but that time is past. I have a .22 rifle, for example, that I used at least once a week between the ages of 13 and 18. I haven't used it once in the past twenty-seven years, but it's stored here and I worry about it being stolen whenever we leave home.

When was the last time I used this? _____

The last time I even *thought* of using it? _____

I'll take it up again:

❑ *next* _____

❑ *as soon as* _____

❑ *someday*

If I were moving, and only allowed to bring 500 pounds, is this one of the things I'd take? _____

How much do I want to do this *now*? _____

Why do I want to do it again?

❑ *I just love it, it makes me feel good to do it.*
❑ *I'm embarrassed that I haven't been doing it.*
❑ *It always sounds good if you can say you do it.*

Of all my hobbies and interests this is # _____

If I were in prison or stranded on a desert island, how long would this keep me happy? _____

What has stopped me from doing it?

❑ *other, newer interests*
❑ *the cost of doing it*
❑ *my age*
❑ *the new circumstances I'm in*
❑ *I wasn't really making any progress / enjoying it as much as I expected / used to*

How many hours of "air time" (actual pleasure) does it give me per week/month, for all the effort and accessories it calls for? _____

"Someday is like tomorrow—it never comes. I've finally decided those silly somedays aren't worth wasting my todays for."

Calculating the Keepables

Some things we keep just don't need to be kept. When I was growing up and our wooden screens at home would get a tear or sag in them, we'd pick up a small box of those blue brad tacks, about thirty of them for 49 cents. We did that maybe three times in my whole childhood and adolescence. Many years later my cleaning company purchased an old bankrupt lumber store and yard to make into a new company office. They left some pretty good stuff behind, I thought. Such as a 6-gallon drum of those blue brad tacks. It weighed 120 pounds and there must have been 8 million screen tacks in there—a real bonanza! I lugged it home feeling I was set for life. I did realize we had 100 percent aluminum screens now, not a single wood one, but I was convinced that somewhere I'd find a use for those brads, so I treasured and stored that drum for thirteen years. I moved it and stored it, spilled some, stepped on more—but I never actually used a single one of them. Then finally when my goal for the year was to rid my life of everything and anything that didn't work, I gave all but a handful of them to the local Boy Scout arts and crafts council (of course, I kept the good drum they were in).

Bad Junk Judgment —Invalid Reasons We Often Keep Things:

- Heft. Just because it's heavy doesn't mean it's healthy.
- Age. Young or old doesn't have any bearing, *use* is the issue.
- Who had it once. Has the object had it, is the real question.
- What it did once. Let bygones be *gone.*
- How long you've had it. Again, *use,* not length of occupancy, is what determines value.
- How much you paid for it. *Use,* not economic value, is the issue.
- Who gave it to you. *Use,* not source, is what matters.
- How much it was marked down. *Use,* not ease of acquisition, determines worth.
- Where (the place) you got it. *Use,* not geography, should rule.

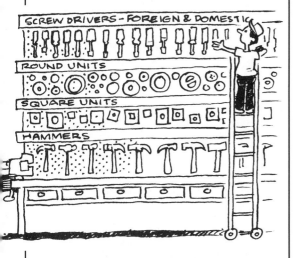

SCREW DRIVERS - FOREIGN & DOMESTIC
ROUND UNITS
SQUARE UNITS
HAMMERS

Ditch Those Duplicates

We all like to have multiples—we even like to brag about them—but the truth usually comes down to the fact that we have six usable racquetball rackets but hate five of them and use only one, but keep the others in case the good one breaks (at which time we will run out and buy another good one we like). Yet we have—and keep—four vacuums, eight tablecloths, three luggage sets, two punch bowls, etc.

Our tendency to collect is the culprit that clogs many a closet and drawer. During our winter stay in Hawaii one year, for example, I set up my sharpening tools and while I was sharpening our shovel and hoe and root ax (badly needed in the jungle), my wife ambled over to our gracious neighbor and asked if *she* had any tools that needed sharpening. She came lugging home an armload, including a couple of things I'd never seen before. I was happy to help out, especially since most of them were as blunt as a boxer's nose. Soon the neighbor and *her* friend (a part-time gardener) came roaring into the yard with a whole pickup load of tools in the back. There was every kind of digger, pruner, cultivator, and weed whacker imaginable—I wasn't sure if some were tools or weapons of war. I was doing the same yard work as they were, on a larger plot of ground, and had only three basic tools.

We all do this with kitchen equipment, sporting goods, hand tools, and computer disks. Just go look. When one doesn't work (or we aren't completely satisfied with it), we get another. Or if we see a new kind in the store or catalogue that looks neater, we get it. And if somebody gives us (or we find) an old, beat-up, or inferior one, we keep that, too. Why should we keep stuff we don't need when someone else might need it now?

Get rid of the nonworkers and the ones you don't really use, weed out the impostors and keep the purely useful.

For many things it makes a lot of sense to **set a limit!**

Limit the amount of anything you keep—do you *need* thirty pots or eighty pairs of pantyhose? You might possibly need forty plastic food storage containers, but not four hundred.

Don't be taken in by the old "save one for spare parts" theory: if the new one breaks, I can get parts from the old one. Eighty-nine percent of the time the same thing breaks on the new one. Or we end up with two thermometers—the bad one and the good one—but we don't know which is which.

> "Nothing that went has been missed and what is left can be found and enjoyed."

But I *Should* Keep This

Are you sure? Listen to what one thoughtful dejunker (who decided to make dejunking her Lenten project) has to say:

"No sooner had my clutter war commenced than I discovered my 'enemies' had infiltrated everywhere—every closet, drawer, and shelf. And many of them had taken on a disguise—the camouflage of 'shoulds.' There were items I *should:* fix, sew, mend, glue, patch, tape, repair, piece, return, match, paint, mount, varnish, frame, rearrange, sort, alphabetize, or tend to in some manner.

"Now, looking at these 'shoulds' from my new perspective, I realized that many of those demands and expectations were capriciously imposed by trends in society, by strangers in the outside world, by tradition or personal pride. They actually had little or nothing to do with 'shoulds' of a more significant nature.

"They were *burdens,* symbols of my failures and dead-ended good intentions. They were not well-chosen inspirational guides that I had kept to spur me on to greater efforts or self-improvement or better organization or more consideration of others. No, they were reminders of how often I had failed in the past and of how I was continuing in my inadequacies.

"There was that highly touted educational toy, purchased ages ago, to be used with parent and child—still untouched. There was that unread bestseller of years passed—now quite dated. Their very presence evoked a vague sense of guilt.

"There were other items that definitely were meant to be tossed, for they were reminders of hurts and disappointments better forgotten. There was that broken knickknack that could never be perfectly mended, which only served to remind me of a child's carelessness. There were mementos of unhappiness and poor judgment and neglected promises, both mine and others. These were reminders of unfulfilled 'shoulds' of long ago that now *should* be forgotten."

—Theresa Cotter, from an article first published in *St. Anthony Messenger*

> Don't love what can't love you back!

Don't Lean Too Much on Deadlines...

...to do your dejunking. Time measurements are fine in the Olympics, but tagging your property with a time limit isn't the answer. "If you don't use it in six months, toss it," says many a junk solutionist. That sounds like sound advice to judge junk by, and lots of people use it, but I disagree. It takes unnecessary chances with what could be good stuff. *Activity,* not frequency, is the right way to calculate keepability. Let's apply the time-trial style to a few things and be generous and give them a year to be put on active duty:

- Smoke alarm
- Family sled or toboggan (no snow last winter)
- Life preserver
- First-aid kit
- Jack and chains and jumper cables for car
- Kerosene lamp (for power failures)
- Touch-up car paint
- Insurance policy

None of these are clutter, yet all would be judged so by the time-allotment principle. As a former scoutmaster I now use my uniform, packs, equipment, etc. (several hundred dollars' worth of stuff) only for jamborees once every four years. You can be sure I'm not going to sacrifice them to the "clock and calendar" decluttering concept.

When's the last time you used your fire extinguisher? Want to toss it in the trash?

> If the stack of keepables seems to be larger than the original pile, it definitely means you are not making progress.

Pulling the Plug on Dying or Dead Junk

It's nice to come across *some* clutter there can't be any argument about. The issue of euthanasia can be a mighty tough one elsewhere, but it should be a cinch when it comes to clutter. Why keep clutter on life support when it's not merely dying but dead? When it may look and weigh the same, but it's worthless?

I do lots of cement work, and short, easy-to-clean rubber boots are a real necessity. I came across several pairs of them once in a clearance bin so I left a pair in my home in Hawaii and two pairs out here in Idaho for me and my wife, plus the pair I wore regularly. I was totally covered, I thought. When I pulled my spare Idaho sets out one day both of them had holes in them, rotted from sitting. I got to Hawaii, and the pair there had disintegrated (and a 9-inch centipede had made a home in the heel). Likewise, we note that no woman will throw out perfume, even when it's down to dark resinous dregs, even when those twelve awkward ornate bottles take up a sorely needed shelf and a half.

All the stories of people going downhill quickly after retirement apply to things, too. When they're in everyday, active use (and view), they stay okay. Once they're stashed they crack, rust, rot, and mildew; they get punctured, mice chew on them, etc. An awful lot of the stuff I've had to move in the course of cleaning closets and bedrooms and garages had died in storage. I thought you might be interested in the following list of items and the toll depreciation takes of them. The type or brand you have might have a slightly different timetable, but these are a pretty good average:

Is It Still Good?

A hard look at the **shelf life** of a lot of stuff we like to keep forever, straight from the manufacturers.

Item	How long it lasts in storage	Remarks
Film	Don't try to ignore the expiration date on the package.	Heat hastens its demise.
Batteries	Zinc carbon, 1 year; alkaline, 3–4 years; lithium, 5 years; mercury, 2.5 years.	If it's crusty or oozing, get rid of it.
Seeds	Over 5 years, forget it; many last half that long, or less.	Vegetables do a little better than flowers.
Flower bulbs	Several months at the most.	So you can't skip a year.
Medicine	The expiration date is printed right on it.	That's why the medicine chest is your medical history at a glance.
Vitamins	2 years.	Forget about "just taking two of them now."
Car wax	A couple of years; longer if never opened.	How many times have you found nothing but a hardened lump in the can?
Hoses	5 years or less.	Sun and weather exposure are hard on them.
Spices	Herbs, 1–2 years; spices, 2–5 years.	All lose flavor with thyme.
Cologne or perfume	2 years.	Beyond this it may still have some scent, but probably not the one intended.
Cosmetics	2 years.	Have you ever tried to apply dried-up lipstick or eye shadow?
Paint	Unopened, up to 5 years.	If it wasn't sealed tightly or has ever been frozen, forget it. Oil base lasts longer.
Polyurethane, varnish	Unopened, up to 5 years.	If it's been opened and not well resealed, it'll cure right in the can.
Spackle	Unopened, 1 year.	How many hardened cans have you been dismayed to discover?
Old cars just parked	10 years in average climate; longer in dry places, shorter in wet.	That's just the body; there are working parts, tires, and fluids to worry about, too.

Item	How long it lasts in storage	Remarks
Rubber boots or waders, etc.	Up to five years if given ideal care.	Rubber cracks in storage; if exposed to ozone, as in a garage, it will go much faster.
Tape	Masking tape starts to get less sticky after 6 months; packaging tape and "foam tapes" after 1 year.	Sunlight will yellow and deteriorate transparent tapes, and heat, cold, and excess humidity will hasten the demise of any type of tape.
Canned food	12–18 months, depending on type of food; meat and vegetables do better than fruit.	The warmer the storage area, the faster it'll go bad.
Frozen food	3 to 12 months, depending on type of food; prepared foods and meats deteriorate quickest.	If you've forgotten what it is, it's probably flavorless by now; in freezer compartment of a refrigerator things go faster.
Rubber bands	About 2 years under normal conditions.	Newspaper bands go faster.
Pre-gummed labels	Ordinary varieties, up to 3 years.	Light and heat make them ungum faster.
Glue	Both water- and solvent-based, 1 year unopened; epoxy longer.	If you don't close the bottle tightly, they'll never see that first anniversary.
Aerosols	Up to 5 years.	If the can's rusty, get rid of it. And remember: just because the container still operates doesn't mean what's in it is any good.
Ballpoints and felt-tip markers	About 18 months.	Dry up quicker in dry climates.
Calendars and datebooks	Until the last day of the year printed at least several inches high on the cover.	You're going to wait 6–14 years till that configuration comes around again?

P.S. Don't get fascinated with (and led astray by) the exceptions. As you're going through thirty-year-old stuff, most of which is dry-rotted or ruined, suddenly you find a tube of airplane glue in perfect condition after all these years! Don't jump to the junkie conclusion that there's hope for the rest of that sad stuff; not so. It's just a trick, a bit of junk bait to get you to cling to everything.

But I Paid Good Money for This!

Certain pieces of junk we can't bring ourselves to get rid of simply because we'd feel guilty about the money we'd be wasting.

Even though we know deep down that we hate it, or that we'll probably never actually use it, we still harbor this nagging need to justify the money we spent on it! So rather than just admitting we made a bad investment, or an impulsive purchase, got snookered, or were slightly overzealous at a sale and bought more than we will *ever* use, we go on punishing ourselves by pretending we'll vindicate the purchase in the future by putting the little jewel to some use:

"I've always hated the way this sweater makes me look—so sawed off! But I paid $25 for it, so maybe I can wear it to jog in this fall."

"They soaked me over two hundred bucks for this Speed Reading Course! All these tapes and lesson outlines, and I've never even opened them. Maybe when the kids reach junior high age we can take it together."

"What a waste this sales sample kit turned out to be! Seventy-five dollars to find out I'm no salesman. Maybe this binder and case will come in handy sometime if I can manage to cover up the insignia."

The smartest thing for us to do when we recognize ourselves failing to get rid of something because we feel guilty about the cost is to forget about the dollar cost and start counting the *emotional* cost. What do we pay in mental harassment every time we see it collecting dust in a needed space? What do we pay in mental energy every time we have to create a new excuse for why we bought it? What do we pay in domestic harmony every time someone says, "I told you

you'd never use it."

Close your eyes, grit your teeth, and just get rid of your bad investments. I promise the time spent will be one of the best investments you ever made!

> **Q:** What's the biggest surprise *all* my dejunking clients and friends have discovered?
> **A:** "Can you believe it, I haven't missed it?"
> **Q:** What's the most common exclamation of ex-clutterers?
> **A:** "I can't believe I really kept that thing all those years!"

New Is Nice and Often Cheaper

The Amish wouldn't find me arguing with the spirit of their message—simplicity! Sometimes, however, a refusal to accept and use the new and better can clutter our lives as easily as mindless fashion-following. Yes, the old has some romance, but why clean with a scrub brush on your hands and knees when there are better tools now that save time and cost even less (and are easier on you and your household surfaces)? Just because the old is "still good" and "still works" doesn't mean it makes sense. I have 1915 farm machinery that still works and antique irons and rifles, but the effort and risk to operate them is a hundred times more taxing than the modern alternatives.

Sound reproduction is a marvelous thing when you think of it. In the eighteenth and nineteenth centuries if you were lucky, once or twice in a lifetime and at great cost and sacrifice you could experience Mozart or one of the other masters, or a cowboy yodeling. Then came the phonograph and the old break-

and-warp records that you played with a needle the size of a nail. Soon there were LPs whose sound quality was not as scratchy; then reel-to-reel tape; then the same was done cheaper and better with 8-track tapes, then with the much more compact cassette. I had all of the above and today own a beautiful Teac reel-to-reel, the finest at its time; it still seems new to me—until I see my son's compact disc. The sound of CDs is fabulous, and they're hard to damage and a cinch to store. Ten times the music of a cassette on a tiny disc. The other day I looked up the purchase date of that reel-to-reel and it was 1966—I couldn't believe it! Lots of things get old and useless slowly, so slowly we don't notice; like gaining weight or starting to use profanity, you suddenly see it—gasp!

Maybe some of your good stuff is only good in your mind and memory. Once upon a time it may have been the top of the line, but now it's only upon something (a shelf or floor space you could find plenty of better uses for).

What Will Happen if I Throw It Out?

Lots of people are really hung up on this, imagining all kinds of dire consequences, but the answer is generally NOTHING.

So don't let yourself be hung up forever in indecision, because you can always think up better answers and excuses for yourself.

Tiebreaking

You're dejunking determinedly, but a certain thing keeps whispering, *"I'm a keeper."* You can't get it out of your mind. So keep it, don't fight it. Only keep it right in the room with you, right in sight, so you really have a chance to be around it, to find out once and for all if it's friend or foe. When something long buried is freshly unearthed, it can have a certain novelty and charm. Leave it out and in the way so you pass it (or dodge it or stumble over it) ten times a day. This forces you to decide whether you love it enough or dislike it more than you thought—things that may be hard to decide when it's packed away. Once you know it well anew, you may find that the ties and emotions were just temporary.

If you bog down with emotion on some item, get another person to help give you perspective. Even if the person just lends moral support or serves as a sounding board for your own weighing of the pros and cons, it can be a real tiebreaker.

No Double Dealing

Double dealing is bad practice in business, and a disaster in decluttering. Once you've dealt with your stuff—where it goes and what you're going to do with it—once you've dropped it from your hand, then whatever happens, Harry, so be it. Don't open the case or box or bag again. If you do, you'll be hit by an uncontrollable urge to reconsider, to backslide, to renege on the nixed, and you'll fail. When you pass sentence on your "inmates," make it capital punishment, not life, or it will be on parole around your place forever and you'll be its guardian and police officer.

Call the Truck and Back It Up to the Door

Line up four boxes (big sturdy cardboard ones, not just bags). Make a large sign and put it up behind the boxes:

Is this enhancing my life now…or will it ever in the future?

Does this love me back?

What's the worst thing that could happen if I chuck it?

Label the four boxes as follows:

Junk. This is the useless, broken, wornout, stupid stuff that even you the owner can't find an excuse to keep. It's valueless to you or anyone, and that's not even hard to figure out if you just take a good look at it, so trash it.

Charity. Stuff that might be useful, but **you** don't need it now—you have too many (or better) of them already; you're not really interested in that anymore; you no longer live where fur slippers are essential. Give it to a needy or interested relative or friend, or pick a good charity, one you know the stuff will be beneficial to, one that will use and appreciate it. One where compassionate hands will go through it and find a new home for it, where it will delight someone or serve a real purpose.

Sort. The box for fully usable stuff that's out of place or you forgot (or never knew) you had. It needs to be put back where it belongs or a place made for it where you'll see it and remember to use it. In here, too, can go things that are perfectly good except that some easily replaceable part is gone. But don't get carried away in this category or you'll end up with a half-roomful of I'm-gonna-fix-it-someday junk. (And a single sock whose mate has been missing for years doesn't qualify!)

Emotional withdrawal. Memorabilia of which the memory is even more faded than the object is no problem. It can be slipped gently into the junk box now. But the tassel off the drill team flag, that freeze-dried fragment of your wedding cake (you're coming up on your twenty-fifth anniversary), the pretty flowered slip you wore to your first prom, may need to go in here for a while. You can start parting with it now, in your mind (you've really wanted to). But you don't have to face the shock of actually getting rid of it right this minute. Seal it up in a box like this and then a month, or two, or three months from now (depending on how dear to your heart it once was), you can take another look at it and probably dispose of it easily, because you've already separated from it in your mind. You may not even want or need to open it up for one last look, because you'll have realized it died years ago!

Probation

You might want to add one more category here, as suggested by one of my readers.

"My wife and I came upon the following idea after reading your first book on clutter. We got quite radical on the first and second round of our dejunking—I reduced my wardrobe by 50 percent in one afternoon, for instance. Yet there were a few things we both knew we didn't need physically or emotionally now but couldn't bear to part with because we *might* need them, might take up silverworking, might do this or that someday, etc. For these borderline cases we came up with 'probationary stickers' listing a date mutually agreed on during our decluttering work. Then if the item is not used regularly or does not reveal itself as clearly part of our lives during the next six or nine months, or whatever the allotted time, it's gone without question. If applied too broadly this could just be procrastination, but in a few limited borderline cases we believe it's valuable."

It won't hurt to take an active or aggressive approach to probationary items, either—don't just identify them but force yourself to wear them or use them or look at them every day until the answer is clear.

You'll have to ask those key questions of each item for a while, and some you may have to really mull over and ponder. Then, like a memorized keyboard, the sorting process will become natural and automatic. And floods of relief will wash over that hoarding heart of yours.

Once you get those boxes filled up, don't get bogged down in one of the biggest traps of dejunking: Don't pack them full and pile them up and then let them lie. Back the truck up and get those boxes out before they back the hearse up and haul you out. Do it!

In any plan of reformation, the only way you can succeed is to overcome the habit or the desire to do it again. So after each toss, taste the victory of clean and pure—savor it, so you won't want to reclutter.

153

CHAPTER 11

An Excuse Is an Excuse:

And None of These Count

There must be at least a thousand excuses for hanging on to junk and clutter.

I'm married to the head packrat.
I paid good money for this.
It's been in the family for years.

But those were Aunt Annie's.
I'm sentimental.
I was raised during the Depression.
My doggie's teeth marks are in it.
We only used it once.

It's my retirement project.
It will be an antique.
It's a conversation piece.
Someday I'll fix it.
I may need it someday.
They aren't making them anymore.
It's an incentive to lose weight.
It might come back in style.
I'm a Dane, and all Danes do it.
It's perfectly good.
I can put it in my vacation home.
It was a gift.
It's handmade.
It was imported.
I'm from a long line of savers.

What has more originality, inventiveness, creativity, and dedication ever gone into than the effort to think up reasons to hold on to the past through things?

"I Might Need It Someday"

Okay, I'll buy that as a legitimate excuse, but only for about *10 percent* of what you keep. As there isn't enough time and space in the universe to consider every junk and clutter excuse, we'll just let this one—"I might need it someday"—stand for all of them. Shortly after we've learned to say mama and dadda, our brains learn and our lips repeat this most famous of all justifications for leading a cluttered life. *But I might need it someday.* Some of the other 999 excuses are clever, if not convincing, but this one is the great-grandaddy of them all. It might even hold water if you wait long enough and look hard enough. In the end, how long is long enough is a question of how much space is available, how long we live, and how tolerant our spouse or boss is. Things do indeed lose their savor, flavor, and for that matter, findability.

I remember once when I ran across some firecrackers I had saved and saved,

hid and rehid as the kids grew up, and we moved and moved again, waiting for that someday occasion when I could pull off a fine firework display or scare someone out of their wits. I felt pretty smug staring down on those nice old explosives (they dated back to the days when they were legal, so they were bigger and neater than anything you can get now). I wanted a little preview, so I lit one. The fuse sputtered mightily and then nothing. A dud, I thought, and picked the crispest one out of the pack and lit it. It looked promising, but again no go. Too many years in that damp basement! *All that time and all that hoarding for nothing!* What a hype! And so goes with all too many of your keepables…there won't be any great show, or bang, for you either.

Sure, like all the excuses, *you might need it someday.* If you can find it, if it's still alive, in style, safe to use, if you remember what it is and what you kept it for.

"It Might Get Me Through Hard Times," or Nest-Egg Junk

You've got it, man! That backlog of litter, that reservoir of rubble, the stuff you've mentally labeled my "desperate days" junk. When everything fails—the economy, your income, your friends, health, or fortune—you'll still have all this to wear, use, eat, or drive. Of course, you've forgotten that you hated it the minute you got it, didn't like the way it looked or worked or was made. But you still have it and if you were in a bind, if you were up against awful odds (a circumstance that surely will come), you could use it—but you won't. You never will. Even if you reached your last hour, you'd still want to look good and be convinced you deserve the best. That old windbreaker would only add to your agony—dump it now. Take it off hold! If you ever get that desperate, you'll be willing to rob or kill for something better anyway, so why not just write off all this invalid inventory?

You don't believe me, eh? I hate to burst the bubble of any of you waste-not-want-nots, but just take a pencil and add to this list all the stored unused things (junk) you intend to reactivate when you learn that the next depression or the invasion force has arrived:

1. Food
2. Extra shoes
3. Aluminum foil scraps
4.
5.
6.
7.
8.
9.
10.

Hard to think of any, isn't it? Most of what isn't used now won't be used then.

> "In an economic crunch—a real depression—I'll be able to save *all* my neighbors!"

> "We're sure to be more depressed by the junk we've accumulated to get us *through* a depression than we'd ever be if we actually had a depression!!"

"I'm Going to Fix It Someday"

"I'm married to Mr. Fix-It (or at least he is when he gets time). The trouble with a fixer is that you never get anything new."

My comment: The real trouble with a fix-it is that it never gets fixed.

A Familiar Scenario —Just Fill in the Blanks

A perfectly good _____, not even close to worn-out. It just quit yesterday (it actually began to quit some time back, but sharp raps or kicks brought it back to life for a while). But now, no pulse; it's gone for sure. There's a strong principle involved here: Has it really served its fair time? (As much as you expected, or as the ad copy said it would?) You take it in for a physical and Dr. Fix-It says it can be resurrected for _____. You are aware (sitting in the store as you are) that new ones are only _____. However, this is an old one and they don't make them like this anymore. Not willing to be tricked or coerced or to spend _____, you bring it home and put it away, hoping for a healing of some kind. Like numerous other things, it has now entered the Gonna-Fix-It Zone.

We all have more than our share of things like dolls with no arms or hair that we are going to fix one of these days. We're sure we'll restore the bad or broken part—ourselves. It's the rugged pioneer spirit, the American way. Then we break a handle and go to get a new one and find that the handle cost more than the complete tool we bought before. Even for expert putterers, computer chips and circuit boards have all but eliminated the baling-wire-glue-and-string school of fixing.

I've seen people have those dropped-in ceiling tiles cleaned for 64 cents a square foot when they only cost 43 cents new. If nothing less than restoration of the original will ever do, go for it. But often (even if we are willing to spend the time and money) we can't find somebody to fix it, or they don't fix it right—so we have double heartburn. Or the repair creates new problems to be dealt with. Or the parts have been discontinued, or the manufacturer no longer exists. Or we end up on a six-letter exchange with the culprit company that leaves us short of satisfaction in the end anyway. Are you sure you shouldn't just cut your losses right now?

"But I Paid Good Money for It"

Yes, you paid good money for it and it darn well better earn its keep, or you'll keep it, dead or alive, until it accounts for itself. The feeling is close to the emotion of revenge, except we don't necessarily want to get even, just our money's worth. Abandoning your illusions about this particular type of junk can save you a lot of grief. A perfectly good TV was totaled, two steel measuring tapes broke on me in one week, smoke rolled out of my new Christmas gift drill, two expensive gas cans sprang leaks, the handle on my heavy-duty outside broom broke —all in the last month of last year. I paid good money for all of this, and most of it only gave me a fifth of the service it should. A true travesty of justice; surely someone has to answer for such mass failure of merchandise. Several evenings of imaginative thinking couldn't come up with a single use for any of these broken items—but I kept them, as we do so often, to take it up with or get satisfaction from somebody. Or for the principle of it. The TV tortured me the most —only two years old, sitting most of the time untouched in our Hawaii guest house. I took it (with the warranty) to the store and soon had the store's owner, the manager of the service department, and a regretful repairman standing around what appeared to be a nearly new set. He knew it well—other guests in my house had brought it in in an at-

tempt to fix it. He showed me the circuit board: a total sheet of rust, it looked like it had been tucked away on the *Titanic* and just pulled out. "Don, you live in the only place in the world where stainless steel rusts (it rains 38 feet a year just 5 miles from me). If a set is played regularly, the heat burns off the moisture. If it's just sitting there, it goes in a year.

So its useful life was over. Too short a life maybe, but over. He told me to buy a timer next time and arrange it so the set would be turned on once a week for twenty-four hours.

The drill suffered a mystery illness, and tracking down the store sixteen states away where it was bought, proving that it wasn't used in any unrecommended way, sending it in to be diagnosed, delaying my project until it was returned, etc., would surely cost more than the original $50 or $60 I'd paid for it. The tapes were the same—a short mission and no recovery. I hung them in effigy from the eucalyptus tree out front. I trashed the gas cans and bought plastic ones the next time. None of it was fair. But trying to get my money's worth would have been worse. We do amazingly unreasonable things in order to get "reasonable recovery."

You've got several things like this right now, in form of a lawn mower, weed whacker, snow blower, hot pot, chop o' matic, electric eyebrow plucker, etc.— often a gadget you got to do a miracle job (under the influence of a TV or county fair demo, probably), and it just never cut the mustard. At first you thought it was you, because others seemed to be able to make it work. So you keep it around to fiddle with it or whip on it or until a new part or mechanic brother-in-law shows up to fix it. Keeping a nonperforming object like this is like keeping a bad play running on Broadway or keeping on a dud employee. They never manage to merit a good review, but you keep them around to get your money's worth for the previous month's training cost. You've already guessed my point. *They don't ever pay up.* The longer you keep them, the more they cost. The more they cost, the more you have invested in them, and the harder to let go. When it's just a heap of rust you paid $1,500 for, you lie awake nights trying to come up with ways to redeem it. No sale, Sally; you lose.

If it's beat you, take the defeat like a good sport. Admit it and toss it. Trying to recoup your loses, to prove you can make it good, will only do you in and get you again and again and again.

> **Do you have any of this deadbeat junk?**
> - Dull things that can't ever be sharpened properly.
> - "They-don't-make-parts-for-it-anymore" equipment or machinery.
> - The old hand-run model kept around in case the electricity ever goes out.

"It Might/Will Be Worth Lots of Money Someday"

Oh, that we would live so long!

Yes, clutter collectors are willing to believe anything—what if telephone pole insulators (or Avon bottles or two-pound coffee cans) go for a grand apiece at an antique store before I head off to the great beyond? Alas, just as with the value of our real estate and the gas mileage our vehicles get, our expectations always exceed reality. In the seven years since I wrote my first book on clutter, I've made a point to ask my audiences (from 800 in person to 8 million on TV) what piece of stuff have they ever kept and sold and made big money from. Not a single person has yet stepped forth and given any hard evidence of great value increase. It's always someone else we hear about on the news who has the baseball card worth $3,000 or finds $5,000 in silver dollars in an old mattress they kept around. I remember doing a "People Are Talking" show in Pennsylvania and the editor of *Life* magazine was being interviewed on the segment just before mine. One of the hosts asked him, "Wow, I have a 1935 issue of *Life*. What's it worth?" "About $1.35" came the quick answer. "What? But it's a 1935." "So?" All this time the host had thought he had prize bullion stashed for a big "someday" cash-in. Don't count on it too much, folks. Great appreciation in junk and clutter is rare; few rusty old buckets are money in the bank.

I still remember the surge of entrepreneurial spirit I felt as a freshman in high school when I heard my favorite radio announcer saying "Casper Keck Hide and Tallow Company is paying $5 a ton for prairie bones." My imagination soared into triple figures: our horses and cattle weighed almost a ton and I knew where the remains of numerous winter-killed critters were from my hours spent riding fence, hunting, or herding. So every night after work and before supper I'd grab a gunny sack, run out on the desert, visit those above-ground burial sites, and fill my bag with those big bones. I collected and carried all summer, those bony bags gouging my back every mile of the way home. The pile behind the shed grew and grew, and finally it was time to collect my well-earned treasure. I had a total of 721 pounds, $1.80 worth of bones (not counting what it cost to haul all this the twenty miles to Casper's Bone Yard).

When someone says "it's valuable" or "it's going to be worth a lot someday," check it out before you construct a storage compartment for it.

"But It's Never Been Used!"

Now, there's a dead giveaway (great pun, eh?). One of the reasons you're keeping the thing is that it's new and never been used. Your logic is a little backwards, isn't it? If it's never been used, there's a good reason for that, like you don't need it or don't like to use it or you have at least four others. But we keep insisting that it's valuable because it's new. Never been worn, what a shame. We need to wear it just for principle, maybe?

"Well, It Isn't Worn Out Yet"

How much of our stuff fits legitimately into that category? About 99 percent of it. I remember wearing out two sets of patches on jeans as a kid, and today people pay an exorbitant price to get them with patches already on them. Then they're abandoned and stored because they're out of style or too tight (or other reasons having nothing to do with wear). It would be a rare thrill to wear something out today. How many of you can produce tie, coat, suit, car, game—anything—that's actually, honestly worn out with use (okay, I'll admit there might be a few TV knobs). I buy other people's used cars and put another 100,000 or 200,000 miles on them and they *still* aren't worn out. We abuse and neglect things, yes, but seldom do we wear them out. And if we store all that's "still good," we'll surely have no space after a while.

"I'm Sure I Can Find a Use for It"

Once an entirely useless piece of something is discovered to be usable for anything, even another useless activity, it suddenly becomes a keeper. So people sit around for hours trying to think of "uses" to transform their trash.

I did the "Wil Shriner Show" in Hollywood once, and Wil did something interesting (for a joke) with old shoes. The real joke was the earnest expressions on the faces of people in the audience who had old shoes they were wondering how to keep around.

Wil had the old shoes under the counter and pulled them up one by one:

- An ultra-high-heeled beauty—with a plant in it (the audience swooned approval)
- A golf shoe—used to beat and tenderize a steak
- Old rubber boot—filled with ice and used as a cooler
- A jogging shoe—made a magnificent Jell-O mold (I actually saw people in the audience write this down)
- Hiking or logger-style boots—the ultimate key chain for those who lose their keys constantly

We all hold this illusion with certain types of clutter. We keep it because someday, when we have a day off, a broken leg, when we retire, get confined to bed (or prison), we'll have the time to do something with all this—and that is a nice thought.

> "This is a collection of socks I've collected over the last ten years. I intended to make sock dolls, rugs, and doll clothes. But as you can see, I never used them. It was getting to be a real addiction until I was prompted to bring something for this lecture series."

I would never discourage the urge to recycle or make light of even old egg cartons or empty toilet paper spools as creative playtime materials for kids. But it's all too easy to salt away more stuff like this than we could ever use, and too many of these "trash to treasures" projects are just trash fused together in a form that's harder to throw away.

"They Don't Make Them Like This Anymore"

Cast iron! Solid wood! Genuine brass! Heavy steel! Heady, almost intoxicating words to us children of the plated metal, thin veneer, and crumbly pressboard age, who drive around in cars with fenders that could be caved in by a fist. But use your head for a minute. Just because it's old and strong and heavy doesn't mean you should drag it home or let it take up our shelf space forever. If it doesn't work, if you'd never use it (even if "the electricity went out"), if you're never going to get around to refinishing it, if no parts are available and you haven't been able to talk any welder relatives into fabricating the missing pieces, and you already have enough conversation pieces and oversize doorstops...*forget it!*

"But These Are Memories!"

Junk for many of us is a memory prop, and letting it go seems to be surrendering memories and the past. Or we're secretly afraid we won't ever amount to anything and so need souvenirs of every salute and tribute we ever got.

Then, too, many a woman still has all her tiny lace bikini underpants stashed somewhere to hold onto her dainty days and prove she is ultrafeminine. Seeing evidence of what we once were (and what once happened to us), having something to touch and feel and show is more powerful than just knowing it in your mind—tangible proof, hard evidence, hard to duplicate by words or thoughts alone. See page 99 for some solutions to this perhaps toughest of all excuses

"But Don, if we all dejunk our houses, the nation's landfill sites will be exhausted much sooner."

(Now is that a bad excuse, or what? Didn't you ever hear of *recycling?*)

Packrat Phobias

We all know that the urge to commit clutter runs deep indeed, but only recently have psychologists begun to be able to isolate and identify the underlying primeval drives that compel us to collect some of the specific things we collect. Here are some of the very first findings to be released on this important topic.

What You Keep/Do	What It Shows
Excess clothes	Closet exhibitionism
Shoes to which the mate is missing	Incurable optimism/ dissatisfaction with mate
Dead batteries, expired coupons, pens that have run out of ink	Deep belief in reincarnation
Old newspapers, magazines	Secret fears of being caught with no toilet paper
More than one of anything you need	Octopus envy
Too many decorations	Overwhelming need to be noticed
Excess furniture	Fear of open spaces
When in doubt, buy one of each	Insecurity
Dropped garments or stuffed giraffes on every available surface	You live just to irritate your spouse

CHAPTER 12

Don't Delay the Funeral:

The Actual Disposal of That Clutter

You can't imagine how many people make the commitment, tear into their piles of junk and clutter, wisely and willingly separate the objects, stack the junk on the path to the dumpster or thrift store, and *then never pull off the final burial.* It's just like laying the coffin by the side of the grave and leaving it there. Doing this to your junk means you'll never release it. And the longer it sits the more tempted you'll be to bring it back to life. As long as it's there, you can rebuild or rekindle affection for it; you have a chance to re-examine and reassess it and to backslide! It will worm its way back into your life, like the stray dog you won't let in the house but continue to feed. (The longer junk sits around in limbo, the more it multiplies your problems.) It gets scattered around, people break into it and get parts, the wind and rain erode whatever worth it still had, and you feel guilty for leaving it out—so you keep it a little longer to make amends.

It almost seems sometimes as if we set this stuff in the garage, attic, cellar, or storage shed to ripen or age to the proper point. When it breaks or shrinks, gets a little duller and uglier, a little more paint chipped off, or maybe a rainstorm or hailstorm finishes it off for us, release is easier and we're willing to let go.

> Failed Errand Junk: "I finally had the guts to do it: I tore down those old dismal drapes and had my husband take them to the trash. Three weeks later I found them stashed in his corner of the garage."

A big dejunking secret is, once something has been clearly designated junk, close the can (coffin) and take it right to its intended sweet by and by... at the Salvation Army, the friend's house, the dumpster, the library, the child-care center. **Take it now**, even if you only have twenty boxes ready and there are forty more coming. Take what you have and get it out of your sight—and off the premises! You'll be amazed how this accelerates the dejunking process.

Last-Clutch Clutter!

You've admitted it's no good, you don't want it, you're throwing it out. You even move it in the direction of the dumpster, but you keep a little anchor line on it—almost like having one last fling, except that you haven't flung it yet! Somehow you come up with a new excuse more ironclad than all the previous, such as "I'm going to get rid of it" or "I've been through it." That may impress most onlookers, but not me. "I'm through with it" isn't strong enough; "It's stacked by the garbage" means next to nothing. (You've probably tipped the garbageman not to take it.) Last-Clutch Clutter is simply delaying it, and when you delay an apology, delivery, or departure, it just gets harder.

The Longer You Wait, the Longer the List of Excuses

Excuse to Collect It:

- It's an antique.
- It's a gift.
- It's just right for my collection.
- I always wanted one.

Understandable!

Excuse to Keep It:

- It's been in the family for years.
- As soon as I throw it away, I'll need it.
- It has sentimental value.

- I paid good money for it.
- I married the head packrat.
- It's a conversation piece.
- They aren't making them like they used to.
- I intend to fix it.
- It hasn't got enough miles on it yet.

Tolerable!

Excuse to Delay Dejunking—Once You Decide It Has to Go:

- I'm still adjusting to the idea of getting rid of it.
- I hate to hurt Aunt Gwen's feelings.
- I'm waiting for Virginia to visit so I can give it to her.
- I haven't had a chance to take it over to the church.
- I can't find the collection box; someone moved it.
- I've gotta get some containers to put it in.
- I haven't had a chance to break it up, cut it up, etc., yet.
- I need to have it appraised by an expert to make sure it isn't valuable.
- I'm waiting for Clean-Up Day.
- I'm waiting till I have enough for a garage sale.
- I haven't taken the good parts off it yet.
- I want to clean it up before I get rid of it.
- I need to borrow a van or truck; it won't fit in my car trunk.
- I need help lifting it.
- No one will come and pick it up for free.

Miserable! (Invalid or easily solved—every single one of them!)

Unloading Options

We all have different systems and methods of dealing with things, and so it is with dejunking. I keep a "to burn" pile out on my ranch; in fact I poured a concrete pad just for the purpose. It's there all the time, for anything combustible that must go. You could have a junk dump bin, a place waiting to welcome stuff on its way out.

Recycle It

An excellent answer for all of us worrying about a proper end for our precious packrat pieces: our stuff—the long-stored, the dead, and the unused (even the unusable)—can come forth and rise again and be useful. It can live again, get back in action—and all we have to do is a little sorting, which is good practice in the number-one skill we need to deal with all or any of our junk anyway.

Recycling can help put our accumulation back into circulation. We can recycle either by seeing that still-good things get into other hands that will really appreciate them—see the pages that follow—or by seeing that recyclable metal, glass, plastic, fabric, paper, engine oil, etc., is sorted out and saved for that purpose.

Your local recycling center or state department of natural resources can let you know exactly which things can be recycled now, where to take them, and what form to deliver them in. (You may even end up with a little cash to recycle into your bank account.)

Recycling—a thrill that sure beats landfill!

Sell It Away

"I lost 125 pounds today—I had a garage sale!"

"We had so much stuff that we had to get rid of, we decided to have a yard sale and we made over $1,000—yes, over one thousand dollars, from items marked 25 cents to $5."

"Have at least one yard or garage sale. I sold some utterly ridiculous things—half bars of soap, nearly empty cologne bottles, nonworking ballpoint pens, and an old iron teakettle with no bottom that my Dad had dug up in a Tennessee game reserve. I also packaged and sold old crochet patterns Mom had torn from magazines over the years. Many things I sold for 10 cents, 25 cents, and 50 cents, but I did sell them and in three sales made $3,000. My relatives were amazed. I put out an old beat-up alarm clock that hadn't worked in years and my aunt said, 'You'll never sell that.' To my amused delight that was the first thing that sold. Also sold an electric iron with the cord cut off. So the old saying is true: One person's trash is another person's treasure. It's worth trying to sell absolutely any of your clutter, broken or not. It is advisable, though, unless you want to have another sale soon, to call a flea market dealer to take the rest, or to give it away or throw it out. Otherwise you'll have a nucleus to begin a whole new pile of clutter."

Garage sales sound good, I admit. You not only get rid of it, but someone pays you to let them take it away. But we hear all about "I made," never anything about "It cost." Reflect a minute on the many expenses involved in almost any garage sale: Usually a large classified ad, signs and posters, tanks of gas, phone calls, babysitters, hired help to lug it around, time spent to wash, iron, sort, arrange, and price. Neighbors that hate you because lots of it got transferred to their house. And then there's the hassle of returned checks and maybe even a family fight or two thrown in for good luck. (Not to mention time spent to restore the trampled lawn and police the litter everywhere, and the aggravation involved in watching total strangers turn up their noses at your treasures.)

In the end it comes down to how much free time you have available, whether time truly is money for you, and whether you mind spending it this way.

If you have a lot of unquestionably high-grade discards (it's easy to kid ourselves here), a simpler course might be to unload it all on a secondhand dealer,

or let an auctioneer help you get rid of it in a single shot.

A Few Signs to Help the Clutter Overflow

- Please haul to the DUMP!
- Free! Help yourself!
- Yard Sale
- Basement Sale
- Moving Sale
- Estate Sale
- Garage Sale
- Carport Sale
- Barn Sale

Give It Away

When something goes to a good cause or a good place, it goes ungrudgingly.

Seeing your kids' precious baby crib (even a well-worn one) crushed into a sour-smelling garbage truck makes you never want to toss another thing. But if someone wants to refinish that crib, or even make it into something else, you'll probably be willing to transport it fifty miles for them.

So look for a home before disposing of something. It brings a real sense of relief and release to give things to someone who wants them and needs them—we'll surrender even good things for that. That's why we were saving it, anyway—because it might be *needed*. Giving like this is a positive, uplifting act that builds a feeling of confidence and control rather than the sinking feeling that something's been taken from us or lost forever.

How to Get Rid of Things and Feel Good About It

- Give some good friends (or members of the family who do **not** share the same address) a junk pre(disposal) viewing. This is sort of like the "charge customer's special private sale" and will really bring out the human urge to get there first. Gather together the stuff you're going to get rid of—or even just the better things—and let them pick whatever they want before you haul it off.

- Call your own or any local church and describe what you've got and ask where and when you can drop it off if they want it. They might even send someone for it.

- Stage a community or neighborhood giveaway, like the one described by one of my Canadian readers:

  "Our school decided to have a 'giveaway.' It was like a rummage sale but nothing was for sale. People brought what they didn't need anymore and took what they wanted. It was for the service of the community, not to raise money. It wasn't much work because there was no time spent pricing, handling money, etc. It worked really well. People were polite and caring, not like at some sales, where people grab the thing right out of your hand.

  "I've been the lucky recipient of many giveaways. When my aunt and uncle moved they had a whole billiard table covered with stuff that we were all invited to look at and take anything we wanted. I'm all in favor of it."

- Donate it (or the best of it) to a young family starting out, someone getting his or her first apartment, or a divorced person who didn't end up with the better half of the community property.

- Charities.

Dejunker's Guide to Intelligent Donation

Here are some simple guidelines to help guarantee that your goodies reach the pearly gate of another appreciative household. The folks who are the adoption agencies for our clutter (the Salvation Army, Goodwill, St. Vincent DePaul, Deseret Industries, etc.) don't want us to make things over or restore them to new, but we shouldn't just heap raw junk on them. A little pretreating and culling of clutter before carrying it in will give it the maximum chance of a new life.

Clothing: Few thrift stores are equipped to clean donated clothing. They hang the good stuff on hangers and hope the wrinkles will fall out, then sell it, "as is." If clothing is soiled, stained, or so wrinkled they don't think it will sell, they just bale it up and send it to a recycler. Clothing is an important part of their inventory, but if you want your donated clothing to wind up on the shoulders of someone in need rather than as a rag rug or industrial wipe, do as follows:

1. If it's no good for anything but rags, just hand it over as is. But do separate it from the usable

clothing—it saves the donee time and helps protect the good clothing from damage.

2. If it's a serviceable piece of clothing (as a rule, the seriously outdated doesn't fall into this category), wash or dry-clean it before sending it in. At the very least, submit it neatly folded or on a hanger. Keep good clothing all by itself in one bag or box, not mixed in with shoes, small appliances, or other things.

3. Don't donate wet or mildewed fabric, or clothing that's been badly stained with body wastes or other organic contaminants. If it stinks, put it in the trash.

Shoes:
Charities like shoes (especially men's shoes, of which they don't get enough), as long as they're in reasonable shape. Don't bother with worn-out shoes or shoes that would have to be repaired to be wearable. Most thrift shops don't repair things like this, they just put them out "as is." If they're too far gone, they just go into the trash. You might as well can them right at home and save the charity the trouble.

Furniture:
Thrift stores will usually do minor handyman stuff, like put a new screw-on leg on a couch, tack down cover fabric that's come loose, or stitch up an open seam. They rarely can do major repairs, though, and some shops aren't even equipped to clean donated furniture. If something is torn, defaced, or worn to the point that it won't readily sell as secondhand, it just gets dumped. If it has large cuts, holes, burns, stains, or springs sticking out, save the thrift shop the trouble and trash it yourself. When you call some thrift stores to pick up furniture, they ask you this question: "Is this item in good enough shape that you'd use it yourself, if you were in need?" If you can't answer yes without hesitation, chances are it won't do anybody any good.

Appliances:
Appliances that don't work don't usually do a thrift store much good. If it's a fairly new appliance and just needs minor fixing, many stores will send it out to have it done. Most of them have service shops they work with to get bids on proposed repairs to see if they're worth doing. But for older appliances, or those needing major repairs, the end value just doesn't justify the investment. These will just end up being trashed. If you have appliances kicking around that don't work or have missing parts, and you're not willing to do what it'll take to fix them up, chances are the thrift store won't, either.

Cameras, Watches, Electronics:
Broken cameras aren't worth anything, unless they're antique or rare, and most aren't. Very few older cameras justify repair, and most thrift stores don't even consider it. The same is true of watches. Stereos, TVs, and other electronic items are handled like appliances. If the unit is basically in good shape and just needs a minor repair, they'll often get it fixed. But if the picture tube or something major is gone—forget it.

Books and Magazines:
Good books—such as hardbound classics, encyclopedia sets, dictionaries, and timeless picture books—are appreciated by thrift stores, but your forty-year-old college psychology text probably won't do them much good. Some like paperbacks and some don't. For a lot of stores, cheap paperbacks require more sorting time and shelf space than they're worth. So check with the one you have in mind. Magazines aren't worth much to them— some stores do like back issues of enduring periodicals like *National Geographic,* but a two-year-old *Time* magazine might as well be used to line the bird cage.

There are some agencies, such as Deseret Industries, that don't turn down anything and are set up to utilize almost anything that comes in, and a number that train the disadvantaged and disabled to restore the restorable for resale. But the preceding guidelines should give you a good idea of how to make sure you're helping, not adding to the disposal expenses of, the charity of your choice. If the charity aspect is important to you, do take the time to be sure that the thrift store or collection box you have in mind is a genuine charity, not a similarly named ripoff. Most charitable agencies will arrange to pick up, if you have a goodly amount, and will provide you with a receipt to record the value of your donation for income-tax purposes.

> Once convinced that her hoards of stuff could help feed hungry children, the woman was able to part with a lot, and said "It was actually pretty selfish of me to hold on to all that when it wasn't doing me any good and could have helped someone else."

Too Big... Too Bad...

Big clutter is still clutter; the fact that no one can lift it or quite knows what to do with it, doesn't amount to permission to permanently ignore it!

We all have something like an old furnace, screen door, or sink leaning against the side of the house, a broken window, an old stove or dilapidated table, the water heater we replaced ourselves, or maybe a dewheeled vehicle or piece of far-gone furniture—none of which fits within the allowances of our town's curb pickup policies. So it waits and weathers and is an eyesore, and a mild mind irritant. What won't fit in a garbage bag, we often don't remove. We just wait for it to perhaps wilt a little or for someone to steal it (we should be so lucky)—or it might rust away (about a half century from now).

Take, for example, that 400-pound Hide-A-Bed we dragged to the backyard because none of the kids wanted it and it wouldn't fit in the station wagon. As the sun, wind, rain, and the neighbor kids work it over, it sheds stuffing, fabric shreds, and springs and is a breeding and recreation spot for all kinds of insects and little animals. Even after it's

168

reduced to a skeleton, it still weighs 350 pounds and we still have the same disposal problem we started with—plus we've littered the entire surrounding half acre.

First, the No-No's

- **Using it:** As a decoration, an angleworm breeding unit, a shade for the strawberries, or a playpen for the baby chickens. Forget it. It'll just rust and look tacky, and all that old paint will flake off and kill the nightcrawlers or the chicks. I've tried all these approaches and I know—these are bad ideas.
- **Burying it:** Only those of you who own a backhoe or a D8 Cat can qualify here, and even if you can manage it you can count on the new sewer line or underground phone cable running right through that spot about six months from now.
- **Burning it:** Anything that's too big to lift always has a frame and about 4,000 tacks, screws, and nails that will be left after you burn it, good for about two centuries' worth of flats and foot stabbings. Plus the fines for unauthorized incineration will be at least $50 more than it would have cost to just have it hauled away.
- **Throwing it in the river:** How'd you feel about the old tires and refrigerators you paddled past on your last canoe trip? Or hiked past on your last wilderness experience?
- **Dumping it into a gully:** Alas, we're no longer gullible enough to believe this "helps prevent erosion."

So How Do I Ditch the Big Stuff?
Dismantle it!

People have moved all kinds of things by reducing them to smaller pieces. They moved London Bridge to Arizona, and it weighed several hundred thousand tons! And we've all heard of murderers who eliminated an incriminating body with a few tools (and fertilized the flowers!). If you can't use a wrench, sledge, crowbar, hacksaw, or cutting torch safely yourself, find a friend who can.

Pickup Owners to the Rescue

At least 10 million macho men are out there with pickups, aching to justify ownership of such utilitarian transit. You only have to mention that you can't get it (whatever it is) into your Honda and most will spin all four wheels to show you how much tonnage their Dakota can tote. Pickup owners are hungry for bona fide pickups! Slip a couple bucks in the pocket of their cowboy shirt if necessary and they'll drive to the toxic dump for you.

Capitalize on Clean-Up Day

A chance to clean out all that stuff you've been procrastinating about, and you only have to travel 40 feet to the curb to do it.

Put it all out, but do the big, heavy, hard-to-get-rid-of things first, while you've still got the energy and ambition—and while it's still that giddy once-or-twice-a-year day when anything goes!

Really pack it out there. It'll all be gone for good—and for free, too!

Then resist the urge to fill those now-empty spaces with your neighbor's junk.

> "I tried to get rid of some old tables, books, and odds and ends. My husband took them to the dump, but brought back an old sled and an old-fashioned chamber pot!"

The Phone Call

It only takes a few minutes to make, and it can eliminate years of suffering, not to mention loss of neighborhood prestige!

You can call places such as scrap-metal dealers or salvage yards. If the booty is big enough, they may be willing to swing by on a scheduled pickup and get it. There are often local people, too, who advertise their services in the classifieds (under headings like "Junk Hauled Away"). Or you can call the garbage company/sanitation department itself and see if you can arrange for them to pick up big stuff. There may be a fee (usually reasonable) involved, but even if they charge you twenty bucks to come, do some math, man…a hernia operation costs at least $5,000, and the cost of the death or injury of a child from an old big piece of clutter is beyond calculation.

If you have a *lot* of big stuff to dispose of, such as from a barn or giant yard cleanup, you can arrange with a garbage removal service to have your very own 20-, 30-, or 40-cubic-yard dumpster delivered. A semi will bring it right where you need it and take it away when it's full, for a one-time charge plus a small rental fee for each day you keep the dumpster.

If all else fails, asking a favor at curbside isn't out of the question. Wave a $10 bill at the trashman if necessary with a please and a thank-you; most are good guys who will deal with it graciously—and you will have got off cheap.

How to Keep the Keepables: Storage

I'm not going to tell you exactly how to store and what to do with what's left. You can look at the room you have and how often you use something and with one of the many storage primers around figure that out. Just be careful with the dejunking helps (tools, equipment, and supplies) that are supposed to force us to be organized.

Files and boxes, baskets and bins don't solve clutter problems. Neither do the magic organizers and handy-dandy doo-dads, most of which just help us hide junk or stack it better. And excess and unneeded storage cans and boxes in themselves can become clutter.

Classy containers are like a dam. Remember, the water is still there, and if enough of it collects and you don't do something with it, it floods!

Storing the really good stuff intelligently is important, and it's an art unto itself. But my goal here is mainly to relieve you of the 4,000 pounds of stuff that obscure the good stuff and make it almost impossible to get to or use.

Whenever the word "store" or "storage" pops into your mind or vocabulary, try replacing it with "throw" or "dispose" and see if it doesn't make a lot more sense. The very fact that you are ready to store it away is usually because—_____ (you answer). I rest my case.

> **Storage:** Getting something up out of sight for a while until you can move it up higher and out of sighter.

Building or adding on or arranging for more storage is like buying a bigger size when you start gaining weight—it's a way of eluding the truth that eventually punishes you severely. Racks and other storage equipment cost money and take up space. If no good stuff is available for them, you'll fill them with junk and clutter. And once something is stored on our premises for a while, it begins the sanctifying process.

More storage, more stuff. Think about it—more storage, more stuff!

Beware of Junk Bunkers

What's a junk bunker? Anything that creates space for more unnecessary stuff. Example: you need maybe four knives in a kitchen to do everything you need to do. Then you get a nice knife holder and it has twelve slots... Or the desk is overflowing with stuff, 90 percent of which is junk. Instead of cleaning it, you buy a desk organizer (i.e., a junk bunker), which allows you to stack things higher and deeper. Unfortunately junk, if stacked neatly enough, even looks valuable. Lots of closet organizers are just junk bunkers. Your closet is loaded, shoes are running over the threshold and out into the creek. Do you sort and unload and get rid of the foot-pinchers and the ankle-breakers? No, you buy a junk bunker, a shoe storage unit. Now you can hang them up one side of the door and down the other (and rip the door off its hinges).

They call the new closet contraptions names like "closet organizer." These and all other bunkers are just innocent pieces of plastic, wood, or metal; they don't organize anything. **You** are the organizer, the king, the controller. You're the one who has to teach your closets and cupboards some discipline to keep them tidy.

This is just **the tighter girdle approach:** there's too much there, too many bulges and rolls, so we move from a 6-ply to an 8-ply girdle and it works (or seems to work) as long as we hold our breath. But the problem isn't gone—it's just out of sight. Beware the:

- Cedar chest: A fragrant way to protect things you never wear.
- File cabinet: A way to store paper junk vertically.
- Garment storage bag: Oxygen tent for dying dresses and comatose coats.
- Bookshelf: One of the more attractive ways of insulating a wall.
- China closet: A piece of furniture that keeps dust off the stuff you never feed anyone out of.
- Spice rack: A study in herbal archaeology.
- Zip disk: An excuse to keep every byte of the leftovers.
- Pegboard organizer: An ingenious way to keep unused things in plain view.
- Industrial shelving: A high-tech way to keep our boxes of useless stuff from being crushed by more of the same.
- Hardware chest: A way to organize your lack of control in hardware stores.
- Desk organizer: A chance to slip things into a slot before ignoring them.
- Tie rack: A short course in tie-style history.
- Toy box: A receptacle for broken toys.
- Banker's box: A high-class way to hide obsolete papers.
- Plastic crate: A petrochemical cage for questionable stuff.
- Desk spike: Death by impalement for pieces of paper you're trying to ignore.
- Video cassette library: A way to store movies you'll never want to see more than twice.
- Drawer organizer: A way to add something plastic to the stuff rattling around in there.
- Trunk: A former piece of working luggage that now only makes trips to obscurity.
- Sewing basket: A decorative enclosure for three or four things you use occasionally, surrounded by snarled thread, unraveling bias tape, antique hooks and eyes, and tangled zippers.
- Whatnot: A handy place to put things you oughtnot have bought.

CHAPTER 13

Professional Organizers:

Getting a Second Opinion on Your Clutter

We let professional decorators and designers and salespeople help fill our house up so why not the reverse? A professional to help empty it out! Pro dejunkers (their proper title is professional organizers) are people who lead you by the hand and work closely with you, in your home or business. They can even get down into the actual sorting and evaluation of your stuff and help you decide what to keep and what to toss and then where and how to keep what's left. Some of us go for professional help and others don't. Libby Edwards, a capable professional from Lubbock, Texas, points out the value of a pro in this very personal matter:

"My real value is that as an outsider I can serve as a mediator between people and their junk and help them feel less overwhelmed by it. They can't see over the hurdles and I can. As a partner I encourage, motivate, and assure them if they really don't want something, it's fine to fling it. Then I can serve as a scapegoat for any family aftermath, too. ('But honey, the professional organizer told me to throw it out.') I'm the target of any adverse reaction; it helps them and doesn't bother me. My other big value is that I can make them aware of what they really have, I can find the invisible baggage **and** the overlooked treasures."

That sounds like pretty solid therapy to me, so if you think you can use the help, get it!

In the last half dozen years of cleaning homes and businesses and collecting thousands of clutter confessionals, I've met a number of these decluttering professionals, and they all seemed sincere, able, and compassionate—not greedy or overly profit-oriented.

But like you, I was curious about the concept of a "professional organizer." I wanted to learn more about this new profession called uncluttering homes, offices, and lives. I discovered you didn't necessarily just find them in the Yellow Pages. You find them profiled in the feature pages of your local newspaper and in radio and TV interviews, teaching local adult-education classes and in local classified ads, and as the authors of books on the subject in the bookstore or library. You can often get the names of professional organizers from closet design and stationery-supply stores, or from the National Association of Professional Organizers, P.O. Box 140647, Austin, TX 78714, www.napo.net, 512-206-0151.

When I tracked down some of these specialists (many of them were women), I asked all of them the same questions. The following is a summary of their answers. You'll enjoy this and might find salvation here for your situation—or someone else's.

What triggered the call to you?

People like to talk about dejunking and want to do it, but often just can't. They may not be quite ready, or they think

173

they don't know how. They finally become desperate and feel that they have lost control of their environment. They feel overwhelmed to the point of admitting they need help. Their activities and the demands on them have increased and increased and take all their time, and so dejunking doesn't get done even though their clutter is choking them. They're busier than they can handle. They're frustrated, they don't know where to begin, and they want a companion in dejunking, to share the load and help.

A lot of people are pressured by someone else to get their house or office in shape.

Moving is another reason we often get calls. A person suddenly *has* to wade through the junk—all at once!

What do they really want out of you? Reassurance and reaffirmation that they're doing the right thing ("I haven't worn this and it still has the price tag on it. Is it really okay to get rid of it?"). They tend to think there must be a certain precise way to declutter or a formula for going about it (which there isn't). They want specific, practical ideas on how to go about it and how to choose what to keep; they want you to inspire and motivate them to do it. They want support through a tough emotional time, and they seem to want someone else to help them make decisions and take the responsibility for the "execution" of their stuff. They want you to absolve them of any guilt and tell them they really can't afford to keep certain things. And unless they are senile or under five, they want to be involved even though you are doing it.

How do other members of the family feel about it? There's often tension, as might be expected. Even if the other household members admit dejunking is overdue, they consider the dejunker an outsider. (Although sometimes they are grateful to have a professional take over where family members have tried to help and failed.) Then, too, there are often conflicts, as you might expect, between the saver and the nonsaver. And you're in the middle. You seldom get cases where both are of the same mind. Some good arguments sure get started. People take their things very personally. It's always important for the professional organizer to put the one who **didn't** call at ease—to assure them that they too will benefit from your presence.

What can a pro organizer really offer them? The strongest thing is reassurance! The second strongest is the motivation to do it—convincing them to let go. Third is to give them steps to follow (like a dieter reporting back). The professional may not have to finish the project, as long as he manages to get it started. After that he may be able to just answer questions and help with specific problems that hang up the process. But if you want them to, a good hands-on organizer will come work side by side with you and help you decide what to get rid of and exactly how to organize what you can't bear to part with.

What is a fair cost per home? project? Any tax deductions? Everyone waffles here: the cost depends on the size and nature of the job. In general, the cost seemed to range from $20 to $60 per hour, and the people with big names and reputations and books out on the subject may quote you up to $100 an hour or more, or $500 or more for a day. Urban areas are, of course, higher. If there turn out to be an excessive num-

ber of phone calls from the client to the professional during nonscheduled sessions, there may be an extra charge for that. Some organizers also offer improved storage devices, boxes, labels, etc., for an extra charge, as a service. Expenses such as travel or lodging are also extra. (Don't be ashamed to discuss price or to shop around until you find someone who fits within your budget.)

Any usable clothing or goods you donate to charities or nonprofit organizations in the course of the process are tax-deductible.

How long (or how many visits) does it take to "dejunk" a place, per square foot or whatever? Longer than you'd think, so you have to encourage people to do a little each day. It isn't done in a couple of afternoons or a weekend, as so many imagine. A typical schedule is one full-day or half-day session a week for 4 to 12 weeks.

Do you refuse any jobs—and why? Yes, if there is a deeper mental problem or great rift between spouse and family and trouble is more evident than progress. If there are deep mental problems, a person will not be able to dejunk unless they get help with the other problems first. We might also refuse if the caller indicates he isn't ready to do it and has called under pressure, or if he is too far away or too far gone. Some people want to get organized, but they aren't willing to get rid of anything. And some people want and need the help but don't really want to pay for it.

Are clients usually able to retain their dejunked status after they achieve it? It depends on how motivated they are, of course. Many of them do adjust and are able to achieve decluttering without repeat consultations or follow-up; however, a lot slip back to where they were before. But even the backsliders don't usually slide all the way back, as dejunking does change their shopping patterns to some extent, which cuts a lot of the flow. If you leave them with written instructions to follow, they tend to do better. In short, professional assistance isn't a cure-all but is a definite help in getting people started and thinking **anti-junk.**

Many organizers offer a package service that includes a three- or six-month "tune-up," or fine tuning of the work done initially. This is especially useful, since the client has lived with the results for a while. By then, the client may also be ready to approach additional projects.

How to Be Sure You Have the Right Professional

My only question would be in the matter of qualification. The flow of letters I've received from people who want to become professional organizers or dejunkers makes me aware of how many beginners there are out there. To help us with decluttering, I'd want someone who has succeeded superbly in her own life—who has run her own home, office, and clutter well. I'd want a doer with a proven record of mastery, someone who's done a lot of one-on-one decluttering, not just someone who only talks, writes, or philosophizes about it. Ask some questions. If they can't answer you satisfactorily, stay away.

- Don't forget to ask about: Length of time in the business. Those who love their work and cut clutter well will last and be busy for a long time. I'd look for at least several years' experience on the job. (Although some may have had prior jobs that gave them good related experience, and sometimes relative newcomers can have exceptional energy and enthusiasm.)

- You want experience and specialization—in the type of job yours is. Describe your own situation as clearly as you can so the professional can get a feel for what needs to be done. Ask her what kinds of jobs she's done, and don't be reluctant to ask for a referral if yours isn't up her alley.

- Ask for references. After all, what she's about to see and learn about you is a peek into your most private space, so take a little peek into her past and call four people she's decluttered.

- Get an advance estimate for the job, once the organizer is well acquainted with what you have in mind. Anyone who really knows the business will have a good idea of what things cost per house, per person, per hour, per job, etc. Then ask for a simple written statement of the basis for all charges. This assures that you'll know what you're in for. (You wouldn't want to start your dejunked life with an overdraft.) But do bear in mind most organizers charge strictly by the hour—for good reason. This is one line of work where the client is involved the entire time. Thus dealing with a roomful of clutter can take five hours or five days, depending on how the client deals with the process. A client who has to agonize over each and every piece of trash or treasure is going to prolong the experience indefinitely, and being charged by the hour may motivate him to abbreviate that tendency so that the project can be completed in a reasonable amount of time.

- Check your own intuition, too. Does it give you a good sense that the organizer is discreet and reliable—will do what she says she will? These are two of the most important qualities. Organizing is a very personal service, so you need to just plain feel comfortable with her, too.

A good pro should help *you* face it, not do it all for you—or she'll only have been a temporary crutch. *You* are the one who has to plan, and own, the new arrangement of your life.

How You Can Help the Pro

The professionals all report that dejunking is hard work, physically and emotionally (and I can say amen to that!).

Professional organizers aren't afraid of hard work, but don't ask them to clean, which is a different thing altogether. Most organizers recommend having a second person (kid, teen, whomever) on hand to do the cleaning and to haul out trash and charity giveaways as they accumulate, so the dejunker—and the organizer—can concentrate on making decisions.

When pricing a client's house as a pro cleaner, I always tell him I will cut the bid (bill) if they do certain things themselves, like take pictures down, clear the floors, cover the furniture, keep activity down (no pets, guests, etc., while we are there). This only takes him minutes but saves us hours. Why not get all the junk under the sink out of the way before the $50-an-hour plumber gets there and has to do it? The same rule goes for getting decluttering help if you need or want it. Always ask the organizer, 'What can I do in advance?" It'll save you money. In general, a pro organizer can move a lot faster if:

- You hand them your treasures, not your trash, to sort. Whenever possible, dispose of obvious garbage before they arrive.
- You prevent other people from causing arbitration on every piece.
- Likewise, keep kids and pets out of the way, turn the TV off, etc., so they can concentrate and you can converse.
- You control the urge (after you and the organizer have a chance to get acquainted) to chat about

extraneous or unnecessary things at $50 or whatever an hour (unless you're rich and just want the company).

- Follow their counsel—you're paying for it!
- Remember that professionals—and that includes organizers—don't have all the answers. If *you* come up with a solution (who, after all, is better acquainted with your deepest desires and needs?), it may well be the best one of all.

And if you need the help but can't afford a pro, or your dejunking agenda is so huge the charges would be astronomical, go talk to the right kind of friend and see if you could help each other out in all the kinds of ways that a professional would. It does help to have someone there beside you in some of these decisions.

Group Therapy Maybe?

"Dear Mr. Aslett:

Your book has helped give me a boost, but unfortunately I need a heck of a bigger boost, something on the order of a Titan rocket. Just before I heard you on the radio, I was more or less seriously considering forming a 'support group' (like AA or Weight Watchers) that could help motivate junkers even more and help them progress. I noted that you give seminars, but frankly I think week-in, week-out support is needed for the lessons to stick and take effect."

"Several years ago I began to collect material to form a support group for declutterers (an exchange of views, not of goods!). I think I need a support group more than an organizer or declutterer to exorcise the demon."

You'll be glad to hear that there are packrat support groups cropping up all over, and there is at least one organization that has been focusing on helping members overcome clutter and disorganization since the early 1980s: Messies Anonymous. For a list of self-help groups and information about starting your own (and a free introductory newsletter), send a self-addressed stamped envelope to:

Messies Anonymous
Department S.H.
5025 SW 14th Avenue
Miami, FL 33165

There's no reason you couldn't start your own group, either—there's nothing like the company of the equally committed to keep you on track!

CHAPTER 14

Helping Someone Else to Declutter

We never hear a sermon without three or four people who could benefit from it popping to mind: "Boy, I wish Jim (or Janie) were here to hear this. They sure need this." We seldom think the advice is for us. Almost every time I'm asked to autograph a clutter book, the requester bends down and says in a low voice, "Would you make this out to my husband [mother, daughter, etc.]—they really need it." One night, unaware, a husband and wife both bought the book and each had me sign it to the other one.

Is others' junk really a problem? I'm sure you already know the answer to that—it's about the hottest topic and the toughest challenge in the whole realm of clutter. So here's a little ammunition to get us in the mood to help cure it:

"My husband likes garage sales. My garage is so full of junk I can't get my new car in it. It's been this way for years. Last hunting season I threatened to clean it out while he was gone, and he

locked it with chains and locks. He threatens divorce if I touch it. He can't find anything in it, and I can't even make it to the freezer. What can I do? HELP! P.S. If cleanliness is next to Godliness, my garage is hell."

"I am a junkee born and raised by junkees. One weekend I helped my mother haul off a pickup load of my dad's junk (while he was out of town). That Monday my dad went to the dump and brought back the pickup—as full as it had been and then some—all excited because now he had matching sets."

"I would dearly love to go through my house and throw out everything that we didn't use in a week's time. My problem is being married to the King Packrat. When he went overseas several years ago, I did throw out a lot and had a ball doing it. However, to this day, he claims he misses what I threw out and has watched the garbage ever since, just in case, and catches me every time. So how do I reform my favorite Packrat? He comes from a long line of the same."

"My seventy-year-old mother is a bonafide junkee. I am a young mother of four who has had a very hard time living a normal life. You would not believe the joy I feel when my kids have their friends over because growing up I can only remember being terrified at the thought that my friends might wander from the front room. It was the only decent room in the house because my sisters kept it nice and clean, even though it too was wall-to-wall furniture. I can remember being terrified at the thought that one of my friends might take a peek behind a strategically placed curtain, go into a closed room, or look into the garage, and believe me there were questions. I could go on and on about the mental strain it has placed on me and my brothers and sisters."

"I come from a long line of savers. And my sweet husband was the 'All High,' the King Saver of them all! Boxes and boxes and boxes of newspapers and books. How we fought over those boxes piled wall to wall, floor to ceiling in the living room!"

"Please send the self-incriminating junkee exam to my wife. She is terminally stricken with clutteritis and does not realize it. This test may show her the light."

"Within a few weeks after my marriage to Prince Charming, his White Charger (motorcycle) was scattered all over the garage and utility room, spilling over into my laundry area I told him he should get rid of his useless junk. He told me if he did that, I'd be the first to go. Thirty-three years later the only thing that's changed is the model of his 'horse.'"

And Now, for the Other Guy's Junk

I had a relative, never knew him well, but all the rest of the family talked about him so much he seemed like a buddy to me. It seems this gentleman of my genealogy was, in his early and middle life, a hard-drinking, loud-swearing, double-dealing dude who was well remembered wherever he chose to exercise those talents. Then, as it happened, he saw the light and turned totally against all his former failings. Although his own salvation was nothing short of a miracle, he was definitely not satisfied with this single conversion. He thought all humankind should follow suit and that it was his duty to pull it off. So he exchanged the title of "town drunk" for "town fanatic," and much to the irritation of all preached everywhere with a (now steady) accusing finger. Reformed junkaholics often fall into the same thing. We see the light, and when we run out of our own (or think we do), we start pointing at others' piles, much to their irritation. But we soon discover junk is not merely holy to those who own it— it's *sacred!*

I'd equate the task of dejunking an unwilling junkee to pulling off a total personality change in them. Junk is part of people's makeup, an extension of their emotional state, a cornerstone of their character. Junk is generally the hottest romance they have going, their (safely stored) security blanket. Couples make compromises in hundreds of areas of human relations—"You snore, so I can have a dog." Not so with junk and clutter. No trades, Teddy—except on biggies like "You can buy the condo if I can keep the collection." But decluttering converts can't let a sleeping pile lie; they bitch and whine and moan, criticize, make snide remarks, threaten, coerce, beg, bribe, impugn others' possessions trying to effect a change in the unrepentant rubble-keeper. "You can lead a horse to water but you can't make him drink" well describes the effect on a hardened junkee. You can establish a credit balance with the trash hauler, give him garbage bags for his birthday, have the church come by begging for a few spare blankets for widows and orphans—but a threatened junkee won't budge. He's firm and you better not even think of tossing any of his stuff while he's away. It's one of the fastest ways to trash a relationship.

> One woman who had her fill of an old motor her husband hung on to through five homes and garages has in her will directed that it be buried beside him, if it's still on the premises. Talk about sweet revenge.

The Logical Approach Doesn't Work!

WIFE: "Honey, your junk is unsafe, unsightly, unhealthy, embarrassing, and a bad example for the kids. We're out of room, it's raising our taxes, lowering the value of our real estate, and unnerving me."

HUSBAND: "So? What's wrong with it?"

You can use intellectual appeal, and that falls as flat as singing by a diesel motor. One of the most intelligent women I've ever known is two steps above a chronic clutterer; she even bought a farm with six outbuildings to accommodate it. I call her a hard case, and she just smiles and picks up the sticks and stones and saves them. Praying doesn't help, either. The Lord made us all free agents, so count that out.

I shake my head every time I hear idealistic statements like: "I knew he was a junker before we got married but was sure that once I had him, I could change his packratty behavior."

That's exactly like the two lovers, each devoted to a different religion, who know they'll never surrender their doctrine but won't get along if they don't—especially when children come. Each is confident they can convert the other. But don't count on it! Seldom do opposites meet in the middle; each generally becomes more unyielding rather than more compromising with time.

Some Definite Don'ts— Others' Stuff

Ever seen a rat take on a giant dog or cat when cornered? Well, packrats (the two-legged variety) can be at least as vicious when you encroach on their territory.

The following tactics will only intensify a junker's resolve or even inspire her to keep more. So stop right now while you have what uncovered ground you have.

It's a bad idea to:

Threaten: "If you don't clean that out, I'm going to do it for you!" It never works. A threat to a junker will only cause them to cling tighter and then distrust you; you're a loser all the way with idle threats. And if you carry out your threat by carrying out some of their stuff, the divorce or lawsuit will cost you more than keeping your mouth closed. Threats will turn a messer into a mule.

Try to intimidate: I remember discovering in grade school that snakes were most girls' number-one horror. So I learned how to catch slithering three-foot-long serpents, grab them by the tail, twirl them around my head like a lasso, and let them descend unmercifully into a group of girls. Would that generate the squeaks and squeals and did I get their full attention! But temporary attention was all I got. The snake was just a weapon to intimidate; it sure didn't make them like me. Intimidating people in an effort to dejunk them is even dumber than my snake trick. If you force people into alarm or to arms you gain about as much as I did with the snakes.

Serve notice: "You have three days to take care of that or else." Or else what? Are you going to kill them or just maim them? What you'll get back with this is: "I'll show you; I won't touch it for at least three months."

Preach: (That includes humphing, snorting, hissing, and eye-rolling, too.)

Nag / criticize / make jokes about it: Especially in public or in third-party conversations. If you keep it up, "Messy Marty, the head packrat of Roberville," will become a sort of hero and get sympathy (if not a round of applause) and will only grow more attached to his junk, which is now projected as a "cause" before the public.

Demean the value of their junk: It will only unleash a fierce defensive dialogue and make their hearts grow all the fonder of the stuff.

Divorce: Not just yet, anyway.

Withhold sex or affection: They might find abstinence is just great—or someone else is a lot better. The only thing that will get tossed is your love life.

Touch their junk: Unless the person him or herself asks you to, or you're court-ordered to, don't ever attempt to deal with or throw someone else's junk out. Nothing can match the raging fury of a junker whose junk has been meddled with. If you intend to go on living with them, don't you ever do it. *Packrats have to make the final decision or the decision will never be final.* What do you know about someone's innermost feelings and memories (which most clutter is connected to)? It'll only cause heartache if you try to do it.

THE WITNESS SAID SHE SAW THE VICTIM GOING THRU MRS. VON GOBBIN'S OLD POLKA RECORDS... AND WHAM-O!!!

In my capacity as "Clutter Expert" I've even had people write to me and ask my professional advice on their (entirely well-intentioned) plans to marshal their forces to totally dejunk some beloved relative's home or apartment in their absence, sparing no effort or expense to save the person in question from the "fire hazard, and physical and mental health hazard" of their overjunked existence.

The following excerpt from my answer to one such inquiry says it all:

Dear ———,

Your desire to help is admirable; however, at any age your mom is still her own person and still has the right to the choices (good or bad) she wishes to make in her life. You and I might hate her junk, but it's *her* junk, and the solace or security she finds in it is real to her. We can't inflict or force our value system onto others, even when it's done in a spirit of love. You people are running a risky venture, and she could easily build the junk back up in a year anyway (good junkers do it faster than that).

We all have the right to choose our own fate. Others may have a right to teach, coax, or convince us, but never to force us or to meddle in our personal possessions. In more than forty years of marriage, I've never opened one of my wife's drawers, or that of any employee in any of the businesses I own. I allow people to harbor what they want, when and where they want—until it interferes with others. And even then I think we should teach others the principle and let them govern themselves.

It's a Good Idea To:

Give a good example they can imitate ("Look at me, I'm free!"). Strange how seldom this most effective technique of all is used to persuade or to change behavior. More than ever these days people listen to what you are, not what you say. Before you beat on them, see to it that all your stuff is squared away. It's only fair, and it has the best chance of working. Jettisoning your junk will reveal rewards they will want.

Then remind: Purge every pile of your stuff into perfection and then not obnoxiously but quietly and subtly flaunt your freedom. This will apply pressure like nothing you've seen.

Salt your conversation: With lots of inspirational, non-nagging gems like: "Did you hear that the Joneses had to rent another storage unit at $80 more a month? Why, that could buy a new bass boat (name one of the listener's favorite nonjunk desires) before you know it."

Offer newer junk: Constantly point out all the new and better and more genuinely interesting stuff they could have—stuff *you* want, too!—if there were only room.

Set up a vacation or trip away from their junk: Help them see they can and would live happily away from it by sending them far away (preferably for an extended period) without it. When it comes time to reunite with their stash, they may not want to.

Offer them an incentive to get rid of it or clean it up, such as something they've always wanted the two of you to do. If the prize is desirable enough, it can move mountains of clutter.

Offer a compromise or a trade-off: ("I'll get rid of this if you get rid of that.") Offers of anything less than self-sacrifice of your own junk may not get anywhere.

Help them become aware: Education, too, is one of the best techniques of all and always the last tried. Other people's stuff is just as invisible to them as ours is to us. Before we can get others to dejunk, we have to get them to see it. They can't and won't come to terms with what they don't realize they have. I have great faith in people. We may have a mean streak in us now and then, but few of us will intentionally hurt anyone. Most people are compassionate and loving, and positive action is usually possible once they're really aware.

Explain—quietly, tactfully, and objectively—what problems their junk and clutter poses. And what it seems their junk is doing to them. You could even hand them a copy of this book ("I found it surprisingly helpful, and fun to read, too").

Call in a "nonhostile" friend or relative—someone the junker can't resist. We all have people we're always at our Sunday best in front of, and an outsider often has lots of strength in swaying. Set them up to help persuade your partner to part with those parasitic piles.

One picture is worth... Film is cheap and effective. Hundred-pound pumpkins or horses are just stories, but when I see a picture of it, it sure changes my reaction and convinces me. Junkscapes that escape the naked eye look twice or three times as tacky and cluttered through that cold camera lens. Snap a centerfold shot or a whole scrapbook of the most gruesome when they aren't around and present it to them in a way—**and this is important!**—that has some supposed other purpose than highlighting junk. But the evidence will be clear even to their eyes. At first they may just chuckle at them, even show them to friends, but gradually guilt will creep over them.

Invite someone awesome or cute/handsome/eligible to visit. Or have the fire inspector visit; or have the place reappraised (pride of property gets us all going, and we all know clutter can reflect badly on us). Or get the local reporter to finally do that feature story on your mate ("The photographer is coming Thursday…").

Plan an event involving the target area—a party, open house, wedding, reunion, barbecue ("If it rains we may have to move to the garage/basement"). Enter the local home tour, garden tour, or Christmas-light contest, or arrange for your child's school class to visit. We all suddenly see our place differently through the imagined eyes of others.

> Ninety percent of the time the garage (I don't know what deed granted it) is the man's domain.
>
> "Get rid of that old paint."
>
> "It's my paint and in my garage, so don't you worry about it."
>
> Women have been dominated and unjustly put upon so long that if you move their stuff your fate will be a little less grim than the doom that will befall if you move a man's stuff. Even if it's total trash, men really get huffy. Treading on others' stuff is touchy and always will be, so forewarned is forearmed.

Try reverse psychology till *they* get horrified and have enough. Offer to help them organize and catalog it all, especially if there's a good chance that once you get into it, they'll see that it really isn't worth saving **or** organizing (or buying all those expensive storage devices for).

Seize the day/hour. We all have moments, hours, or days when we're more vulnerable and submissive and in general more open to suggestion. Your beloved junker will have these too, so be prepared to capitalize on them when they come—to pounce and fling like mad.

Limit the area (or confine the clutter zone): Easier said than done, but effective! When you remove shelves, shed, etc., junk will disappear with them. Tell that unrepentant packrat at home or in the office what boundaries their junk can't creep beyond. You may not own the house alone, but you do have some authority in the disbursement of space and storage. The woman has a little edge here, because she's usually in charge of the "inner space" in a home. Limiting the amount of space people have to stash stuff always helps—when they run out of room or it gets really inconvenient to clutter, people will ease up. Or at least condense or organize their belongings better.

Set up something to force them to move it (in moving, we often review and reevaluate): A remodeling job, change of storage station, or warning that mice or cockroaches have invaded their hoard.

Do something to take advantage of the fact that a junkee will do anything to get to his stuff before you or something else does (junkees are very quick to perceive any threat to their junk): "Cousin Pete is coming over Saturday to help me clean out the toolshed."

Make some improvement in your shared environs that involves quietly organizing, moving, or condensing some particularly bothersome piece of the junk: "I'm just doing this for now." (For some reason that involves preventing harm to their junk, such as "So your radiator collection won't get dripped on while I repaint the garage.") Then just leave things that way afterward, in hopes that they will see how much better it is (or at least be too lazy to put it back the way it was).

Make it easy for them to join in. Establish a family discard day, or say, "I'm going to the dump/to have a garage sale. Would you like to add anything?" (Even one item is a victory.)

When you come across something you suspect they might part with, ask them "Do you still want those rusted-out stovepipes? Would you like me to get rid of them?" The bother of actually disposing of things stops a lot of us. (This must be a sincere request, not lightly veiled aggression.)

Don't steal their thunder when they do get rolling. Avoid overenthusiastically seconding the idea, reminding them of how long you've wished they would do this, etc. Let dejunking quietly proceed as *their* idea.

Don't fail to praise every bit of progress: Really jump and snort and roll around when even a morsel of the mess goes—we all do more to get more praise.

Last: Don't give up and change your name to Mr. or Mrs. Rat. You can't wean someone from something that took ten, twenty, thirty, or more years to squirrel away with one magic word or a single week of effort.

What Has Worked for You?

This is such a tough subject I would really like to hear your suggestions, any strategies or approaches that worked for you. Write to me aslettdon@aol.com or:

Don Aslett
PO Box 700
Pocatello, ID 83204

Offer to help them: ("Would you like me to come over and help?" "I'll clean and haul while you dejunk." "Want to use my wheelbarrow/pickup?") Or just keep them company and offer advice if and when they ask for it while they do it all. A woman could offer to help a man with the small stuff and nuisance details, a man to help a woman with the heavy stuff. A little opposite sex attraction never hurts decluttering chemistry.

If they need reassurance, let them stay with you every minute so they can satisfy themselves you're not throwing anything out they don't want thrown out.

Neighbors' Junk

Definition of a good neighbor: one who doesn't share with us his noise, pets, smells, weeds... or clutter!

Talk about a helpless position in life—that's having a junker for a neighbor (and they're probably nice folks, too, so you can't even hate them). Their stuff is the plague of Pilgrim's Pride Place, offending the eye and inching everyone's real-estate values downward. They're content to collect, never conceal or can anything, but it's their property. A neighborhood petition would crush them but probably not a cubic yard of their clutter, or they might ask how we determined *our* clutter and junk was all good. Or their family and forefathers back eight generations were taught the fine art of keeping and conserving, so you're attacking a whole genealogy instead of a front yard or a few junk cars. Love thy neighbor was the commandment, however, not love his or her stuff—so you have the right to try and reduce it. Use all the diplomacy you can muster and any of the techniques on pages 182-185. If all else fails, move.

CHAPTER 15

Kids Have Clutter, Too!

To all of you who gave birth to a human and now have a squirrel, don't panic... yet. It's going to get worse and then worse...when they leave for college or marriage you are going to get it... their junk! If you don't want those cold chills to run up your spine, you have to face the cold facts about kids' crammed corners... now.

I've raised six kids of my own, but to get some up-to-the-moment information on the kiddie clutter scene I decided my four-year-old granddaughter, Amanda, was a good place to start. I had a little time alone with her while her mother and grandmother were out buying more junk for her. So I gave her her first official book writer's assignment: "Amanda, let's count all your toys, and your little brother Jason's [age two]. How many toys do you think you have?" "A thousand," she said without a blink or hesitation. What a cute exaggeration, I thought; just what I needed to dramatize my story. "Show me the whole thousand," I said—and she did. We should have entitled our tour "falling over evidence."

Upstairs in her room I counted thirty-five toy units (not separate pieces) and thirteen more major toys in the closet. There were nine teddy bears secure in the window casements; sixty-five books blessed one shelf in her room; there were nine mini-toys in one bathtub alone, forty-seven different units in the basement on hold (retired for the moment). These were only the obvious toys and clutter, not counting crayons, balloons, coloring books, junior jewelry, puzzles, and other small items. My daughter Elizabeth (a neat, conservative college graduate) then informed me there were a few toys boxed and put away in the attic and forty more boxed books, too! My final tally for this average house of a couple married five years with two little ones: 120 big toy units, 107 books, and twenty videos.

And since we're talking clutter, let's consider what these individual units actually mean; Amanda's Little Miss Kitchen Set, which I counted as one unit in the tally, has thirty-six pieces; the Barbies, those beyond-belief Barbies, also counted as single toys in the tally—even though each had sports cars, full-scale wardrobes and furnishings, and pets. The games had all kinds of balls, jacks, cards, game pieces, spinners—a toy's true junking factor isn't the unit alone but how many pieces to lose and get in the vacuum and underfoot. The final total of units, parts, and books together exceeded Amanda's thousand estimate by a third. Over 1,300 pieces of kid toys and stuff and gadfreys! I forgot clothes, boots, and wall hangings, and never got outside to dig in the snowdrifts for wagons and trikes and their parts. Oh well, you get the idea. One kid today very possibly has more toys and clutter than an entire town of thirty years ago.

The Cure Is the Cause

Finding out where and when all this stuff came from is a good place to start when considering how to control and get rid of it.

My daughter said, for example, that of the nine teddy bears, she had bought *zero!* (It's those lousy grandparents who cause all the problems, and aunts and uncles, godmothers and godfathers.) She also said that having a boy and a girl instead of a matching set almost doubles the toys and accessories needed. She also blamed those ever more inventive fast-food lunch packs that contain ever more indigestible things (and by some miracle of design, these cheap plastic and rubber things outlast the expensive "intelligent toys" every time).

They say by age six our values are formed... and we wonder why they sniff and snuff and are unhappy and want more. When a child wants something, say *another* new Nintendo game (because their friends all have it), the parents will give rousing lectures on covetousness—then next week buy a $28,000 van or pickup to keep up with the neighbors. When kids get a card or Valentine, they rejoice, snatch the bill inside, and that's that. Then an adult comes in and says, "What did you do with that card from Grandma?" The kid looks up guiltily and says, "But I read it, Mom!" "You will show some respect and keep it." (If they fail to do so, we file it away for them.) Our double standard of junk must be awfully confusing to kids when we lay the junk on them at Christmastime and then tell them to lay off.

We warn them about matches, germs, strangers, rapists, and crossing the street but never about the danger of the *stuff* that teaches us greed, poisons our personality, and steals our time.

The "Kid" Is an Easy Cure... You're Not

I hate to keep going back to this, but the problem is adults. Kids don't really have much control over their junk situation. It's all in our hands—until they're about eight years old, they're actually only boarders at our place.

Ninety percent of the problem is our example. We control kids and their surroundings, we are the landlord and superintendent of their lodgings and their things. We are master of the house. We determine what and how much there is and where it stays!

In my dejunking seminar presentations, as I'm heaping on the guilt about the excess junk in the average home, I make the statement "...and your children have 75 percent more toys than they need." That always gets instant, affirmative head nodding from the crowd. Even relieved looks of "See, Don, it isn't just me" until I say, "Yes, folks, and you know why? *You gave them all that...* In

the spirit of "Be good and Daddy will bring you home or buy you some junk" millions of parents each day heap on little Herman and Heidi some of the most worthless stuff imaginable. The undivided attention we give our kids is on the average 37 seconds a day, they say, and parents and grandparents who seldom spend the time they want with a child feel they should pick up a toy to replace themselves.

How to Keep Down Kiddie Clutter

• Get rid of the stuff the *you* saved for them! A lot of this they would never want and they still don't know what some of it even is. I'd flush this away first... fast!

• Practice regular rotation (but make sure no kids are around when you do it, because like us they will automatically cling to anything you want to take). Then just like the tyrant who thinned the soldiers he didn't want to feed all winter, do that to the toys. Box those babies and pack or hide them away for the next generation (or at least the next couple of months).

• Many young parents have semiannual kid dejunking days: Before birthday and before Christmas to clear out the old, the broken, and the outgrown and make way for the new.

• Make sure you give them a *place*. Many of us don't stop to think that a kid's room has to be his or her whole house. We only allow them one room, so it's really a combined sleeping and recreation area, living room, hobby shop, dining room and storage area—no wonder it's cluttered. Make sure they have space and a clearly defined place to put it all—toys, clothes, games and books, computer stuff, art and craft supplies.

A few ideas here:

Multipart playthings. Store in clear plastic sweater or shoeboxes or plastic dishpans on shelves, one for each set.

Toys in general. Put a toybox in every major play area, such as each kid's room and the family room. You could even use something that matches the decor in nonkid rooms, but if you do make sure it's fitted with special (safety) toybox hinges.

Stuffed animals. The nets (such as Pet Net and Teddy Bed) that you hang across the corner of the room do a good job of getting these hard-to-stack critters up and out of the way.

Bathroom toys. These need containment even more, for *safety's sake*— a zippered net lingerie bag is great, with a suction cup on a hook stuck right through it. (As long as you stick the suction cup somewhere out of the soap-scum zone!) Or you can hang the bag on a plastic hanger over the faucet or shower head.

Art supplies. Crayons, markers, brushes, scissors, etc., fit neatly and compactly into one of those lazy-susan-like artist's bins available at art-supply stores.

Books. Built-in bookcases with shelves divided into narrow (about twelve-inch) sections are best for holding up those skinny kids' books. Far better than bookends, which are forever falling over.

Children's hair accessories (incredible clutter potential). Try one of those small plastic chests with divided drawers for these, or a fishing tackle box or the like.

PG (Parental Guidance) Dejunking

When it comes to the actual pruning or thinning, just remember that once kids are old enough to speak, there is some honor of ownership as to exactly what is the stuff that's got to go. Forty years later, there are kids who still haven't forgiven their parents for those "toss time" invasions on their stuff, after finding their old doll or train set in the garbage. For the sake of future relationships (and a great chance to teach the concept to our kids), dejunking should be a team effort, with you coaching and the kids calling the shots. A few sneaky secret confiscation raids might have merit, but remember if you choose what they lose, they also lose the experience of dealing with their own problems. If not now, when and where do they learn?

Give each child their own personal storage area(s)—a box, shelf, whatever—and when it overflows have *them* choose what should go. Kids' interests change and only *they* know when something has ceased to be a fascination. Kids soon forget what's gone if you let them make the decisions and choose. And they usually choose better than we do.

This process can even help make dejunking an exercise in compassion. You might be surprised at what a kid will surrender to a friend or poorer kid.

You could even offer to let them include some outgrown treasures of their own in your next garage sale (and let them keep the proceeds).

If a child has something they feel is very important that doesn't fit in their everyday storage area, you could tell them we'll put it in a box (in the attic or wherever) and see if they feel the same about it six months from now. This may not work with preschoolers, who feel anything they can't see doesn't exist and is never coming back (that's the reason they cling to Mom when she leaves), but it's fine for bigger kids.

> "The hardest dejunking came in my son's room. I couldn't face doing it myself, so I gave him a huge box and told him to fill it with toys he no longer wanted and ones that were broken or had pieces missing he could put in the large garbage can also in his room. I had to bite my tongue several times while he threw *my* favorite toys in the box. When he was finished, we took the box to his preschool (he is only five years old) and donated them to his class. The teacher was so thrilled to have some new toys for the class she treated us to ice cream and also wrote me a check for one million thanks! Now my son can keep his room straight all the time, and he has **his** favorite toys at easy grasp."

Dealing with the Daily Drag-In

Every day, from school or play, something comes home with a kid (all junk to you, but not to them), and you have to process all this. Put whatever they bring home right up on the fridge, bulletin board, or wall immediately, taking down and disposing of what was there. The current piece of prose or art is what's important; yesterday's can go.

Kids have paper, too, much of it—hero junk, posters and cards of every kind, awards, trophies, school papers, certificates for good smiling or no cavities, plaques and photo treasures enough to clutter a hundred dresser tops. Again, after hanging them for a while, you can put the more important and worth keeping of these into one of those plastic file crates with a folder for each category.

P.S. Taking your kids to the junkyard isn't real bright or conducive to dejunking.

Advice for Parents and Grandparents for Coping with Children's Christmas Demands

"We do not pretend to have any expertise in child psychology, but we here at the SCROOGE organization (see page 109) are sometimes asked for advice on how to respond when children make demands for Christmas gifts that parents or grandparents don't approve of or can't afford. Our advice, for what it's worth, is:

- Take a good look at yourself first. If you are a 'super consumer,' if *you* run right out and buy every fad item for yourself, if *you* are overly concerned about accumulating material goods and status symbols, how can you expect your children to be any different?
- Try to exert some control over *how much* TV your kids watch and *what* they watch. Saturday mornings are the worst; that's when children are bombarded by commercials cleverly designed to whet their appetites for all sorts of costly junk.
- Offer alternatives to gifts that you know to be overpriced and shoddy. ('No Santa won't be able to bring you the Super Killer Robot Doll That Walks and Talks and Mugs Old Ladies in the Park, but you might like a small telescope to look at the stars and planets or a soccer practice goal.') Tell them *why* an item isn't practical—it's dangerous, you know from experience that it will break in the first hour, or it just costs too much.
- Get across the idea early that you have your own rules and principles and that your decisions will not be governed by what other parents do or what the voice on TV says.
- And the hardest one for most of us: learn to say *no* to your children while they are young. Kids seem to get over little disappointments fairly quickly, but it gets more difficult as they get older. If you *always* give in and buy the expensive hunk-of-junk toy when they're six, you may find yourself sending them on ski trips to Switzerland when they're twenty, making their house down payments when they're twenty-five, and paying for their divorces when they're thirty."

CHAPTER 16

Dear but Not Departed:

Deceased People's Possessions

Your junk and clutter will survive you, count on it!

Picture yourself breathing your last today, and let's make your end as dramatic as possible. One day the upstairs ceiling supporting your 33 r.p.m. record collection, your library of Uncle Scrooge comics, and your lifetime accumulation of steins and mugs caves in and crushes you, instantly, with no suffering whatsoever. The records, cups, and comics aren't hurt, only you. The family gets the news and stands outside the house as the forklift is raising the floor to get out your flattened remains, saying, "He (she) was so young," "She had so much (stuff) to live for." They are, of course (since there's nothing they can do for you), directing the recovery crew to not break any of the records or mugs. By now all your family, friends, neighbors, and associates have been called and come to what's left of your house to pay their condolences and case out what you no longer need (well, it does have to go *somewhere*). No one really says anything about all your treasures, but you can bet their concern to confiscate a goodly portion of them is ten times keener than their concern for you.

A Realist's Lament
I think about the future and the years that lie ahead,
I wonder what will happen to my things when I am dead.
The things I have collected that have meant so much to me,
The things I love, to someone else, a pile of Junk will be.
—Hazel Turner Hamblin

The obituary is kind, listing your departure simply as a "home accident," rather than the truth—"Local Citizen Crushed by Cache of Half-Century-Old Cartoons." The funeral is over; many mourners paid tribute and now will pay dearly for what you left behind. It was bad enough that you went and died on everybody and left a vacancy in your family, job, bowling team, the IRS rolls, and the scout troop, but to leave all your rooms, drawers, closets, files, garages, and shops full of junk was pretty low down.

You wanted your kids to have what you didn't, but you botched it. Instead, they have exactly *what you did!*

> "I keep it because when I die, I'll finally get even with my four kids for all their messes. They'll have to sort it all out and throw it away."

It all starts after your burial, when the stuff you didn't take with you (which is all of it) is gone through. "They" will always start with your papers, to see what bills you got out of by dying and whether or not you had a million-dollar insurance policy somewhere. More than one person does this to "witness any finding" (so no one person will get all the good stuff). Your papers: wait a min-ute, imagine right now what your private papers might do to your family and friends.

"Gasp! Daddy had an intimate friend on the side!"

"Gasp! He was paying off a racing debt!"

"Gasp! Mother never told us about this operation!"

Unless your intent is to torture your survivors, you need to start dealing with your junk now, today. It's 1,000 percent inefficient to let others deal with it!

Families are together for only a few days after a death, a shame—because there's so much stuff to fight over before going back to California. No feelings or love can be shown or expressed... the junk you left behind has made it utterly impossible.

Attorneys and the perennially greedy relatives seem to handle the money too quickly and efficiently for most of the survivors to get involved in, but the *things*—the aftermath of a lifetime of collection—are the real killer. There's so much jealousy, jousting, claim jumping, and jabbing over it that even the Grim Reaper is repulsed!

One family (of three ministers!) haven't spoken to each other since their mother's death... all because of a pocket knife! Another family was split apart by an imported cuckoo clock! How many people do you know have quit speaking since the spoils were divided?

I can see you nodding your head. Yes, Don, you're right. You also know that you have some real swoopers (those who attack free stuff first) in your family who will be quick to apply the law of least deserving: the ones who get the most are usually the least deserving, and they have all the nerve because they have the least affection.

You still aren't completely convinced to act *now?*

Suddenly your death isn't a sweet sorrow, it's a sorry mess. There's a fast fight over your four tennis rackets, and two family members get keys made and sneak in at night (right past the National Guard) and snitch your camping gear and JanSport backpack. By now the word is out and everyone is plundering your possessions. Twelve Swiss-made mugs gone already, and an in-law (not direct family, mind you) had the nerve to make off with your portable speaking platform. Everyone proceeds to politely pressure the couple who stupidly volunteered to be executor or arbitrator of your junk, and they begin to mistrust

and dislike everyone (besides, being in charge, they can't do any obvious pilfering). Your innocent junk has suddenly made liars, thieves, cutthroats, sneaks, and bitter enemies out of those you most cared about. You have them hot with anger before you're cold in the ground. As you look down you see them—your family, reduced to casting lots, drawing straws over your junk. Two of your aunts will never speak to one another again over an old Austrian lace hanky you got from Grandma in 1931. Your son and daughter are dishing out insults over a dish you once fed Walter Cronkite out of. And they haven't even got out of the house yet to the storage bin, the chicken coop, and what's stored at the "folks."

You wanted your good stuff to carry on in life, to live on, and now it's being carried off.

You are waiting to be told by the doctor to "get your affairs in order," you say? Only a tiny percent of us will ever hear those words; the rest of us will never know what hit us. Our affairs will be someone else's. *Zap!* That quick! And people don't just die old—it could happen anytime. If you're the kind of person who says, "Big deal, it won't be my worry," you're not only a packrat, you're a dirty rat. Why not respond to the inevitable before it's inevitable?

Leaving your junk and clutter for someone else to wade through is worse than leaving a live mine field. Just think of the peace and tranquillity you'll have in your last forty years of living, knowing you've dealt justly with the things you're directly responsible for.

There's nothing sadder than going to an aged or terminally ill person's home (or the hospital) and helping them square things away. It's awful to see a person who has only three months or three weeks left spend all of their remaining time and energy worrying about their radial arm saw or their collection of antique oddments. Much sweeter to see someone with a twinkle in their eye, not worrying about *things,* but savoring the final loving and caring of family and friends. Let it go early—clutter is one cancer you can cut out by yourself, and doing so might add ten years to your life!

Right now, in mere minutes, you can distribute all your stuff in a way that will create love and harmony and benefit everyone. It will save years of grief and there's no secret to it, no mysterious fine print to create future problems. If there aren't mountains left around and what's there is earmarked, arbitration is eliminated, guilty consciences are gone, and the swoopers (whom we all hate) never get off the ground!

One wise woman gives some of her life's accumulation away every Christmas. She simply puts a piece of tape on the back of the platter, painting, book, album, or whatever and writes a name on it. Then she continues to enjoy the object now, more so because she knows it will never become a burden to anyone.

Some families have a tradition that the person who gave a present to a family member is the person who gets it back after they pass on. That's a nice idea and justice all around as the generous and the stingy both get what's coming to them.

Write It Down

Anything you want done in this area, don't say it—write it.

Start by being sure that you have a will, and don't just see that all your financial assets

and real estate, etc., are assigned therein. Make a list of all the specific objects too small or purely sentimental to detail in a will—or at least all the ones you're particularly concerned about—and who you want them to go to. Be sure to reference this list in the will. Update it from time to time and always sign and date the additions. If you don't want to be bothered with a list, make clear somewhere in your will who "all the rest and residue" of your estate (which means everything not spelled out) should go to.

I keep my list in an envelope in my desk at all times. In case of my untimely exit from this life, each and every one of my unfinished manuscripts, cameras, guns, souvenirs, collections, etc., is assigned to someone. I update this no less than once a year—a little exercise which reminds me of mortality and to appreciate the life I have now.

A few last thoughts here:

• Cash is a lot easier to divide than clutter. Greed, poor judgment, deceit, and other vices get involved in its ownership, but money doesn't keep emotion alive nearly as long as stuff. Arranging in your later years to sell or liquidate some "stuff" (such as jewelry or antiques) will definitely cut the complications of distribution. Cash is easy to deal with and lets people select their own time, place, and passion. Stuff can rule from the grave. Cash is colder, but In the long run, kinder.

• Pick a popular executor. A family member or close friend that everyone likes and respects is a good choice for executor. He or she has the battle half won. His or her reputation and standing will carry lots of force to cut complaints. Any whiners run the risk of the others thinking they're just being greedy. Who loves an umpire, judge, referee? Everyone—if they are fair and likable.

> "The meanest thing you can do is die and leave your loved ones to deal with all your junk. I don't want to do this to my family. I bought a household inventory book, in which I am listing all the really valuable things in the house. The items have a peel-off white sticker on the bottom, with a corresponding number in the book. Any item can then be easily identified, and I put an approximate value on it, or if I don't' know, I put 'valuable' or 'very valuable' or whatever."

Death Is Final...
for Only One Person

(Disposing of Other People's Treasures and Junk, Too)

"I inherited three bushel baskets of pictures. I don't know who most of the people in them are, but they must be valuable, so I'll hang on to them."

"I inherited my junk fever from parents, who never threw anything away. After they died, we cleaned their home and they had telephone receipts back to 1932.... Now we have them."

"My parents-in-law lived in a small house with a full basement. My husband is an only child, so when they died, he inherited everything. He had to work and asked me to take care of sorting through the house and disposing of their goods. He told me to keep only the books, papers, a couple of other specific things, and 'anything valuable.'

"The house was one of the older ones and the closets, cupboards, and much of the basement were filled front to back and top to bottom. After I had given away about two pickup loads of clothing and sold some antiques I knew I didn't want and made the charities happy with a generous supply of things, we took

back with us an 18-foot truck filled with 'valuables.' We filled our previously usable two-car garage with them. Then we had to have a garage sale to get rid of things like the second dining room suite, the couch, and so on and on. We did keep a lot of very useful things, but there still was no space in our garage for our cars because of the rest of the junk. It was about ten years before we could finally use our garage again."

"Last April my mother died suddenly and unexpectedly, and I spent from then until Christmas in another state trying to sort through and get rid of all her belongings. What a chore! And it still isn't done. It would probably be unbelievable to anyone outside our family—except you—how much Mom had accumulated in a two-bedroom mobile home and one small storage shed. She had nearly every drawer filled with fabric scraps saved for quilt-making (some were pinky-finger-sized), plus a four-drawer chestful in the storage shed. She had every card we had ever sent her and Dad (who died in 1977), had hundreds, maybe thousands of them, including every get-well card he got during his ten-month hospital stay before he died. My mother had evidently never thrown away a jar of any sort—I found boxes and bags full of jars of every size and description. She had my dad's carpentry tools as well as some of his father's farm tools, mostly broken, and Dad's shoes, and a back brace from his hospital stay—and on and on I could go. With record-breaking heat and poor health as a deterrent, it took me all summer long to go through it all.

"I *am* glad she kept some of the letters, cards, and other papers, but as for the rest she could have gotten rid of much of it years ago. What a job it would have saved me.

"Getting rid of things that belong to a loved one who has died is extremely painful emotionally. One has the feeling of betrayal. Because all five children live in other states, we had to begin sorting through Mom's belongings the day after her funeral. It was without a doubt the hardest thing I have ever had to do. I asked one of my sisters if she felt, as I did, that we were intruding where we had no business, and she said, 'Yes I do.' None of us can get rid of everything we own before we die, but if we had less excess baggage, it certainly would make the job easier for our families."

In the course of my research for this book, deceased people's possessions emerged as about the most unsettling of all clutter. Without exception every person I interviewed (by letter, phone, on TV or radio, etc.) came forth with a horror story on the subject. Coping with our own collection of clutter is bad enough—but imagine having to deal with someone else's. Without the insights you have as the actual owner and originator of it all, it's ten times more difficult and indecisive.

Then, too, no matter how it's dealt with, even divided into fractionally perfect shares by an accountant, "deservingness" rears its ugly head. "He's rich already." "She never helped while they were alive." "He's an in-law (or outlaw) (or bum)."

There are two different problems to deal with here—our own reaction to the situation, and the actual logistics of going through it all and disposing of it intelligently. Let's consider the emotional quagmire first.

After a death, we're in shock: we refuse to believe it, we feel out of control, and we don't want to deal with it. How many times have you heard, or even had the experience, of someone leaving a loved one's room, etc., exactly as they left it? It's our way of holding on to that person, to the belief that things haven't changed. We also know, instinctively, how painful going through so many reminders of the person will be—and so, by putting off the disposal process, we put off all that pain. It's not at all uncommon for a survivor to say they would rather have someone come and cart it all away than face sorting through it and inspecting it.

But by putting off this hurt we also put off our own healing. We need to go through all those possessions—ourselves if at all possible—but only when we're ready. Reaching the point that we're ready to do it—and then deciding to do it—is part of the grieving process. We need to reach it at our own rate, no matter how long that takes. The most important thing to remember here is that when we get rid of things, we're not erasing that person's existence. As Dr. Sharon Katz, who has a great deal of experience in grief counseling, says: "A departed person's things are an extension of themselves, and they can help the person live on, through the good they do for others. We *need* physical reminders of our loved ones, mementos of them, things that were special to them—but it's okay not to keep all of it.

"Do it in steps and stages if necessary—month by month or box by box. It's going to hurt doing this—you may cry the whole time you're sorting. Let yourself cry and feel the feelings you feel.

"If it's a family inheritance situation, don't do anything at all for about six months afterward, if possible; let things cool down and give everyone a chance to become a little more detached. Then it's critical for all the family to communicate: sit down together, if possible, and talk and reason it out. It's important that all family members have a chance to have their say; leave no one out. If just one person goes through it all and gets rid of things, they may never realize what certain things might have meant to certain people."

A few more ideas for keeping this a positive and manageable process:

- If at all possible, give to family and friends what is most meaningful to them. At least let them each take one favorite thing as a special remembrance, or choose one for them.

- Distribute these things at a special gathering that celebrates the departed person's life, not merely regrets their death. Use it as an opportunity to give each other support and help each other heal.

- Keep only certain things and use them as often as possible to help keep the person an active part of your life.

- Keep the most important things and give them to relatives and close friends as the occasion comes up or they need them over time. For example, you could give a child a piece of her mother's jewelry on each birthday after a certain age.

- As for the deceased person's wardrobe—always a special problem—you could take pieces from all their favorite garments and make them into a memory quilt. Then give away all the rest.

- Donate it all to some person or establishment that will do good for others and be a permanent reflection of who that person was.

- Auction or sell it and donate the money to the favorite cause of the deceased.

- Reduce it to the most meaningful, and eliminate the rest. Then review the collection after time has passed and weed it down further, and so on until you've reached a reasonable size.

- If it's a child's possessions, give them to the child of a dear relative or close friend or a needy child of the same age.

The following letter from one of my readers lets us end here with an inspirational example of enlightened disposal of other people's possessions.

"I've had a lot of experience dealing with departed persons' possessions and have arrived at the following conclusion. Depending on the personality of the individual, usually one of three things is done:

1. Indiscriminate disposal of almost everything soon after the death of the loved one.
2. Keeping everything, including income taxes, for the past thirty years.
3. Greedily poking through boxes, bags, trunks, etc., for the good things.

"I feel that all of these approaches are wrong. The first because, all too often, after the wounds begin to heal and the grieving is less severe, one finds that too much was disposed of. The second and third are wrong for obvious reasons.

"I have been directly involved with the disposal of my parents' property and also the sole heir of all the household goods of an aunt for whom I cared and whom I helped for years prior to her death.

"My brother, sister, and I did the following after our parents' death:

1. As a threesome, objectively evaluated each of our own and our married children's actual needs, as we saw them.
   a. made a list of the things we felt each could use, gave each their list, and let them mark off the things they wanted.
   b. prepared cartons of things such as pots and pans, dishes, silverware, linens, bedding, and small appliances for those children ready to branch off into apartments of their own.
2. Boxed the things we felt were family keepsakes—pictures, jewelry, certain dishes and collectibles, genealogical information, etc. These were thought about and then dispersed or disposed of at a later date—after wounds had healed and good sense prevailed.
3. Had a garage sale for all that remained, including the leftovers from categories 1 and 2.
4. Sent all unsold items to charity.

"When my aunt died, I did basically the same thing. I gave much of her clothing to her older friends, all living on limited incomes. Out of a whole house of furniture and belongings I kept two end tables, a cedar chest, a desk chair, and two wood chairs. And two pieces of glassware for personal keepsakes. Not too bad! Again, I assessed the needs of my children, made lists for each, and let them mark off what they each wanted on their individual lists. Then I did the same with what was left for my sister and brother. The balance, which was a lot, went to charity."

Living Clutter-Free Thereafter

CHAPTER 17

Staying on the Wagon

How to Keep Yourself Uncluttered

Congratulations! I know it was quite a struggle; getting rid of all that clutter was rough—but you did it. But don't turn your back or go back to sleep. The hour, the minute—in fact, the very second—you finally feel you've *done* it (cleansed your life of junk and clutter), all the forces that gave it to you are regrouping for another attack. Temptation never takes any time out. Every billboard bribes, every magazine promises to remake us; the radio reminds us of stuff, our friends fill us in on more, the TV puts it all in color, parents pile it on us, stores stack up ever more delicious marked-down merchandise. Misery likes company—yours—and it always wants to come back to an old familiar friend. And it won't come with announcements or a fanfare parade. It will slide and sneak, creep and crawl in the form of gifts, low payments, special sales, inheritances, vacations, new projects, and attractions. And the wonderful, free, powerful feeling you have is threatened, especially now, while you're still weak from the effort of it all.

This is a crucial time, because the sinking sense of slipping back into something once you've gained ground is worse than any punishment ever inflicted. It feels so good to conquer yourself, to accomplish something—to lose the weight, drop a bad habit, end a nonconstructive friendship, gain ground on the battlefield, quit smoking or drinking, get to work on time or attend church regularly, put an end to family fights. And then, if you start falling back into it all, you hate yourself and feel weak and spineless. It's absolutely awful—*so don't let it happen.* Remember how much work it was to shed the stuff.

So many of us start something out well and begin to get results and enthusiasm about it, and then it winds down and we're back where we started, fighting the problem instead of fixing it. In dejunking it's even more important to carry the momentum all the way through, all the time, because junk and clutter aren't just going to cease once we make that first big cleansing. It's just

that now we have stable ground to fight them on. Our first big dejunking session or onslaught is a lot like winning the first two games of a playoff or world series, we're likely to think we have it made and let our guard down—and suddenly the underdog (or under-the-bed storage) sneaks past us and steals the day.

Will the junk flow continue? You can bet your empty garage on it!

But moving to a monastery or an A-frame in Alaska isn't the answer. If you're going to live, you've got to live with temptation—without yielding to it. Then you'll respect yourself, others will respect you, and gradually the temptation (if you don't nurture it) will leave you and go look for a more hospitable host.

The joy of being junk-free is the biggest weapon you have here. It may have taken you a year to dejunk; it took me that long to get out of the habit of eating a pile of popcorn or quart of ice cream before bed each night. I hated waking up in the morning feeling like an army had camped in my mouth during the night. When I finally stopped eating the food, I felt so good that it was actually a joy to get up in the morning. In fact, it began to be a more sensual experience than gulping the goodies.

Once you're pure, staying that way is a hundred times more pleasant and efficient and rewarding than backsliding and then having to battle the results again—so don't slip back. Before you know it you'll be up to your collarbones in clutter and have to go through another "place lift."

Controlling junk once it gets a foothold is like trying to contain wild morning glory. You seldom gain ground, and if you do it's expensive! As the weedkiller can says, catch it in the "sprouting stage" and you have a chance. This is good gardening wisdom for junk.

Cutting the Junk Flow Sources

The best and first thing to do is cut the source of new stuff coming in, head it off at the pass. Otherwise, any empty space will be refilled in no time at all, just as sand on a beach refills the tracks.

Junk and clutter don't materialize by magic; they have a source, they come from somewhere. Just run through the house now, and when you spot a piece of junk or clutter, check the source. Where did I get this? Scanning that whole shelf of silver salamanders, for example, you realize you didn't buy a single one of them—where did they come from, then? Once you pinpoint the source, you can overcome it. If someone is shooting at you, the first thing is to find out where he is, then you duck behind something, hide, etc. Otherwise you'll never know what hit you!

My Junk-Source Locater

Before you dispose, take a minute to tabulate. This will tip you off as to how things are slipping into the house and tell you where to put up your biggest barricades.

Item:

A Gift
❑ From family or friend (who?) ____
❑ From business acquaintance/associate.

I Bought It Myself
❑ Because it was the rage/a friend or rival had one.
❑ Because it would do something for my image.
❑ Because it was on sale or a bargain.
❑ For a souvenir.
❑ Because I was out shopping for recreation.
❑ Because I was depressed.
❑ Because I saw it in a catalogue.
❑ At a garage sale or flea market.
❑ Because I needed it for a few hours (or a few minutes).
❑ Because _____
(any other reason, such as I had the money; there wouldn't be any left; two were as cheap as one; I had space to fill, etc.).

It Was Free
❑ Someone gave it to me.
❑ I found it.
❑ I got it in the mail.
❑ The former occupant left it behind.
❑ I inherited it.
❑ Because _____
(any other reason, such as they were left over; it came free with a purchase; if I saved or collected ____ , I got it).

It Isn't Mine
❑ I borrowed it.
❑ Someone left/stored/parked it here. (Who?)

Some Ways to Reduce the Inflow

There are probably thousands of ways to prevent junk, but the following will do a lot to reduce reaccumulation. They're all based on that big basic truth about dieting—the surest way to reduce hips and stomach is to take in less!

- **Let everyone know you despise junk and clutter.** If you cultivate the reputation of clutterbuster and it gets around, people will lay a lot less junk on you. They'll think twice about buying you cute, useless little whatnots, and they won't automatically expect you to be interested in their cellar cleanout surplus. They might be relieved to have an excuse not to buy you a gift, too. Public pronouncements will get around like wildfire (and it won't hurt to exaggerate a little): "I've tossed every single bit of nonessential stuff in the house and I think we could do without a lot of the furniture, too." You might even consider a "I don't brake for garage sales" sticker.
- **Toss all the junk bunkers**. Remember that the basic human drives are greed, power, hunger, sex, and filling available space. Take a perfectly happy home or business where all is well and everyone is content and add to it a table, some new shelves, a dresser, a credenza, or a wardrobe—something no one wanted or needed—and then watch. Within hours it will become a magnet for stuff. In a couple of days it'll be covered; within weeks, crammed! It will become a headquarters of hunting, thrashing, and arguing. And then someone will begin to protect the stuff with plastic covers, signs, keys, and insurance, and punish anyone who moves or alters it. So cancel the storage unit, dismantle the no-longer-needed shelves, burn the boxes, ban the bunkers.
- **Tiptoe past the free trap.** (Yes, I said Free, not flea, although this stuff can infest you as badly.) Free traps are set everywhere, claiming to give us something for nothing. Think of that: something for nothing. But you already have too

many somethings that do nothing. Even if they pay you to take a freebie, it isn't free, no matter what you get or where you got it. You pay for it with your time, space, and efforts to preserve it. Free? There is a catch. You!

I've gotten letters from my radio audience saying, "I didn't hear what it was you were giving away, but send me one." Think! It's like taking a free puppy or kitten home. You gain control and responsibility and hundreds of decisions. There's lots of free cheese at a mousetrap, but did you ever see a happy mouse there?

When it's free, cautious be!

Taking extra toothpicks or mints or matches at a restaurant because they are there and free is a seemingly harmless act. But when you do the same with brochures, samples, and everything else you come across, you can stop wondering what clutters up your drawers and closets.

Is it impolite not to take something handed to you? Not on your junk-jettisoning life, it isn't. I wouldn't refuse an after-dinner appreciation award in front of the appreciative crowd, but I *would* come home from convention and trade show without any shopping bags.

- **Say no**. We may once have felt obligated to accept any kindly offer, resulting in the possession of three sideboards, two Victorian wardrobes, four moth-eaten fur coats, and a second gas stove. But no more!

Curb Shopping

by Don Aslett

MAN, I COULD FIX THAT WITH A LITTLE PAINT.

WELL I'LL BE... I'VE BEEN LOOKIN' FOR ONE OF THEM FOR YEARS.

OH, JAMES... STOP AT ONCE! ...THAT WOULD GO SPLENDIDLY IN LITTLE ERIC'S ROOM.

I'D BETTER TAKE THAT HOME BEFORE SOMEONE STEALS IT!

THAT'S FUNNY, OLD MAN HORN SAID HE HAD A WHOLE LOAD TO PICK UP.

ACME TRASH

- **Control that passion for OPJ (Other People's Junk).** What is it with our incredible obsession for other people's possessions? The Lord caught it early and called it coveting.

  We only need to spot someone's castoffs sunbathing in the alley to feel the uncontrollable urge to check them out—so we do. And which of the five boxes of on-its-way-out offal do we paw through first? That's easy; Our choice is made when the owner tells us, "Oh, that box is all trash." We know as sure as the sun comes up that something valuable they missed is in there. So we grab the box and dive in. I've driven past garage sales of pure unadulterated junk and my wife, mother, and daughter-in-law in the car all screamed, let us out, let us out. They have all they want, their rooms and storage areas are overstuffed, but they love to go and search through stuff that other people had. Curiosity killed the cat, and curiosity sure collects the clutter—warped TV trays, percolators with missing parts, souvenir spoon rests from places you've never been, broken record players, rockerless rockers, scorched pans with no lids, awful armchairs. Get serious! (Or at least, get a smaller sack.)

Here are some more categories of stuff that have contributed mightily to the pile:

- **The traditions trap.** The subscription is due for renewal. I don't really get around to reading the magazine/ newsletter anymore, but I've been a member so long it would be a shame to drop it now. I'll just keep one more year and then I'll forget it. Cut those roots now—remember, they're growing

- **Book and music clubs.** By far the most dependable followup folks around—a wonderful way to get things you don't want. They thrive on your indecisiveness and procrastination. The deal might be fair and good, but if your capacity to handle it isn't, stay away, cancel!

- **Garage sales** (of course).

- **Mail** (junk mail).
- **Fashion fixation.** This one is real dangerous. Everything you own is obsolete the minute someone in L.A. or Paris gets tired of baggy pants, or frost nips a fashionably exposed kneecap. Fashion will junk you faster than anything going, including several neighbors having simultaneous garage sales.
- **I'm-bored-today clutter.** A lot of clutter is picked up when we're unbusy and undirected in life. We buy something to give ourselves a lift, but it never works—we're soon bored and frustrated again.
- **Vacations.** (See page 103.)
- **Softie junk.** "Charity," believe it or not, can make donations to our clutter fund, too. How many outfits—through the mail or at the door—offer us some unwanted object or fragile freebie in return for a "modest contribution"? Just give the money! You'll both be better off! Have you ever tried to throw one of those poignant little poppies away? (The same goes for artwork or crafts you buy mainly to encourage an artist or craftsperson.)
- **Holiday clutter.** By 2020 the calendar will surely be solid with special days. The big eight were bad enough, but then we began to add: Father's Day, Grandparents' Day, Secretary's Day, Boss's Day, Sweetest Day, Arbor Day, Dairy Products Day, Save the Chub Day. What next? Every other saint already had one, and then we added every other president's birthday. Amazingly enough, they almost all merit a sale, even Election Day.

Public holidays are bad enough, but things like our own birthday are worse. They can't just be marked by a hunk of cake; they have to involve *things to* recognize their arrival and mark their passing until next year.

Resolve this year to pull off a miracle: see how many days you can observe without adding to the pile of special-day fallout. I know every store and organization including the corner grocery and your club are lying awake right now coming up with mementos for those coming occasions—aisles lined with luscious shortcuts to affection and memory. Don't do it! **Try to savor the spirit instead of the stuff of the occasion.**

10 Smart Ways to Refuse Junk and Clutter

- I can't—it will raise my tax bracket.
- Gosh, I'd like it, but we're moving into a mobile home.
- I've already got one just like it!
- Alas, I'm allergic to…
- My mate/the landlord would never let me.
- I have such bad luck with _____.
- Unfortunately, it's against my religion.
- I'm afraid my pets would shred it.
- It's too (damp/dry, etc.) where I live.
- Every time I take one of those, something terrible happens to it.

Shopping, One of the World's Few Unsolved Mysteries

Suddenly:

- You have cold chills
- Your teeth chatter
- Your muscles tense
- You may find yourself sweating

It's **mall**eria! A terrible disease, striking far more women than men. All reason leaves and a serious mental condition develops, along with the fever that leads to any number of clutter complications. No cure yet has been discovered.

When cash insufficiency appeared to cure it, a secondary infection called credit set in. **Mall**eria is junk and clutter's biggest ally, and sad to say, in a playoff, the world's champion dejunker couldn't keep up with a seasoned passionate shopper. I interviewed a typical victim—an attractive, enthusiastic young woman in her mid-twenties (not even a veteran yet).

"Could you think of a substitute for shopping?"

"Yes, eating."

"When you go on vacation, can you rest from it?"

"Heck no, we plan our vacation around it!"

"Your husband, does he like to shop?"

"Oh, yes, he goes along—" (Husband interrupts: "Only to protect my money!").

"Could you think of anything that would make you stop?"

"Well, if I died!"

"You have more than plenty now. Why do you do it?"

"Man, it's like the hunt!"

At this point in the interview I, who would choose the electric chair over a shopping cart, gained a glimpse of understanding. Never before in my wildest imagination could I comprehend why anyone would fight traffic, climb in and out of cars, trudge for miles through crowds of cranky, elbowing people in noisy aisles and concourses, carry heavy bags and bundles around for hours, and spend perfectly good money for all kinds of things they don't really need. Comparing shopping to hunting was a low blow indeed, but right on target.

When I used to hunt, I fought biting wind and subzero weather, jumped in and out of trucks, trudged uphill and down for mile upon mile, fought brutal brush and briars, carried heavy arms, ammo, and supplies all over, wore all kinds of weird and uncomfortable cloth-

ing, and ended up spending $25 a pound for meat I could buy a block away at the supermarket for $2.50 a pound. *It was the hunt.*

If decluttering doesn't come easy, don't let it get you down and discouraged. Lots of habits we have to blame ourselves, not society, for. But junking, well, we've had lots of help with it. A top advertising executive told me that the average person is shotgunned with over 5,000 messages daily, urging them to: do, buy, take, go, get, get more. Every corner of every communication probes for a weak spot in our psyche, and it never lets up, we have no time to digest, just ingest. Our clutter congestion is understandable considering all the coaching and coaxing we get—we're in the game 24 hours a day. The junk disease is highly contagious, and we're inoculated daily with glamorous catalogues, easy payment plans, and that incredibly convenient 800-credit-order number.

All of these compelling clutter seductions come down to: Your place or mine. And once in our place, it's in our life.

Human impulses and drives have remained pretty much the same throughout history, but the array and allure of temptation around today has grown astronomically. And the ability to buy has been multiplied and perfected. A few years ago, if you wanted to cut off a chronic shopper, all you had to do was hide the Sears catalogue and the saddle. To cover all the bases today you'd have to stop the mail and phone, confiscate all the newspapers and circulars, remove the radio and TV and computer, incapacitate all four cars, never let a neighbor in, and prevent the shopper from ever finding out about a home party, garage sale, or auction.

I realize that our modern life's major entertainment is shopping; it's about the only action and adventure many of us have these days. But if you don't curb unnecessary shopping, if you shop for recreation, you will never cut the clutter stream. Probably 80 percent of the clutter you give and receive is the result of excessive shopping.

Helps to Hang on to the Wagon

- Read *Clutter's Last Stand* after this book if you're not fully convinced or activated.
- Cut down your credit card collection. People seem to get a sense of security or even status out of having tons of credit. But easy, instant credit pushes us over the edge on many a questionable purchase. And once we get it paid off, we know the account is still there, a clean, empty, tempting slate just waiting to be filled up again. And then, too, credit cards mean bills with stuffers and postcards letting us in on special sales and deals, etc.
- Become a renter or borrower of rarely used items.
- Don't go to the devil's workshop if you don't want to do business with him—remember malls use landscaping, color, music, etc., to soften you for the kill.
- Think about facing your mate's wrath when you get home.
- Think of how you're going to feel when the bills start coming in at the end of the month.
- Don't shop with a friend.
- Don't shop carrying more cash than you intend to spend. And leave your credit cards home!
- Don't shop just for the fun of it, or to kill time. (Tearful wife to angry husband: "But dear, it wasn't my fault, I was forced to shop because they [Sears Car Care] didn't have my car ready!")

"I got carried away." (Is that you or your junk speaking?)

- Idle shopping is cruising, looking for action, looking for something in all that's served up to you, so you can bring it home and try to fit it in somewhere. Don't just "shop." Don't buy till you feel the *need* for a certain something. Forget about the thrill of wondering how you're going to cover it in your checking account and focus on the freedom of using what you already have instead.
- For this same reason, don't automatically read all the sales pages. (You can't believe them all anyway. And why should you read them if you don't *need* anything?)
- Always do the Old Double Take. Never buy on the first approach. If you think you like it, tuck it in a corner of your mind (not your car trunk) and see if you still feel the same a few days later. I'll bet there are several thousand of you reading this right now who upon first seeing those 30-inch long monkeypod wood forks and spoons really liked and wanted them. I did, and my wife tells me she did, too. Now I couldn't even imagine those oversized utensils hanging on my wall. The first impression is often "want" but the second is often "why?" Go with your second guesses.
- Never bring it home (or have it delivered) while you think about it. Have you ever in your whole life seen anyone who brought a stray dog or cat home, actually get rid of it later? Never! Once clutter comes home with us, it sprouts instant roots and we can't kick it out—so never bring it home to debate about it. Even if we do decide to

get rid of it, it's a lot of bother to find the invoice and pack it all up and ship it back. Many a person has a whole shelf full of stuff "to take back." The allowable return period has probably passed or the store you bought it in has gone out of business—so you can toss it all out or give it away!

• Beware, too, of the following clutter catalysts:

Price break junk. We need a dab of axle grease or a couple brushfuls of paint, but we buy five gallons, because the price was so good we got four gallons (that will curdle on the garage shelf) free.

"Barely above cost" and "wholesale" are more choice clutter snares.

> "My mother can't resist a bargain, but when she bought a dressmaker's dummy cover because it was $25.98 marked down to only $5 and gave it to me to wear, because it was such good material—well, that was the last straw!!"

Overkill junk. We buy a $47 tool (and three attachments for it) to make a $14.24 repair.

The bag will hold more junk. We don't really need it, want it, or have a place for it at home, but it's cheap or free and there's room left in the trunk, bag, or our arms for it.

It's too good to ignore. All too often we see something good, at a good price at a garage sale or store, and feel a twinge of genuine missionary zeal to find a home for it, seek out an owner. (We, of course, are the ones who end up with it.)

Likewise, most of us like to match things up. We'd make marriages if it were legal. When we keep old useless things, we start feeling sorry for them and look for a companion for them. We have a worthless wood chessboard (We don't even play chess), but when we run across an almost complete set of chessmen at a garage sale we buy it and bring it home to keep company with our battered old board and live happily ever after. (And we'll continue to hunt for the lone knight and one pawn that are missing, even though we don't play).

Spare-part syndrome. "I should buy at least one extra set of drill bits, or food-processor attachments, in case this one breaks, or I run out someday." (The vacuum will probably wear out before we have a chance to use up all 96 bags.)

Coupons. Deadlier than most come-on clutter because they're carryable! Notice how many coupons are for things we don't really need, "add on" or "sometime" things that don't sell by themselves. How many coupons do you see for the staples like bread, butter, or milk? But for exotic desserts, sometime sauces, and experimental cereals, there are coupons galore (so you can make an extra trip to the store to save 50 cents on a $5 item you wouldn't otherwise have bought). Buying what you don't need is the core of most clutter collections.

Pushy salespeople. Push right back. Do you want to be paying something off for months—or years—because you didn't want to disappoint the guy in the bright red blazer?

> "I found that if I could stop buying cute little things, I'd have enough money saved, eventually, to buy the one elegant thing I really wanted."

When shopping fever strikes suddenly!

• Examine your last four credit-card statements.
• Spend five minutes meditating on the part that tells you how much the interest alone was last month.
• Balance your checkbook.
• Go see what's available in the "free store" (your stash)—take the time to dig out and savor some of your buried and forgotten treasures.

- Since cruising around and writing out checks is part of shopophilia, go pay all your bills in person.
- Confine yourself to brisk comparison shopping for strict necessities: the new hinges you need or a new mixer to replace the one that died.
- Shop at a mall with a food store, buy the groceries first, then go shop the rest of the mall. We tend to stop buying when we get tired of walking and carrying.
- If all else fails, go to the five-and-dime. If you lose your head, at least it won't be as serious.

"I find the 'money fast' a very useful antijunk tool. I often take two- to three-week vacations from spending paycheck money (it gets deposited directly into an account). With no cash readily at hand, I'm forced to use every food scrap, turn in all recyclable items for emergency pocket money, and utilize existing resources for recreation (board games, bicycle, walking, contact with friends). I always emerge from my money fasts with a clean refrigerator, an uncluttered carport, and an increased appreciation for low-cost noncluttering diversions."

Now Just How Often Must I Dejunk?

In dejunking, just as in housecleaning, tooth care, car care, and plant care, a little daily discipline is better than a save-it-up onslaught.

If you attend to those rotted boards, bent bolts, toeless socks, old magazines, and abandoned projects on a regular basis, you'll always have a clean, lean pile. McDonald's calls this "clean as you go." It's a lot easier to keep things clean as you go than to do a big end-of-the-year clean up or throw out (or throw up and

clean out). I do my dejunking mostly on Sunday, because unloading a burden is a spiritual experience. Choose any day you like, but do it regularly and you'll head off awesome accumulations.

One false doctrine of dejunking: *One in and one out.* Now think about this, you're already drowning in stuff, and your family size may be shrinking. One in and one out is actually adding junk; one in and *six* out might make a little sense.

Clutter-Control Center

Ninety-nine percent of what ends up clutter and litter in a home is stuff we carry through the door and don't have an immediate use or place for. So we set it down "wherever," or in the proximity of its possible use, whence it kind of creeps, sneaks, and wanders into everyone's way or onto any available surface. Stuff, just like people who have no real home or destination, can easily be sidetracked or sidelined. And stuff tossed in a "maybe" pile will end up a mayday situation.

One way to keep a grip on all this is a box or drawer where you can put all the in-transit or undecided the minute you come in. Then you have it contained and controlled. It can stay in there while you decide where it goes or until you use it. This is kind of an improved junk drawer; at least you know where all the loose stuff is. Or better yet, set up a clutter-control center with a marked set of drawers or containers (sized to the amount of loose stuff you usually have in each category) and then chuck the stuff in there instead of just anywhere. Then your next move is to put it back where it belongs next time you're headed that way anyway.

CHAPTER 18

The Rewards of Living of Living Without Junk:

Enjoying the Vacant Ache

Well, okay, it might feel a little lonely at first, that "vacant ache." Being uncluttered and dejunked will be uncomfortable, for a minute or two.

Nothing to move around thirty times a day, nothing to dust every other day, very little wrestling with and transferring of stuff, no one getting cut or poisoned from old paint or machinery, no more sprung door hinges (from closing on overcrowded closets), hardly a thing to worry about. We won't be seeing the friendly doctor as much because we have fewer head bumps and cracked shins. The ulcers have left, too, now that most of the clutter is gone.

You might miss the frantic free-for-all of cleaning up for company—it seems odd, I'm sure, just calmly meeting them at the door instead of stopping to shovel everything into the back bedroom. The echo from the empty space might be a little strange to your ears at first, and conversation has a few bare spots where you once compared the merits of your new nutmeg grater over the old and the rates of storage rental. Your family fights are lots duller now that one of the main aggravations (and a lot of the ammunition) is gone. You've had to come up with some new reading material, too, now that you aren't constantly studying the classifieds. A lot of mice, rats, and roaches are adrift since you've taken their home—the old shed out back—away.

Adjusting to the absence of guilt and embarrassment, and of friends, relatives, and strangers who used to use you as a junk depot, takes a while. And though almost everyone else seems to have a lot more respect for you these days, the neighborhood shopping team has been snubbing you since you cut your daily shopping routine down to once a week. It is a little unsettling, I admit, to actually have room to live and move, and to have to figure out what to do with all the extra money you have now that once was used to acquire and maintain junk. Don't worry though; you'll heal with no scars.

The really big adjustment—I don't know if you can make it—is to all the free time you now have. Not only because you don't have to tend junk endlessly but also because cleaning and maintenance of everything is much easier now that all that junk is out of the way. Your housework is cut at least 40 percent, you have several extra days a month that you used to spend swimming in junk. It's all yours now—all the time it used to take you to fidget with and find a place for stuff you never needed or wanted but that kept pouring in because of your cluttered condition. Your family may even be a little irritated at you because dejunking was such an exhilarating experience you don't really feel the need to go to Acapulco now. You're almost tired of passionate approaches from your mate (now that he or she can find you—uncluttered and unoccupied).

It's true what you've heard: the pure joy of having neat rooms and drawers and closets and lawns on every side can cause a violent enthusiasm of mind and body—and you might not be able to contain such vibrant emotion and might need to take it easy until you get used to it.

Selecting a few short testimonials that say it best (out of the hundreds that have been sent to me) was a pleasure. I thought these would leave you with a real sense of the rewards:

"I can't begin to tell you what a difference dejunking has made in my life."

"I knew I had changed when with great joy in my heart I pitched two oversize Grand Ole Opry mugs, which I had kept and couldn't find a use for! My body is twenty pounds lighter, my drawers open, and even more important, they close!"

"We spend a lot less money on rent and utilities and *junk* so we have more money and time to spend on things that really matter. (I used to spend *two days* cleaning house and now I only spend one hour each week, and the apartment is spotless most of the time.) Instead of working extra hours to pay for junk and larger houses, etc., we go to the park and have picnics, have pizza dinners and go to the movies, and the zoo and science center and the library and visit family members and are planning a trip to Disneyland in the spring (from the junk sale money)."

"With your help we have dejunked our lives, and with simplicity came peace and harmony. My husband and I get along much better now and because our relationship has improved our son also benefits from having a stable family life."

"Many thanks for the inspiration, guidance, and pleasure you have provided us. The feelings of freedom, of letting go, and the satisfaction of seeing the basement emptying are, as you know, difficult to explain but immensely satisfying. We have been applying the principles to many other areas and activities in our lives, with equally spectacular results. In addition, we are experiencing those wonderful feelings of closeness that couples seem to feel after dejunking.

"We can't think of a nicer way to help people improve their lives and feel good about themselves."

"We're having the time of our lives! I've been more places and done more fun things with my wife and the kids in the last year than I did in the whole twenty-three years previous. We never went anywhere or did anything with our kids.

We couldn't. Instead we were paying off the grand piano and buying grandfather clocks. I honestly can't remember a fun vacation we ever took with our kids. My vacations every year were spent hanging new wallpaper and planting fancier shrubs out front or laying expensive tiles in the entryway.

"It's like a second chance. This time I want to do it right. Before this we always thought happiness was 'acquired' and that status was a worthy aspiration. Now I see we spent our whole lives and all our money trying to impress people who don't even matter! In the meantime, the people who really *did* matter were ignored. We aren't going to make that same mistake again!"

"Our church made $700 at the garage sale we had after the three of us read your book. I can chuckle now as I pass garage sales and homes full of clutter. I am indeed free from it. This book should be in every high school as recommended reading. Maybe this country wouldn't have such a deficit."

Final statement and disclaimer:

I'm not asking you or telling you to throw history, memories, or even stupid stuff away. What you decide to eliminate and what you do with it is totally *your decision.* You are a free agent and the only expert on your own junk! I've tried to give you the timetable, but as for what's under your table, it's your move.

I'm just leaning on you for *when* to declutter—and that is *now*.

Well, that's the final dose/chapter of the cure, and I leave with you the final question to ask at any clutter confrontation:

What's the worst thing that could happen if I get rid of it?

Your Success Report

Your chance to tell your story. Be the dejunker of the year! How did you do it? Share your experience! Send your report to me: Don Aslett, PO Box 700, Pocatello, ID 83204 or aslettdon@aol.com.

- How much junk did you have?
- How long did it take you to dejunk?
- Did you do it all at once, or in installments?
- What was the hardest thing about it/were the worst problem areas?
- Was any part of it easier than you expected?
- What did you find the hardest to part with?
- How did you manage to do it?
- What was the biggest surprise to you?
- Did you find anything that worked especially well to help others decide to dejunk?
- Anything you wish I'd said more about?
- How do you feel you most benefited from the process?
- Would you mind being quoted in future books or articles on this subject?

INDEX